THE HYBRID CHURCH IN THE CITY

Christopher Baker offers a refreshing and authoritative look at the opportunities and challenges facing the urban church. This book is a great blend of cultural analysis, local voices and theological reflection. It marks a new wave of thinking about what it means to live as people of faith amidst the complexities of the contemporary city.
Elaine Graham, Samuel Ferguson Professor of Social & Pastoral Theology, University of Manchester, UK

In this fascinating and prescient study, Chris Baker argues for a new kind of engagement and connectedness for theology and the churches. By focusing attention on space, urbanisation and marginalisation, new possibilities for practical theology are opened up that invite a fundamental reconsideration of the churches and their location within postmodern society. This book is essential reading for all those who want to understand the Christianity and culture debate in more depth, and tackle it with imagination, flair and thought.
Canon Professor Martyn Percy, Principal, Ripon College Cuddesdon, UK

The era of post-colonialism and globalization has brought new intensities of debate concerning the existence of diversity and plurality, and the need to work in partnerships to resolve major problems of injustice and marginalization now facing local and global communities. The Church is struggling to connect with these significant economic, political and cultural changes, which are having an impact on all types of urban context, but especially city centres, inner rings and outer estates, and the new ex-urban communities being developed beyond the suburbs.

This book argues that theology and the Church need to engage more seriously with postmodern reality and thought, if points of connection (both theologically and pastorally) are going to be created. The author proposes a sustained engagement with a key concept to emerge from postmodern experience – the concept of the Third Space. Drawing primarily on examples from Europe and the United States, this book examines examples of Third Space methodologies to ask questions about hybrid identities, and methods that churches might adopt to connect effectively with postmodern cities and civil society.

The author's particular areas of focus include: the role and identity of the Church in postmodern urban space; the role of public theology in addressing key issues of the impact of marginalization and urbanization in the 21st century; and the nature and role of local civil society as a local response to globalized patterns of urban, economic, social and cultural change.

The Hybrid Church in the City

Third Space Thinking

CHRISTOPHER BAKER
William Temple Foundation/University of Manchester

scm press

© Christopher Baker 2007, 2009

First published in 2007 by Ashgate Publishing Limited in the UK and
Ashgate Publishing Company in the USA.

This Second Edition published in 2009 by SCM Press
Editorial office
13–17 Long Lane,
London, EC1A 9PN, UK

SCM Press is an imprint of Hymns Ancient and Modern Ltd (a registered charity)
St Mary's Works, St Mary's Plain,
Norwich, NR3 3BH, UK
www.scm-canterburypress.co.uk

British Library Cataloguing in Publication data

A catalogue record for this book is available
from the British Library

978-0-334-04186-3

Typeset by N²productions
Printed and bound by
CPI Antony Rowe, Chippenham, Wiltshire

Contents

To John Atherton – mentor and friend

Acknowledgements

This book has been a long time in the writing and delivery, and due to the rapidly changing situations affecting its subject matter, has been constantly evolving. However, key places and people have helped enormously in the creative process. First, the city of Manchester, whose culture, history, architecture and sense of identity have held a strong grip over me for the past 25 years. I am fortunate that Manchester also happens to be the place where so many equally dynamic and contradictory people live and work. I am grateful to Frankie Ward for introducing me to ideas of hybridity and the work of Homi Bhabha and Kwok Pui-lan. I am indebted to Elaine Graham for her passion for, and knowledge of, cities and public theology, and whose ideas shared during the teaching of our Theology and Contemporary Society course have been so influential. I am fortunate to know so many resourceful clergy, community development workers, church leaders, academics, students and communities who live, work and try to make sense of the enormous changes affecting Manchester, and refuse to let go of the issues of justice and human dignity implied in those changes. In particular (and in no particular order), Lesley Husselbee, Clare MacBeath, Stephen Lowe, Alison Peacock, Anne Stewart, Ed Cox, Peter Rouch, Community Pride, SEDI, Ardwick Deanery and Eden, Alan Simpson Jr, Peter Scott, Martin Miller, John Devine. Friends and colleagues outside Manchester whose reflection on their own context and friendship have been absorbed in this book include Peter Robinson, Rob Furbey, John Fielding and especially John Reader, whose innovative thinking on 'blurred encounters' has resonated so strongly with hybridity. My thanks are extended to the Executive and Council of the William Temple Foundation for giving me the opportunity to pursue my theological passions, and especially to my two work colleagues – Hilary Bichovsky, who is technically our Administrator but whose surreal humour has been important to the creative process, and Hannah Skinner, whose perceptive research and writing is clearly evident in this volume. My penultimate final thanks goes to John Atherton, whose humour, exhaustive knowledge of Manchester and instinctive ability to evolve new thinking and make connections has been fundamental to my resources. Finally, my thanks to the Scargill Community for their love and hospitality to me, and to Dilly, Flossie and Theo for being a smaller but significant community from which so much flows.

Preface to Second Edition

I am very grateful to SCM Press for its encouragement and support in seeing this book through to a second edition, and in particular I would like to express my thanks to Natalie Watson, Commissioning Editor, for her enthusiasm in allowing this volume to come to pass.

Since the first edition was published in 2007, interest in the ideas contained in *Hybrid Church* have developed and coalesced. There were three main themes that the book attempted to address. First was the description of the context with which twenty-first-century public theology and ecclesiology has to engage – namely the Hybrid City. The Hybrid City is the fluid, postcolonial and globalized locality in which diversity and cultural creativity emerge alongside growing extremes of wealth, poverty and opportunity. It is the place *par excellence* where the old binary certainties of modernity have been overwhelmed by the unsettling and persistent presence of the Other. It is also the place where we recognize the renewed sense of an interdependent global community, the flourishing and survival of which is beyond the capabilities of either the State or Market to resolve. It is above all, a space of negotiated identities, whereby the essentials of one's identity have to accommodate and engage with a plurality of other identities. Out of these encounters a new identity is forged which draws on both tradition and innovation and local and global sources. These encounters also create a process by which one's current experience and insight are pushed beyond previously defined boundaries of significance.

The Hybrid City reminds us that change, innovation and adaptability are the prerequisites for today's urban citizen, and that finding a new moral consensus and sense of common belonging are increasingly active and important tasks. I believe the same priorities apply to the church, which has unparalleled opportunities to evolve into innovative and exciting forms and take root in new and hitherto unimagined spaces, for example the Third Space between binary polarities. These themes of innovation and opportunity continue to resonate in a number of areas, especially in relation to the emergence of the concept of the postsecular as applied to both urban space and public life. This concept suggests that processes of both secularization and re-sacralizing are occurring simultaneously. It is therefore not a return to an *either/or* context, with secularism in retreat before the rampant forces of globalized religion, but an engagement with a complex and nuanced *both/and* situation in which both faith and secularity need to learn new skills of discernment and communication and demonstrate the ability to work together to revive the public square.

Second, there was an attempt to bring the insights of Third Space/Hybrid thinking, as developed over the past 20 years in political theory and cultural studies, into critical dialogue with Christian theology. This was enabled by suggesting the possibility of a radically reformulated tradition of Christian realism, building substantially on the legacy of such thinkers in the mid twentieth century as Bonhoeffer, Temple, Niebuhr, and further enunciated in the 1970s and 80s by theologians such as Preston and Atherton. Christian realism steers a middle course between both disabling utopianism and pessimism regarding human attempts to build the Kingdom of God in human history. Rather it sees partnership and reconciliation as the way forward, including rigorous interdisciplinary dialogue between theology and the disciplines of political theory, economics, and increasingly sociology, human psychology and urban theory. Within the increasingly urgent global problems facing humankind, the emphasis of a radical Christian realism is even more directed at working on contextual solutions to local problems while at the same time taking the lead in defining the key principles from a Christian theological tradition by which faith-based initiatives can be articulated and assessed. In attempting to reformulate Christian realism for the demands of the twenty-first century I am pleased to see that realism in other disciplines (notably philosophy) is making a comeback as a necessary prophylactic against the temptation to resort to political and religious utopias in times of global stress and uncertainty. John Gray, in *Black Mass – Apocalyptic Religion and the Death of Utopia* (Penguin, 2008), concludes that 'the pursuit of Utopia must be replaced by an attempt to cope with reality' and that living in an 'intractable world' imposes on us the discipline (in the words of Hedley Bull) of 'not ... taking a single dramatic step of sweeping difficulties aside, but the constant surmounting of new crises and facing of fresh difficulties'.[1]

Finally, a key element of this book was to try and earth some complex and leading edge theory in actual case-studies of church-based engagement in urban contexts. This element is best reflected in the description of what I call local performative theologies, in which the church takes the risk of adapting its performance and identity in a critically reflective way that fits in which local conditions on the ground. This praxis holds in tension local flexibility, multi-disciplinary engagement, learning and reflection alongside established institutional norms and wisdom. This is an ongoing debate stimulated in recent reports such as *Faithful Cities* (Methodist Publishing House, 2006) and *Mission-shaped Church* (Church House Publishing, 2004). Meanwhile I have recently taken some of the issues raised by this book in publications with other fellow travellers in this field – notable Bishop Laurie Green and John Reader.[2]
I hope that the issues and methodologies raised by this book will continue to provoke radical and creative questions about the future forms of church engagement in our rapidly evolving urban areas.

Chris Baker
Feast of the Epiphany 2009

Notes

1 pp. 271–2.
2 *Building Utopia? Seeking the Authentic Church for the New Communities* (co-edited with Laurie Green), London, SPCK, 2008. *Entering the New Theological Space – Blurred Encounters of Faith, Politics and Community* (co-edited with John Reader) Aldershot, Ashgate, 2009.

Introduction

As this text neared completion in the warm serenity of a seaside garden in Brittany in the summer of 2005, news of darker and more shocking events back in the UK began to filter through. A series of bomb blasts had unleashed death, injury, fear and mayhem on London's rush-hour transport system. It appeared that the initial shock and anger at the attacks of 7 July slipped quickly into stunned disbelief when it emerged that the attacks were carried out not only by suicide bombers (the first attack of its kind in mainland Britain), but British-born suicide bombers at that. Shortly after these attacks the British authorities compounded the emotional intensity and complexity of the events by shooting dead, in full public view, an innocent Brazilian man – Jean Charles de Menezes – whose only obvious crime in the panic-filled aftermath was to look and apparently behave like a terrorist.

What followed the events of '7/7' has been a convulsive tangle of soul-searching, recrimination, policy intervention and government legislation on anti-terrorism measures and incitement to religious hatred. But at the heart of the flurry of activity and debate following July 2005 more long-term questions continue to reverberate uncomfortably. How could British-born Muslims, whose victims included young men and women like themselves, come to inhabit a frame of mind that could coldly plan and execute this level of deliberate carnage over a period of several months? What turned Mohammed Sidique Khan, known as 'Sid' to his many white friends and a skilled and caring teaching assistant singled out for special praise in an OFSTED report, into the ringleader of a sophisticated terrorist cell?

Possible answers to these questions have been suggested by a number of theories. Commentators on the left stress the role of poverty and social exclusion as the cause of radical disaffection. While this may be a contributory factor in other parts of the world, it doesn't seem an adequate analysis for the emergence of UK-based bombers and other suspects who tend to come from university-educated and mainstream backgrounds. Those on the right might refer to Muslim unease at the power of the free market, but while Muslims would never endorse laissez-faire liberal economics and probably see it as a corrosive influence on family and community cohesion, it is not in itself a reason for the mass killing of innocent people. Much suspicion rests on UK foreign policy as being the main culprit, especially in relation to ongoing armed intervention in Iraq and Afghanistan and apparent support for Israeli policy in Palestine and Lebanon. But this theory seems not to take into account wider factors; for example, that the majority of suicide bombing is now internal to Islam (for example, retaliation attacks between Shia and Sunni Muslims in Iraq) and that the most recent NATO-led operation within Europe was designed specifically to save Muslims from genocide in Bosnia and Kosovo. Elsewhere, some suspect a more deep-seated and long-term alienation from British culture which expresses itself as a specific form of religious extremism tied to the areas of Pakistan from which the families of several British suspects have originated, and which communicates itself as a heightened expression of puritanism linked to a messianic nationalism. However, moderate mainstream voices within British Islam also express disquiet at hedonistic aspects of Western liberal culture such as binge drinking, loutish behaviour, promiscuity and drug abuse, and which they perceive as being allied to an aggressive secularism. Any clarity on these post-7/7 events is therefore complex and provisional.

This book unearths some of the wider issues that might help answer some of these keenly felt and disturbing questions. Because at the heart of these questions is the issue of identity. What processes prevented these British-born Muslim men from reconciling the different elements of their identity into a more functional form of humanity? What made them decide to reject a working compromise between their British identity and Muslim culture? And within a globalized city such as London, where so much economic, cultural, political and religious energy is derived from largely tolerant interactions of many ethnic groups in close proximity, a bomb placed by ideological purists seems all the more desperate, outdated and absurd – though none the less devastating for all that.

But then all these questions are generated by the tension that lies at the heart of our postmodern, post-industrial and globalized society – the tension between embracing the comfort of a supposedly pure identity (even though, as this book will reiterate, there is no such thing) and experiencing the discomfort caused by the complexity of a hybrid one. Elsewhere this tension is expressed between welcoming the stranger and the fear of the stranger (or the Other).

This book, largely written before the events of 7/7, is about exploring the many dimensions of hybridity that the events outlined above have raised in particularly acute form. This is because the world in which we live is hybrid as never before, and increasingly so. Hybridity is here to stay and there is no going back. My passionate argument in this book is that it is a category of human thought and experience that profoundly influences how we 'do' our politics, live in our cities and consume culture and spirituality. It is therefore time for theology and the church to enter into creative and critical dialogue with hybridity, and no longer to ignore it as a difficult word or unpleasant word. Above all, it is time to explore the positive opportunities that understanding hybridity provides for the creative connection between new forms of church and new forms of urban community.

As already stated, hybridity is a multilayered concept expressing a growing number of influences that now pervade all aspects of our lives, including the communities we live in, the urban spaces we inhabit, the food we eat, the music we listen to, and the people we see around us. However, these surface signs and symbols also represent a deeper philosophical and epistemological change. They tell us clearly that as we move beyond the cusp of the twenty-first century, we are moving further and further away from the binary 'either/or' definitions that the Enlightenment and Marxism bequeathed to the nineteenth and twentieth centuries.

According to these definitions we were simply black or white, gay or straight, working class or bourgeoisie, evangelical or liberal. The community you lived in had similarly well-defined indicators to indicate your social status. In the small industrial railway town of Wolverton, in the South Midlands, near where I used to live, the social and cultural demarcations of how people were expected to live in previous centuries are still preserved intact by the planning and the architecture. Closest to the railway works are the rectangular arrangements of terraced housing with their small back yards, for the workers. A little further away are slightly larger terraces with small gardens and the odd bay window, denoting the accommodation of the foremen and shop-floor managers. A considerable distance away at the top of the hill leading up from the works one finds semi-detached housing and detached villas in leafy curved streets. This was the domain of the upper management of the workshops and factories; houses with well stocked gardens and pleasant views across the rolling Buckinghamshire countryside. Simply by walking around Wolverton, it is still obvious which socio-cultural territory one is located in. I sometimes wondered how many railway workers ever ventured the few hundred metres up the hill to where the managers lived. Were there parts of their town that they never visited?

Today, binary systems and hierarchies have lost considerable power to influence and dictate behaviour and identity. Take, for example, the 'black' vs. 'white' debate. The 2001 UK census had, for example, no less than seven choices for defining ethnic identity at Level 1, building up to 20 choices at Levels 2 and 3. It is interesting how many of the categories offer split definitions of ethnicity, rather than 'pure' categories. So for example, the category of *Mixed* makes its first appearance in the 2001 census as one of the Level 1 categories. The Level 2 options for those people who tick this box include:

- White and Black Caribbean
- White and Black African
- White and Asian
- Other Mixed background
- All Mixed background

The numbers of UK citizens filling out these categories came to 677,177; a 150 per cent increase in ten years. In the 1991 census people born of mixed race households had to fill out their details under *Black – Other* or *Any Other Ethnic Group*. There were 228,504 who described themselves in this category in 1991.

In the domain of human sexuality a greater mainstreaming of gay lifestyles and concerns has emerged in the last two decades, expressed in countless sitcoms, makeover shows, dramas and reality-TV formats. This apparently greater tolerance of gay and lesbian identity within mainstream UK society has led to a deliberate blurring of sexual and cultural identities, especially in urban societies. Thus, for example, the concept of the *metrosexual* man or woman has emerged in the last ten years, an identity that currently has over 100 web-based definitions. From a male gender perspective, it is often used as a deliberate attempt to expand traditional, binary understandings of male heterosexuality into a more ambivalent, hybrid area that is neither gay nor straight. A typical definition of this type would be 'A straight man who embraces the homosexual lifestyle, that is refined tastes in clothing, excessive use of designer hygiene products, etc' (www.urbandictionary.com). Other definitions explicitly link the image of *metrosexuality* to a new from of *urban identity* that is open to both men and women. 'Metrosexuality can be used to describe any person who is in love with both their self and their urban lifestyle' (www.urbandictionary.com).

Some definitions go as far to claim that metrosexuality is a form of 'gender-bending' that '*almost* redefines masculinity and femininity by adding elements that are not characteristic of the traditional definitions of gender roles and behaviours' (emphasis mine). So for example:

> A metrosexual can be lesbian, straight, gay, bi or trans because it is the love of self that conquers all others. But there is a subtle message of ambiguous sexuality in this image and lifestyle. It could be attached to the desire to be attractive to all. Or perhaps, it's the desire to be catered to and pleased by all. The metrosexual may adopt different sexual personas to match their look.
>
> (www.urbandictionary.com)

Thus the idea is created of the metrosexual as an ultra-discerning urban consumer who flirts with deliberate ambiguity as an expression of both the right to choose and the right to be desirable to all. Therefore, within this concept of metrosexuality, very 'postmodern' features involving individualism, consumerism and sexual identity are conflated. Interestingly, my adopted home city of Manchester has provided two 'metrosexual icons'. Morrissey, lead singer of seminal Manchester group The Smiths, whose first hit single was a song entitled 'This Charming Man' back in the early 1980s, has recently found his sexually ambiguous persona back in favour as a global solo artist. David Beckham is a similar global 'icon' whose metrosexual image was cultivated while captain of Manchester United in the late 1990s. Although presenting the image of a tough footballer and contented, married father of three children, he also appeared on the front of the *Gay Times*, and much of his merchandising iconography has been aimed at the gay market.

Unfortunately it is not within the scope of this book to explore the deeper cultural and gender-based analyses of what is being expressed by the concept of metrosexuality. I simply use it as a current case study of an exercise in urban-based hybridity.

But what of city space itself? Two examples, also from Manchester, help to illustrate the developing hybridity of much urban space.

My analysis of Wolverton, for example, could also be applied to a huge peripheral estate of 50,000 people called Wythenshawe, nine miles from Manchester's city centre but less than two miles from its rapidly expanding International Airport. Wythenshawe, like Wolverton, was a pure industrial community, although a much later example, with various types of public housing for workers employed on nearby industrial estates. These ranged from well built and substantial semidetached housing in the Garden City tradition of the early 1930s through to the generic types of high density deck-access housing and tower blocks of the 1950s and 1960s. However, during this latter period the fortunes of this cohesive and relatively prosperous white working-class enclave went into drastic decline. The availability of manufacturing jobs was decimated by deindustrialization from the late 1960s onwards, and the local authority adopted a housing policy that denied second-generation Wythenshawe residents the right to live on the estate. In their place, the local council drafted in its most troublesome and rent-defaulting tenants from other parts of Manchester in the misguided belief that the Garden City environment would improve their moral behaviour. Instead, it broke up the cohesion of the estate and introduced a large element of gang-related crime just as the local economy was going into melt down. For the next three decades Wythenshawe went into severe economic, social and environmental decline with the result that by the mid 1990s, parts of it were designated by New Labour's Indices of Multiple Deprivation as the most deprived community in England and Wales.

This designation prompted a redoubling of efforts to regenerate the community via a public/private partnership, which has been primarily concerned to revive the housing market. Taking advantage of Wythenshawe's close proximity to Manchester's expanding global hub (its airport), developers have started to build large amounts of private housing in cheap areas of land previously occupied by demolished public housing. Gated communities are now being built with executive-style homes that cost five times the price of the original housing stock. There is evidence to suggest that these new residents are using Wythenshawe as a transport hub location, and that their lifestyles and use of services barely mesh with those of the existing local community. The local town centre in Wythenshawe is still populated with 'pound shops' (where nothing costs more than £1), while those with more money and mobility shop at nearby retail parks.

Wythenshawe has in effect become a hybrid community. Its once strongly homogeneous white, Irish and predominantly Catholic identity has been broken down into a series of disparate communities that live in close proximity but share nothing in terms of identity and experience. These include new communities from the global market, particularly Indian and Filipino immigrants who have been recruited to work in the nearby public health service hospital, which has been expanded to cover larger parts of south Manchester. Local communities now live alongside global communities, but rarely do they seem to connect. The previously close connections between urban space and cultural identity (white, working-class) have been broken, and as yet there is no new identity that has emerged. At the local elections in 2004 members of the far-right British National Party were seen on the streets of Wythenshawe for the first time, in what has traditionally been an overwhelmingly Labour area.

Moving from the fragmentation and gentrification of working-class suburbs, what of city space itself? My second example is observed from my office in Manchester, which is less than a quarter of a mile from Manchester's famous 'curry mile' which is good news for my taste buds but constantly precarious for my waistline. The curry mile is a long 'main drag' just south of the university, with over forty curry restaurants whose owners have to outdo each other in neon signs in order to attract customers – at night it seems more like Las Vegas than Manchester. There are also huge global food stores, halal butchers, small Asian food stores, sari and sweet shops, Islamic bookshops, and countless Bollywood and bhangra music and DVD stores. The casual passer-by or curry punter would see perhaps a rather obvious and shallow hybridity (which could be summed up, for example, as 'East meets West') that is now well marketed by the city authorities to the point where £85 million is spent each year on curry in this area alone.

This is apparently a story of 'hybridity as cultural diversity'. When I was an undergraduate in this area two decades earlier, it had the feel of a run-down inner suburb which used to house manufacturing workers, mainly of Irish origin, with authentic Irish pubs along the main road. It has now been turned into an exotic space for the consumption of food and alcohol, with special incentives for students to travel half a mile down from the university as part of the weekend ritual of clubbing and parties.

Yet on closer inspection, a deeper process of hybridity is underway. The simple geographical/ethnic adjective 'Indian', as in 'Let's go and have an Indian' (that is, a curry) is a hugely inaccurate generalization. Those who have immigrated to Manchester to set up curry restaurants have come predominantly from Bangladesh and Pakistan, and have been joined by those who would classify themselves primarily as Punjabi or Bengali rather than Indian, as well as others from outside India altogether, such as Iranians and Nepalese. Their menus offer the now well marketed Vindaloo, Madras and Tikka Masala dishes, but also many dozen hybrids based on their own national or regional culinary customs.

It would also be easy to assume that because of the recent 'curry explosion', curry eating is a new phenomenon in the British Isles. Researchers at the John Rylands Library in Manchester have found a recipe for curry dating back to 1769, written by the housekeeper of Arley Hall in nearby Cheshire. The first English curry house, called the Hindustani Coffee House, was opened in London's Portman Square in 1809. Meanwhile, the first curry houses in the North-west of England were simple cafes opened up to cater for the new influx of textile workers to the UK from the Indian subcontinent in the 1950s, a far cry from the glitzy and sophisticated experience offered today by increasing numbers of city-centre restaurants.

However, not even the origins of curry itself are purely unambiguous. Although the origins of the word can be traced back to the Tamil word *kari*, meaning spiced sauce, recipes containing the basic ingredients of curry, such as spices, oil, pureed onions, garlic and ginger have been discovered in Mesopotamia dating from 1700 BCE, and from seventeenth-century Portugal.

Other aspects of the 'curry mile' experience offer still deeper layers of ambiguity and complexity. The new Asian dance and pop music emanating from the video shops, and thudding at sub-woofer frequencies from the souped-up Honda Civics of British-born young Asian men cruising the streets, is a mixture of bhangra drumbeats, traditional Asian folk melodies, and Bollywood cinema songs, mixed with New York hip-hop, drum and bass, or even dancehall reggae. For those of softer musical persuasion, British-born Asian singers croon in pastiche of American-style R&B/Flava hip-hop. The gold chains and the flash cars speak of American 'gangsta' culture, a not always convincing hybrid identity as lampooned by the comic character Ali G, a creation of the British-born, Cambridge educated comedian Sasha Baron Cohen, who is himself of Jewish stock.

These are the second- and third-generation Islamic-British citizens who sometimes struggle to find an identity that is authentically British and authentically Islamic (for example, see Lewis, 2002). Many such young people find themselves drawn towards what they see as a pure Islamic identity, which will often reject the West as culturally inferior and spiritually corrupting. Young men and women struggle to be accepted by mainstream British society, processes that have been exacerbated by the terrorist bomb attacks in London in July 2005. Even well-educated and partially secularized Muslims in the UK have found that recent events have reawakened a belief in the importance of their faith as part of their cultural and spiritual identity. In an article entitled 'I'm a Believer', Bradford-born journalist Zaiba Malik recalls going to an East London mosque the day after the 7 July bombing in London to interview some women about Islam. She hadn't stepped inside a mosque for 20 years, since she left home for university. A young woman asked her if she was going to join Friday prayers. Malik recalls, 'I immediately replied "yes". It was partly out of respect, and partly embarrassment.' She continues:

> My memory of the da'wah, or prayer, was hazy. My slightly unsuitable top kept riding up my back, exposing my flesh every time I bowed to the floor. But recalling the Arabic that my father had taught me came easier than I expected. Suddenly, tears started to roll down my cheeks. I sneaked a glance at the other women. They were all dry-eyed. At first I thought it was guilt, remorse at not having stepped inside a mosque for so long. Then I realised – I was crying for my faith. Islam was a way of life for these women and now that way of life was being analysed, debated, criticised and even distorted.
>
> (*The Guardian*, 30 August 2005)

British-born Muslims are the group most likely to face the poorest educational achievements, the poorest-paid jobs, the highest unemployment rates and so on (for example, see Ethnic Minority Employment Division, Dept. for Work and Pensions, 2004). Like some of their British-born Afro-Caribbean counterparts, the way to status and money is often the life of petty or serious crime, linked to gang- and drug-related cultures.

This fundamental ambivalence about identity within British society is reflected in the posters adorning the curry shops and takeaways. Some are happy to display the images of hedonistic excess that promote the various club nights or drinks promotions available at the innumerable venues catering for Manchester's 70,000 students. Others however, prefer to advertise rallies against the war in Iraq, the plight of refugees in Palestine or those local cases of alleged human rights abuses under Britain's increasingly tough 'anti-terrorist' legislation. Some leaflets and posters are in Arabic, thus excluding English-speakers from their meaning. Often, live news from Arabic news stations can be seen on TV sets in the corner.

Meanwhile a darker side to the glitz and entertainment of locations like the 'curry mile' emerges in the growing evidence of slave wages and conditions for many of those employed as waiters and kitchen staff. These are often people illegally brought into Britain as cheap labour by gangmasters who smuggle them into the country. A recent Department of Trade and Industry report suggested that informal recruiting techniques by small- to medium-sized catering businesses within small, ethnic-minority communities was throwing up an increasing supply of 'illegals' who were meeting the shortfall in British-born labour caused by low wages and poor job satisfaction. These workers were typically employed for 50–70 hours a week at a rate of pay often no more than £2–3 an hour (Ram et al., 2002: 15–21). The global dimensions of this pernicious form of human suffering are increasing all the time and offer a particularly striking example of how the economic needs of local spaces are supplied by the global market.

Pulling these case studies together one begins to build up a profile of some of the key features of hybridity. These are:

- a deliberate playing with identities such as gender and sexuality as an expression of individual desirability, consumerism and flexible identity
- an expansion of 'official' ethnic categories in the last ten years that recognize many more 'mixed categories' of identity
- a complete 'rebranding' of urban space in terms of function and identity (for example, a space once used for industry and industrial housing being converted to leisure and cultural uses)
- other urban spaces now contain a mixture of populations, some of which are locally based, others of which are highly mobile and globally based
- the apparent disconnection between local and global communities is reinforced by spatial arrangements such as gated communities and retail/leisure hubs that are located away from local centres
- previously homogeneous space is fragmented into the smaller pieces of a 'mosaic'
- a deeper hybridity is often contained within a deceptively simple adjective, such as 'Indian', that includes many more cultural and ethnic strands
- entertainment space is used in a variety of ways – for example, political action and consciousness raising
- global flows of investment and immigration have an impact on the local space in both obvious and hidden ways (for example, largely invisible and illegal workforces) that reinforce problems of marginalization and oppression
- British-born citizens from ethnic minorities often experience an acute sense of dislocation and identity crisis as they attempt to reconcile global and local identities
- other British-born citizens embrace the potential of mixed or hybrid identities to create new forms of cultural identity and expression that genuinely invent original artistic forms – for example, music, art, film and cuisine
- hybridity, while associated with processes of globalization, urbanization and decolonization within the last two or three decades, does in fact contain strands that have been in operation for at least two or three centuries.

In short, hybridity is a dynamic and complex process that impinges on all arenas of human activity: social, cultural, political, ethnic and lived space. It works in ways that are exciting and creative while simultaneously reinforcing marginalization and poverty. It is thus highly ambiguous in both its causes and effects.

This introduction is intended as a 'launch pad' for a theological and practically based exploration of hybridity and its possibilities for the flourishing of creative postmodern Christian communities in postmodern urban space. The argument contained in the rest of this book will unfold as follows.

Part 1 sets the scene for developing the argument justifying the significance of hybridity within our twenty-first-century experience at the level of the philosophical, the urban/cultural and the political. These are some of the arenas in which a publicly accountable theology needs to engage.

Thus, Chapter 1 will include a brief introduction to some of the biological, literary, philosophical and political roots of hybridity, and introduce the key concept of the *Third Space*, which is intimately related to ideas about hybridity and how it operates. Chapter 2 will explore some of the key debates concerning the development of hybrid or 'mongrel' cities and how that helps expand important understandings of plurality and diversity at the levels of culture, belonging and identity as well as the use of urban space itself. Chapter 3 will build on the above arguments to discuss the relationship between changing urban space and changing understandings of civil society and political governance, which are moving towards hybrid and plural forms of participation and methodology. A key concept that will emerge in this chapter is the fluid relationship between *bonding* and *bridging* forms of social capital and between *participative* and *representative* forms of democracy. The case studies illuminating these processes will come from a variety of UK and US examples.

Part 2 will represent a Christian-based response to the complexities, challenges and opportunities offered by urban hybridity and Third Space thinking.

Chapters 4 and 5 will thus explore a methodology for public theological engagement with the complexity of postmodern living. Based on the traditions and insights of the Christian Realism tradition of social ethics, it will attempt to make the case for a radically reformulated Christian Realism that is willing to engage with the plurality and ambiguity of our postmodern context in an interdisciplinary and contextual way that, I hope, will nevertheless be strongly grounded. This, I argue, will steer a middle course between the unwarranted utopianism – or dystopianism – that often clouds the debates between postmodernity, hybridity and theology.

Chapter 6 will be more praxis-oriented, containing a number of case studies of global contexts in which churches are adapting to rapidly changing urban and social situations by adapting their methodology to contain a hybrid/Third Space way of working that incorporates what Peter Ward (2002) describes as both *solid* and *liquid* forms of social engagement. Other arguments introduced into this chapter will be the relationship between *institutional* and *network* forms of organization, and how churches engage in the processes of *translation* and *negotiation* in the construction of local practical theologies that are central to the concepts of Third Space thinking.

Chapter 7 will combine insights from chapters 5 and 6 to construct a theology of the Third Space. This will develop the concepts of a *blurred edges theology* and a new *concept of catholicity* that will also move the theological debate into areas of discussion as to what a post-liberal theology might look like in theory and practice.

It will also develop the powerful ideas contained within the hybridity of Jesus' own identity as *Jesus* and *Christ*, and how a focus on this perspective illuminates other key theological motifs such as the Kingdom of God, Pentecost and the Cross.

PART 1
THIRD SPACE THINKING

Chapter 1

The Significance of the Third Space and Hybridity for Understanding the Postmodern World

The purpose of this chapter is to examine the centrality of the concept of Third Space Hybridity within postmodern discourse under a variety of overlapping headings, with a view to establishing it as a key concept with which theology needs to engage. A key figure in this discussion will be Homi Bhabha, whose book *The Location of Culture* (1994) is a definitive analysis of the Third Space and its origins in post-colonial hybridity (see Soja, 2000, Brah and Coombes, 2000, Sandercock, 2003 and Papastergiadis, 2000)

This chapter will describe some of the important practical origins of hybridity (derived from biological and colonial discourses) before examining some of the epistemological ones (emerging from literature and post-colonial political philosophy). It is in this latter section that we will explore the close relationship between hybridity and the concept of the Third Space, which emerges as a major conceptual tool in understanding how hybridity works. Having set up the broad parameters of discussion, we will then be able to explore in subsequent chapters the impact of Third Space Hybridity thinking on postmodern urban studies, and on civil society and governance debates.

The Concept of Hybridity

The concept of hybridity, according to Brah and Coombes's edited collection of essays (2000) is far from a modern one, although its extensive usage since the early 1990s in such disparate fields as music, political science, cultural criticism and planning theory might lead one to think so (Brah and Coombes, 2000: 3–4). It first emerged as a concept in modern Western thought during the eighteenth century with the development of the natural sciences, and in particular, botany and zoology, where it referred to the outcome of a cross between two separate varieties of plant and animal. However, in the nineteenth century it emerged as a form of categorization of the human species into taxonomies of race, with increasingly vigorous debate about the origin of the species itself. For example, the monogenesists held that all humankind belonged to the same species. The polygenesists held that diverse skin colour denoted different species, which they arranged in a racist hierarchy with the white species at the top of the ethnic tree (Young, 1995: 150). These questions were intimately linked, indeed 'fuelled', by the needs of Western colonialism and imperialism, and its need to 'manage' the colonized subject. Coombes and Brah identify two management strategies that emerge during the nineteenth century: either to promote assimilation of the colonized to the norms and values of the West, or to ensure strict codes of segregation. A particularly shocking example of the former, which survived well into the latter half of the twentieth century, was the practice, required by Australian law, whereby mixed-race Aboriginal children up to the age of four were forcibly taken from Aboriginal homes and placed in adoptive white families. This approach was designed to allow full-blood Aborigines to die out, while the selected mixed-race section would breed with white people whose descendants, over several generations, would ultimately become completely absorbed into the white population. This policy was the subject of a film, *Rabbit-Proof Fence* (2002) directed by Philip Noyce.

Within colonialist discourse therefore, *hybridity* is seen as a potentially dangerous condition that needs to be carefully managed. Strong warnings were issued on the dangers of weakening genetic purity and cultural identity through the persistence of ethnic assimilation due to sexual unions between Western peoples and those of other ethnic or social origins. People from such unions were thought to be more infertile because they had crossed 'species' boundaries. Thus warnings against interracial union voiced by British colonial rulers in the Caribbean in the 1770s and French administrators in South East Asia in the 1930s (Brah and Coombes, 2000: 4) finds its current counterpart in the language of 'swamping' within British politics and the tabloid press in debates about immigration policy. In the United States, Harvard professor Samuel Huntington has raised serious anxieties about the erosion of American culture and identity by the 'persistent inflow' and much higher fertility rates of Hispanic populations from Mexico and other Latino communities, which threatens to divide America into two nations. Hispanic families average 3 children compared to 1.8 in non-Hispanic white communities, and he estimates that by 2050, 25 per cent of the US population will be of Hispanic origin. More particularly, Huntington is concerned that the foundational purity of American identity will be lost:

> America was created by seventeenth and eighteenth century settlers who were overwhelmingly white, British and Protestant ... Would the United States be the country that it has been and that it largely remains today if it had been settled by French, Spanish or Portuguese Catholics? The answer is clearly no. It would not be the United States; it would be Quebec, Mexico or Brazil.
>
> (Huntington, 2004: 2)

Meanwhile, there emerges from the UK some disturbing research into how young people who define themselves as *Mixed* (see discussion of the 2001 Census in the Introduction, p. 000) are treated by the wider society. Because they have, say, one black parent, it appears that society expects them to think of themselves as black, which some are willing to do, but others are not. However, all mixed race young people are subject to deep-seated racial discrimination, epitomized in such phrases as 'peanut', 'yellow-belly', 'half-breed' and 'redskin', which are not used of children with two black parents. And it is also apparent that they experience racist discrimination at the hands of black as well as white people, despite efforts from some of them to identify with black culture and ways of life (Brah and Coombes, 2000: 89).

From this brief overview, it is possible to say how 'anxieties about miscegenation [that is, interbreeding] and the preservation of racial purity' (Brah and Coombes, 2000: 4) remain at a high level and reflect negative notions of hybridity.

The Legacy of Colonial Anthropology

The previous relationships between the West and the world 'colonized' by European powers had been characterized by statements about culture that appeared neutral, universal and self-evidently true. In fact, according to Homi Bhabha, they designated 'institutional power and ideological Eurocentricity' in what he refers to as the 'familiar traditions and conditions of colonial anthropology' (Bhabha, 1994: 31). By this he means the constant framing of the colonized as the Other, the object of study, thus exacerbating the difference, otherness and often supposed 'inferiority' of the object as a case study in cultural difference – a mindset dubbed 'orientalism' by Edward Said (1978) for its frequent application to societies in the Middle East, South Asia, and the Far East.

The purpose of this colonial anthropology was threefold. First, it justified the main tenets of colonial capitalism as the antidote to the 'primitivism' that was supposed to have existed in colonized cultures before the advent of the white man's rule. Within this propaganda, major ideas concerning the nature and purpose of human history were held as self-evident. For example, the linear and predictable progress of history which, as it unfolds, produces increased understanding in technology, culture, democracy and economics – 'gifts' of understanding that the West 'passed on' to the East. It is a heroic and rationalistic view of history that Bhabha and others call 'historicism' (Bhabha, 1994: 194); a grand narrative of nineteenth-century colonialization predicated on 'evolutionism, utilitarianism, evangelism ... the technologies of colonialist and imperialist governance'(Bhabha, 1994: 194).

Second, the close study and evaluation of the Other supplied the justification for colonial anthropology to evolve into *cultural* anthropology as a respectable and credible discipline within the overall genealogy of social sciences. Bhabha describes the process thus:

This is a familiar manoeuvre of theoretical knowledge, where having opened up the chasm of cultural difference, a mediator or metaphor of otherness must be found to contain the effects of difference. In order to be institutionally effective as a discipline, the knowledge of cultural difference must be made to foreclose on the Other; difference and otherness thus become the fantasy of a certain cultural space ...

(Bhabha, 1994: 31)

In other words, cultural anthropology functions in a monopolistic way by choosing an unnecessarily stark and binary analysis of indigenous histories and cultures and then proposing itself as part of the solution to the cultural problematic it has identified.

The third reason is more subtle and complex, and reflects later developments within post-colonial studies. Although at one level post-colonial disciplines are more conscious of past issues of power and exploitation, they still *define* the Other. They still seek to explain and speak on behalf of those who experience marginalization and exploitation. Bhabha is critical of moves towards liberal notions of multiculturalism. This focus on cultural diversity uses pre-given cultural contents and customs on the assumption that cultures are separated and live uncorrupted by other influences, 'safe in the Utopianism of a mythic memory of a unique, collective identity' (Bhabha, 1994: 34). The limitations of this approach are exemplified for Bhabha when the rhetoric of cultural diversity is held within the 'well-intentioned moralist polemics against prejudice or stereotype, or the blanket assertion of individual or institutional racism' (Bhabha, 1994: 35), which he claims describes the effects of the problem rather than its structure.

Despite these trappings of tolerance and post-colonial cultural sensitivity, the Other is still the object of its own experience rather than the subject. The liberal Enlightenment project of categorization and objectivization continues as part of what Pierre Bourdieu has called the 'symbolic capital' of the West, which ensures that new cultural openness and tolerance never actually upset the cultural dominance of the West (see Bhabha, 1994: 21). The very language and theory of cultural anthropology and post-colonialism can be used as a 'power-ploy of the culturally privileged Western world ... a discourse on the Other that reinforces its own power-knowledge equation' (Bhabha, 1994: 34). The effect Bhabha is conveying is a notion of static preservation; the supremacy of the West is represented by its power to culturally represent others, while its 'authoritative address' relies on the codification of experience in its desire to reflect culture and history as 'a homogenizing unifying force' (Bhabha, 1994: 35).

There are close parallels between these processes of cultural commodification by the West and modernist planning, as identified by Leonie Sandercock, whereby planners attempted to create homogeneous urban space via masterplans reflecting the concept of a 'common good' or common identity. These masterplans created zoned spaces and high-density public housing that suppressed plurality and diversity, or simply reinforced structural inequality and prejudice. We shall explore the impact of these modernist masterplans, and the alternative discourses proposed by postmodernist planners, in Chapter 2.

The rise of Postcolonial Hybridity and the Emergence of the Third Space

Homi Bhabha identifies the Third Space as the space produced by the collapse of the previously defining narratives of modernity based on colonialism, class and patriarchy. These narratives labelled and defined the Other on grounds such as race, gender and sexual orientation. The epistemological and cultural collapse of the hegemony of the West has been brought on in the latter half of the twentieth century, says Leonie Sandercock, by four interconnected socio-cultural processes. She defines these as:

- **International migration**, which has been intensified since the 1980s by the growing inequalities of wealth between the North and the South, thus impelling people to search for work opportunities, as well as ethnic and religious struggles, political, ecological and demographic pressures, and the creation of new free trade areas.
- **The resurgence of indigenous peoples**, after colonial planning and farming policies had displaced or excluded indigenous peoples from their ancestral lands. This spatial displacement was never successful, and semi-permeable arrangements emerged whereby individuals or groups found their way into the edges or unincorporated parts of the city. Since the 1970s, there has been a global justice movement on the part of indigenous peoples to reverse the original displacements, with land claims being lodged on behalf of sites that were once sacred or ancestral.
- **The rise of organized civil society**, which emerged during the 1970s and 1980s from feminist inspired social movements demanding better access to transport, child care, community facilities, safe public spaces etc. Other movements also emerged during this period to combat racism, homophobia and environmental issues and these movements have become increasingly influential.
- **The discourse of post-colonialism**, which has exposed the persisting historical connections between empire, immigration, labour markets and racism, and the inherent racialism of liberal democracies. This legacy makes the growing diversity of populations faced by globalizing cities of the twenty-first century more problematic because of the embedded nature of the 'already-racialized western liberal democracies' in these cities, that have been used to seeing 'race relations' as a problem, and through a sequence of policies ranging from assimilation to multiculturalism, have attempted to integrate the 'inferior, less civilized' Other.

(Sandercock, 2003: 20–27)

The combined impact of these four processes has led to the rise of the Other as the carrier of its own self-liberating story. The Other is now no longer willing to be labelled and defined by the West. Rather the Other has become the subject of its own experience, which has created a process by which new identities and cultures have been forged.

Third Space Theory – the Difference Between the Saying and the Said

The above terms are based on the structure of linguistic theory and symbolic representation. Bhabha uses them (1994: 36–37) to describe the cultural position of the object of enunciation (the cultural Other or *énoncé*). Its cultural position always lies outside the statement; that is, its specificity can never be fully covered by the generality of what is assumed by the proposer (or the one doing the enunciating – usually the colonizer). Rather, the way the two parties of the proposition are related (that is, the I and You designated in a statement) is through being mobilized in the passage of the Third Space, 'which represents both the *general* conditions of language, and the *specific* implication of the utterance' (Bhabha, 1994: 37 – emphasis mine). In other words, the linguistic liminality of the Third Space is an area where neither the general nor the specific hold sway, but any symbolic, cultural or linguistic interpretation is an 'ambivalent' process that needs to be negotiated between the two.

Bhabha appears to be strongly influenced by the work of the Lithuanian philosopher Emmanuel Lévinas, who, following his experience as a prisoner during World War II, was keen to develop an anti-universalist and non-prescriptive ethics derived from a respect and responsibility for the Other. He became disillusioned with the dialectical and ontological nature of Hegelian philosophy, which saw reality as separated by sharp edges and ordered into hierarchical categories. He saw how this philosophical position could validate a political ideology like fascism. Instead he advocated an understanding of reality based on face-to-face encounter, whereby the essential unknowability of the Other is affirmed and respected. According to this world view, whenever we encounter the Other – another individual, another culture, even God – we attempt to define that encounter for ourselves, for our own consumption. For Lévinas, this attempted definition represents the Said (Lévinas, 1969). The Said strives for universality and solidity. But the nature of speech and language is that it is fluid and unstable, and the Other is an unknowable mystery. Therefore our striving for complete definition always falls short. This is the Saying. There is always a residue of the Other that resists the Said, but this relationship between definition and the attempt to define is itself a fluid one; a to-and-fro conversation that hopefully becomes a dialogue.

The erosion of national and cultural identity caused in the last twenty years by the upheaval of so many of the world's populations has also been instrumental in causing a transitional feeling in many of our cities. Leonie Sandercock identifies a fundamental ambivalence about these 'post-colonial' times. Are we living in a post-colonial era, she asks, characterized by a rejection of racism and ethnic stereotyping and an embracing of plurality, diversity and equality? Or is the spirit of colonialism still lurking within our supposedly more tolerant and diverse cities? She finds plenty of evidence to support the latter view, giving examples of fortified zoning against the poor and the migrant in northern US cities, São Paulo, and Cape Town (Sandercock, 2003: 115–22) as well as the rise of the far right in European countries such as the UK, France, Denmark and the Netherlands (Sandercock, 2003: 22). Previously dominant cultural discourses are being eroded and adapted by 'insurgent discourses' (Sandercock, 1998: 129) emanating from newly confident and insistent groups that were previously marginalized. Insurgent discourses are those stories and practices of planning and civil society that emerge from outside the control or influence of the state and represent the perspectives of disempowered communities. They also acknowledge 'the politics of difference ... a belief in inclusive democracy ... and the diverse claims of social justice' (Sandercock, 1998: 44).

The location of these new discourses is often from what Sandercock calls the 'Voices from the Borderlands'; those already living in the marginal spaces of our globe who have been uprooted or have chosen to settle in host urban spaces that would often prefer not to acknowledge their presence. These voices belong to women, people of colour, gay and lesbian communities, those of mixed ethnic heritage, children, the elderly, the poor and homeless, those living with physical or mental disability; in other words, any group whose experience has been 'marginalized, displaced, oppressed or dominated' (Sandercock, 1998: 110).

The ambivalence and instability caused by the enunciation of experiences and identities from insurgent practices and borderland voices has created the conditions necessary for the growth of hybridity; the fusion of identity and practice between old and new, colonizers and colonized, Occident and Orient. Within our postmodern culture, we now have stories, theories, cultures and urban spaces that are fusions of gender, sexuality and different degrees of mobility as well as race, culture and ethnic identity.

Some Examples of Entering the Third Space

We now explore a little further what it means to leave the confined 'space' of a colonial past and enter into a Third Space that is controlled by neither a colonial power nor a mythic traditionalist identity (both of which are predicated on notions of pure identity). This will be done with reference to new understandings of 'being at home' and examples of hybrid literary protagonists from US and UK literature. It will also feature an exploration of black British Christian experience and identity in urban Britain.

Womanist writer bell hooks (Gloria Watkins) powerfully redefines the concept of home from the perspective of post-colonialism. 'Home' for her is no longer a precise geographical location, but a non-physical space, liberated from any constraints of spatiality or culture. It is the space of emotional and intellectual freedom in which she can feel empowered to be what she feels called to be; a new identity forged from various different aspects of her personal past, the history of her gender and (African-American) people, and also created by the opportunities of the present – especially education and a degree of political tolerance (hooks, 1990). In terms reminiscent of Ferdinand Tönnies and his sociological categories of *Gemeinschaft* (the socially and geographically restrictive but supportive relationships of the agrarian or village community) and *Gesellschaft* (the more liberating but anonymous associations available in the city) hooks refers to the freedom encountered in her journey away from her Southern roots in Kentucky to the University of Wisconsin and then on to the University of California. She is currently Professor of English at City College in New York. This newfound freedom she attributes to her willingness to be flexible and adaptable to new opportunities without losing her sense of who she is and the importance of re-engaging with a past that never forgets previous injustice and exploitation, but also refuses to be bound by it.

Similar stories of personal journeys are to be found in examples of fictional protagonists in post-colonial literature, such as Toni Harrison's *Beloved* and Salman Rushdie's *Satanic Verses*, where there emerges what Bhabha calls the 'unhomely' moment (1994: 9), when identities that have been imposed by oppressing ideologies are transformed either through pain or subversion. What these protagonists had once called 'home' in both the physical and cultural sense is made strange by changes in political and identity consciousness, a process that Bhabha calls the 'postcolonial condition' (1994: 9).

Toni Morrison's *Beloved* (1987) is set in Ohio in 1873, with flashbacks to Kentucky in the 1850s, just as the era of slavery is coming to a close. Sethe, a mother accused of murdering her daughter, is incarcerated in a punishment home, 124 Bluestone Road, with its 'one high, mean window'. The motivation for her infanticide many years before is described as a desperate act of rebellion and resistance against the slavery system; an act against the master's property and his surplus profits. In an even more desperate sense, the murder is a way for the mother to reclaim the killed infant as her own. Through the haunting by her murdered daughter, Beloved, who has come to free herself of the violence and stigma attached to the conditions of her death, Sethe is awakened to her own fate as a projected-upon victim of her oppressor's racist fears and anxieties and the destructive madness contained within it. Through a painful and fragmented, but ultimately healing, dialogue between herself, her surviving daughter Denver, and her dead daughter Beloved, Sethe comes to understanding that they are all beloved – they can be at home with themselves as women of immense value and dignity while at the same time journeying away from the mad 'home' of the oppressors' labelling.

Salman Rushdie's' *Satanic Verses* (1988) revolves around the daily lives of a collection of fantastical and deliberately emblematic figures that exist within a stylized contemporary East End of London, with its large Indian-Pakistani-Bangladeshi Muslim community. All these figures are semi-mythical and protean, enfleshing the processes of identity change brought about by migration and the coexistence of multiple cultures and histories within the post-colonial 'melting pot' of a global city like London. The story's main protagonist is Saladin Chamcha, a London-based voiceover artist who has turned into a goat. He is caught between the advice of his landlady Hind, who eats the dishes of both Kashmir and Lucknow (that is, from regions of both Pakistan and India) and extols the virtues of gastronomic pluralism via her increasingly large frame, and his landlord Sufyan, who represents the voice of secular metropolitanism. His advice to his tenant Saladin offers him the classical contrast between Lucretius and Ovid that Bhabha describes thus: '… the problem consists in whether the crossing of cultural frontiers permits freedom from the essence of the self (Lucretius), or whether, like wax, migration only changes the surface of the soul, preserving identity under its protean forms (Ovid)' (1994: 224).

The problem for post-colonial migrants can be summarized as a 'survival' based on 'living in the interstices of a nationalist atavism and a postcolonial assimilation' (Bhabha, 1994: 224). Hybridity, in Rushdie's novel, is therefore seen as an act of survival (although more comically represented than the harrowing scenario presented by Morrison's *Beloved*). However there is a further dimension to this discussion of hybridity, illustrated by the real-life twist following the publication of Rushdie's novel. Following the denunciation of the novel as blasphemous by some sections of the Muslim global community, and the subsequent fatwa issued by the Iranian supreme leader, Ayatollah Khomeini, condemning Rushdie to death in February 1989, some commentators suggested that hybridity is, of itself, blasphemous. In his attempt to want to escape the overwhelming presence of his landlady Hind, Chamcha is guilty of the sin of 'deracination' – literally, the desire to uproot oneself and enjoy the freedom of a new identity, a theme that is constantly reiterated in the novel. The main sin from the perspective of those keen to uphold religious and cultural purity, especially in situations of diaspora, is to allow the purity of tradition to be overwhelmed or alienated by the act of translation into other cultural idioms. This act of translation makes contingent and indeterminate the institutions (such as religious traditions) that express and embody the 'shared standpoint of the community, its traditions of belief and enquiry' (Bhabha, 1994: 225).

These examples from literature throw up two main activities associated with hybridity that we will explore in more detail later when we look at the role of the church in postmodern urban contexts. These are the interlinked tasks of negotiation and translation.

Negotiation and Translation in Third Space Thinking

By *translation*, Bhabha refers to a new process of understanding history. Under 'metanarratives' such as colonialism, Marxism and global capitalism, history is understood to be rolled out to a preordained masterplan – what Bhabha calls the 'pure teleology of analysis' (1994: 27). With the partial collapse of these metanarratives, Bhabha believes that history is now allowed to unfold in an open-ended and non-teleological way by opening up what he calls a 'space of translation: a place of hybridity ... where the construction of a political object that is new, neither the one or the other, properly alienates our political expectations, and changes ... the very forms of our recognition of the moment of politics.' In memorable language, he says: 'The language of critique is effective not because it keeps forever separate the terms of the master and the slave, the mercantilist and the Marxist, but to the extent to which it overcomes the given grounds of opposition ...' (Bhabha, 1994: 25).

The main activity of this translation is *negotiation*, whereby antagonistic or contradictory elements are brought together, not in order to negate one another, but are negotiated through agonistic but also pragmatic discourses that will lead to new hybrid discourses and identities. This idea owes an obvious debt to G.W.F. Hegel's concept of the dialectical process by which ideas emerge and develop, in which a *thesis* is opposed by an *antithesis*, with the resulting consensus between them being labelled the *synthesis*. Bhabha's refinement is to see negotiation as a counter-hegemonic process against the static readings of history that Marxism derived from Hegel, which saw synthesis as a once-and-for-all event within human history and the eventual downfall of capitalism. Bhabha suggests instead that negotiation is a continuous process of micro-adjustment that treats even syntheses as being no less fluid and provisional than the original positions they seem to reconcile.

An example of this process is the work of British black theologian Robert Beckford, who as a second generation member of the Black Pentecostal Church is aware of a number of influences that have shaped his identity and world view. Within the Afro-Caribbean Christian diaspora of which Beckford is part (his parents immigrated to the UK from Jamaica in the 1950s) will be the influence of African religious culture brought to Jamaica by the African slaves. Jamaica was then subjected to the European influence of white missionaries in the eighteenth to mid-nineteenth centuries. Then, towards the end of the nineteenth and the start of the twentieth centuries, Jamaica and other Caribbean islands were strongly influenced by Black and White Pentecostal movements from America. In Beckford's view this produces a tension within Black Pentecostalism between the liberative elements of Pentecostal worship, with its roots in African worship of the Spirit, and the culturally white elements that still exist within it, such as references to 'white' being the state of sinlessness within worship. (However, second and third generation Black Christians have now moved away from the pictures of the blue-eyed Christ their parents had on the walls.)

This fluidity of identity finds its parallels within Beckford's own experiences of the labelling he has received growing up in the UK. 'On my British birth certificate, I am defined as a "Jamaican boy". In my junior school reports, I am described as "West Indian" and in my secondary school reports, "Afro-Caribbean". As an undergraduate I called myself, "Black British".' (Beckford, 2000: 20)

He refers to these parallel shifts within the identity of the Black Pentecostal church and his own identity as black British as a process of *mobilization*, namely phases in which black communities in Britain have had to adapt to living in a society in which the host community has not welcomed them. In this process of mobilization, Beckford sees the Black Pentecostal church as 'an arena in which new ethnicity is worked out, as new generations determine what it means to belong, based on new presuppositions about being Black' (2000: 20). Because there is a spectrum of thinking across Black Pentecostal churches on this issue, he implies that not all Black Pentecostal churches have yet become such arenas. For Beckford, and others of his generation, the key question for Black Pentecostals is the extent to which it is possible to be Christian and black in a properly owned, post-colonial sense. That ontological essence of black identity is contained within the Rastafari concept of *dread*, a multi-level concept that functions across culture, politics, language and spirituality. One of the main understandings of dread is, in Beckford's formulation, 'the Black experience of finding one's "true" identity, consciousness and place in the world'. For Beckford, dread is one of the foundations for constructing a liberation theology for black British Christians, based on a hybrid identity of dread and Pentecostal Christianity. He acknowledges the difficulties in doing this (not least cultural difficulties Black Pentecostals would have with the use of the 'holy herb' and the idea of the deity of Selassie). But there are also many points of connection and overlap in terms of history, 'inaugurated eschatology' and being energized by the Spirit of God (2000: 177). For him, the process by which he constructs an identity for himself, and also a political theology for black British Christians, is a fluid but proactive one; 'a holding in creative dialogue the tension between Christian and ethnic identity so that neither is submerged beneath the other'. This is the painful, but subtle and ultimately rewarding task of hybridity – a holding together and integration of different strands to create an empowered and countercultural identity, rather than a denial or fragmentation of essential parts of one's identity and heritage. Beckford gently chides Pentecostal churches for, by and large, not having the courage to integrate these two dimensions into a creative third possibility. In their worship, the liberative content of the working of the Spirit, powerfully expressed within music, prayer and teaching is held within the safe confines of the church. It seldom moves beyond the walls of the church to provide an empowering critique for black people outside, which is why some black sections of the community perceive the church as a conservative force of quietism in the face of ongoing hostility and racism within British society.

Within Bhabha's ideas of translation and negotiation I suggest that Beckford sees Black Pentecostal churches as possible arenas where debate can be mobilized about the new empowered ethnicity that bridges more confidently and assertively to British society. This mobilization of debate and praxis (translation) is negotiated through the use of dread philosophy and identity with similarly liberative elements within Black Pentecostal Christianity.

Beckford's case study represents a series of events in personal and social history of a type that Bhabha calls the 'hybrid moment of political change' (1994: 28). In another example, Bhabha references the work of British sociologist Stuart Hall, who proposed an interesting interpretation of what happened to the British Labour movement after the national miner's strike of 1984–85. It was an emblematic struggle, portrayed as the defeat of an Old Labour nationalized industry by the force of the neoliberal Market which epitomized the political economy of Margaret Thatcher's Conservative government. It was also portrayed as the death of a certain type of male-dominated, white working-class culture and identity. According to Hall, there was a subsequent attempt to produce an alliance of progressive forces ranged across 'a range of class, culture and occupational forces' that no longer required 'a unifying sense of class for itself' (Hall, 1987). This new network reflected a counter-hegemonic power bloc that moved beyond the traditional Labour Party image based on white, male, working-class and trade-union identities to create an alternative political cartel based on the experiences of unemployed, male and female semi-skilled and unskilled part-time workers, and black citizens. The variety of voices emerging as an alternative to the predominant hegemony of the time represented the fragmentation of class and cultural identity in postcolonial Britain. Hall saw this moment as the time to try to create a collective will based on new forms of identification and belonging. History shows that such an alliance never formally emerged as an effective political alternative to traditional industrial socialism, a fact that was doubtless becoming obvious in the early 1990s at the time that Bhabha wrote *Location of Culture*.

The rather complex point that Bhabha makes from this example is that the messiness of the counter-hegemonic power bloc means it will never achieve the cohesiveness of hard-edged opposition to the hegemonic tradition. Rather, the messiness and difficulty involved in creating new alliances based on fragmented constituencies represents of itself the struggle to judge and identify 'the political space in its enunciation', comprised as it is of 'split subjects and differentiated social movements' (Bhabha, 1994: 31). Bhabha appears to be saying that, in effect, the medium is the message. The Third Space that allows for the emergence of hybrid forms through the activities of translation and negotiation is not especially open to teleological analysis. Those looking for straightforward solutions or alternatives to complex problems will be disappointed. The Third Space is, in its essence, epistemologically unstable and politically enigmatic, not open to dissection by the Enlightenment inheritance and its rationalism. If it were such, it would not be able to produce the necessary imagination and impetus by which to critique the existing power structures and open up possibilities based on new methodologies and the mixing of identities. Hybridity is thus, in Bhabha's words, more 'interrogatory' than strategic, a point amplified (as we shall see later) in the difficulty encountered by the disciplines of both community development and political science when it comes to actually describing *how* hybridity is sustainable as a viable long-term alternative to existing hegemonies. Attempts to build coherent political and community-development planning programmes on the basis of hybridity and multi-discourse politics are notoriously difficult.

However, the significance of interrogation (that is, asking the right questions and thus creating space for new possibilities) should not be minimized. The interrogatory nature of Third Space post-colonial epistemology is part of the performativity that is required of the church and theology if it is to engage more coherently with the complexity of postmodern urban space and civil society. We shall explore these issues in greater depth in Part 2.

Conclusion

Bhabha's endorsement of Third Space theory and hybridity is not without its critics. Kraniauskas (2000) for example, accuses Bhabha of applying too much of a Freudian and linguistic reading to ideas of post-colonial disruption of modernism, whereby that which is repressed (the Other) returns to 'haunt' the conscious rational aspect of culture. This robs hybridity of the necessary political intentionality it needs if it is to really change structures for the better. Jan Pieterse (1995) points out that many hybridities end up simply reinforcing the power of the hegemony by 'assimilating' themselves to the prevailing power structures. And Bhabha himself has come in for criticism for his elitist perspective on hybridity in which he is likened to a 'cosmopolitan' as part of a group of Third World diasporic intellectuals who consume global culture at a rarefied level that tends to minimize the suffering of those caught at the sharp end of migratory experience (Friedman, 1997).

However, despite these criticisms, I would still argue for the centrality of Third Space hybridity thinking within postmodern ways of looking at the urban and political world in which we live. As a way of summing up this opening chapter on the origins and nature of Third Space hybridity, I would like to amplify three themes that have emerged during the course of the discussion.

The first is to re-emphasize the close connections between the concepts of the Third Space and hybridity. The Third Space of enunciation represents the entry into colonial discourse of post-colonial experience. In seeking to express its essential character, the Other rejects both the static labelling by the colonial power (dealing in mythic absolutes) of an inferior or defective culture in need of enlightenment, and the traditionalist agenda of a return to a pure culture. It also, in passing, rejects the liberal agenda of multiculturalism, which still seeks to define the experience of others on their behalf, albeit from the perspective of a more liberal social agenda. The interruption of the stately flow of myth, stereotype and enlightened social policy by the voices of those liberating themselves from the colonial past creates an unstable but potentially creative space – a Third Space. This space emerges through acts of negotiation and translation by which new hybridities emerge and existing hybridities are affirmed. It is *this* space, rather than the space on the binary poles of the One vs. the Other (for example the Colonizer or the Colonized, the Oppressor or the Victim) that, in Bhabha's words, 'carries the burden of the meaning of culture' (1994: 34). Thus the concept of hybridity is closely aligned to the notion of Third Space, being both a consequence of it, but also the overall context within which a Third Space can operate.

A second theme that has emerged from this chapter is the recognition that the refusal of the Other to be labelled and controlled is for many in the world today a threat rather than an opportunity. This will be further elaborated in the next chapter, when we look at the concept of hybridity with respect to postmodern urbanization, but for now it seems important that we agree with Leonie Sandercock when she identifies the fear of the Other and the anxieties caused by rapid cultural and spatial change as the main cause of urban violence and segregation:

> The multi-cultural city/region is perceived … as more of a threat than an opportunity. The threats are multiple: psychological, economic, religious, cultural. It is a complicated experiencing of fear of 'the Other' alongside fear of losing one's job, fear of a whole way of life being eroded, fear of change itself.
>
> (Sandercock, 2003: 4)

The fear of the Other is the main pastoral problem she identifies in the postmodern city. It implies there will be difficulties in trying to create sustainable local civil societies and urban spaces where everyone has, in the words of Henri Lefebvre (1991–2005), 'the right to the city'. It is this pastoral problematic that is the entry point for the engagement and involvement of churches and other faith groups in postmodern urban space, while honestly acknowledging their own potential for creating social breakdown as well as social cohesion.

The final point I would like to express is the pervasiveness of the concept of hybridity as a universal condition that affects us all, regardless of our previous status as colonizers or colonized. *All* parties are changed by the post-colonial encounter with each other, a point made by Salman Rushdie himself in the aftermath of the furore caused by his novel *Satanic Verses*. Although written from the perspective of the 'migrant', and in particular British Muslims living in late 1980s Britain, '... the very experience of uprooting, disjuncture and metamorphosis (slow or rapid, painful or pleasurable) that is the migrant condition is ... a paradigmatic experience from which ... can be derived a metaphor for all humanity' (1991: 394). The point he is making is that even those communities stable and wealthy enough not to have to uproot themselves in search of work, or from fear of persecution or exploitation, are being changed radically by the forces of globalized immigration so as to feel 'the uprooting, disjuncture and metamorphosis' of their own cultural context.

Hybridity, the fusion of two or more identities into a new identity, is thus the cultural norm that informs all our identities as individuals and urban dwellers, and the spatial and political realities that shape our daily existence. As Rushdie says of *The Satanic Verses*, 'It celebrates hybridity, impurity, intermingling ... It is a love song to our mongrel selves' (1991: 394).

Chapter 2

The Hybrid City

At the end of the previous chapter I identified some of the dynamics of post-colonial culture; namely the emergence of the Other as the source of its own defining and enunciation; the potential for these voices to create alternative 'blocs' (which Bhabha refers to as 'counter-hegemonic') that radically question traditional hierarchies and perceived ways of understanding the world based on colonialism and other Enlightenment sources; and the alleged fear of the Other that now pervades post-colonial society as a counter-reaction to this new assertiveness on the part of the previously dispossessed. We concluded with Rushdie's striking assertion that due to the velocity of cultural change in the past thirty years, that all citizens of the West are strangers, or perhaps 'visitors', to their own understanding of culture and society. Familiar signposts reflecting cultural stability and unequivocal understandings of identity are dissolving, to be replaced by perceptions of identity that have to acknowledge understandings of hybridity and so-called impurity. Rushdie claims that, culturally at least, we are now all 'mongrels'. Whether we can learn to love ourselves as such we will leave for now as an open question.

It is now time to deepen our understandings of cultural hybridity by looking in more detail at how cities have evolved in the last thirty years. We will do this by looking at clusters of current thinking that can be characterized under four headings: Network City, Mongrel City, Bohemian City and Locally Liveable City. All four clusters are interconnected, and derive from the basic premise that economic globalization (namely the ability of late capitalism to harness communication and knowledge technologies to create a real-time utility within a networked global market) has powerfully influenced the function and form of cities.

The Network City

This concept is one that has emerged and become pervasive since the late 1980s, following important observations within the discipline of economic and geographic sociology, in particular the work of the neo-Marxist tradition as espoused by Manuel Castells, Saskia Sassen and David Harvey. Castells was one of the first researchers to link the emerging technology of the computer and then the internet (originally developed for the American defence industry) with emerging patterns of urban space and its function. He observed that the growing ability to transmit knowledge, innovation and information 'virtually' (that is, non-physically) in ever-increasing amounts and at greater speeds, was leading to the creation of clusters of specialized research and development industries, which he called *technopoles* (1989). As a

27

The Hybrid Church in the City

prime example of this concept, he describes the growth of the complex of computer technology and other hi-tech businesses on the edge of San Francisco in the early 1980s, which became known as Silicon Valley.

He observed three key facets of this new form of industrialization, which neo-Marxists began to label as post-Fordist. First, the juxtaposition of different industries in close proximity based on developing new knowledge and research allowed for creative synergy, and more effective sharing of ideas and knowledge, but in a way that preserved identity and intellectual property. (In other words, the phenomenon of clustering within manufacturing sectors, long observed in industrial societies, is now occurring between different sectors.)

Secondly, the choice of location on the edge of conurbations was cheaper and more efficient than locating in expensive and hard-to-access downtown areas that were also perceived as crime-ridden and dangerous. It increasingly met the lifestyle preferences of the new technical and managerial elite who developed these businesses, and eventually encouraged further growth of housing and amenities, such as leisure and shopping, that came to characterize a type of community that in the late 1980s was identified as Edge City (Garreau, 1991).

Thirdly, this Edge City location also allowed greater connectivity via airports and interstate highways with other emerging technopoles, both in the United States and globally.

As the intellectual and commercial value of this activity increased, so these new spatial processes became more widespread and pervasive. The most commercially viable processes of the new industrialism (namely research and development, financial investment, marketing etc.) became increasingly separated from the surrounding physical locations in which they chose to be placed. This was because the advantages of physical location were being increasingly diminished by the greater need for connectivity via the Network; namely the World Wide Web (since 1991). Technopoles, and the financial districts that supported them, could now communicate directly via satellites and underground cables that bypassed the need for national or local protocols. This direct and privileged form of communication also became synonymous with the increasingly fragmented and dislocated way the global market worked with respect to the production of ideas, goods and services. The linked-up and increasingly homogenized nature of the market now allowed strategic decisions taken within the citadels of research and financial power to be implemented anywhere in the globe where market conditions were most amenable – namely, efficient but flexible capacity at the most competitive price. Castells describes the process thus: 'Capital investment and the new service industry no longer depends on the characteristics of any specific location for the fulfilment of their fundamental goals.' Rather, businesses merely adopt 'the dynamics of information-gathering units while connecting their different functions to disparate spaces assigned to each task to be performed' (1989: 348).

Each part of the manufacturing process – conception of product idea, research and development, design and marketing, actual production and then distribution – is now a series of disaggregated processes controlled from command centres within post-industrial cities to occur in a variety of global settings according to the logic of the market.

The theme of the global city as the new node of connection (or command centre) within a global network is a seminal point of connection between the work of Sassen and Castells. Ed Soja identifies 21 cities, most of which are in the global South, that by 2000 had passed the ten-million-inhabitant mark (2000: 236). But he refers to them as megacities rather than global cities because he agrees with Sassen's definition of a global city (1991) as referring not to size but to role within the global economy. Global cities are those elite cities that have the critical mass of research, innovation and knowledge-based capital, backed up by control of the financial markets with the communications infrastructure, to process the trillions of dollars transacted daily on the global market. Sassen describes the four functions of the global city. First, they are highly concentrated command points in the organization of the world economy. Second, they are key locations for finance and specialized service firms, which have replaced manufacturing as the leading economic sectors. Third, they are sites of production, but chiefly the production of innovation in these leading sectors. Finally, they are the markets for the products and innovation that have been produced (1991: 3).

According to her criteria in the early 1990s, only three cities could be labelled as global: New York, London and Tokyo. Each city has become the nodal point of communication between the three main relays of the global market: North America, Europe and the Far East. As transactions pass through each city so they pass through the time zones of the world, thus enabling a continuous loop of investment, information, product innovation and knowledge to circulate globally.

Sassen points out that in many ways her description of a global city hasn't changed since the era of the Renaissance. But what clearly has changed is the intensity and velocity with which globalization processes occur. She also identifies the flexibility with which these global cities have had to restructure their function and spatiality within a short period of time, which has become the template that all cities who now wish to compete in the global economy need to fulfil. The role of the global city has shifted from being an industrialized city based on the exportation of manufactured products to a city based on the provision of what Sassen calls 'advanced services'. These include finance, real estate, consulting, legal services, advertising, design, marketing, public relations, security, information gathering and management of information systems, research and development and scientific innovation (1991: 11).

However, it is not only the purpose of the post-industrial city that is restructured. It is social space that is reconstructed as well. Castells identifies the process of physical disengagement from local space that occurs when the new urban elite (researchers, innovators, higher managers, commanders of networks, the nouveau riche) perceives that their priority is now to connect with the global network. 'The new professional managerial class colonizes exclusive spatial segments that connect one another across the city, the country and the world; they isolate themselves from the fragments of local societies.' (1989: 384)

Sassen describes some of the further implications of this selective disengagement, namely the processes of gentrification, which convert previously run-down areas close to the city centre into areas that meet the service needs of the better-off who use the city centre as a place of work, entertainment or, increasingly as we shall see later on, residential space:

The expansion of the high-income workforce, in conjunction with the emergence of new cultural forms in everyday living, has led to a process of high-income gentrification, which rests, in the last analysis, on the availability of a vast supply of low-wage workers ... High-income gentrification in the city ... is labour intensive. Renovation of townhouses and storefronts and designer furniture and woodwork all require workers directly and indirectly. Behind the gourmet food stores and speciality boutiques lies an organization of the work process that differs from that of the self-service supermarket and department store. High-income urban residences in luxury apartment buildings depend to a much larger extent on hired maintenance staff than do the less-urban homes of middle-level-income workers.

(1991: 279)

This breaking down of urban space into closely packed and divergent sectors of business activity represents a form of hybridity, but a hybridity based on service delivery. It is not a genuine mingling of cultures, classes, gender and age. Rather, some have argued that it represents a fragmentation and dislocation of urban spaces, and thus social space, into a mosaic of differentiated niches or experiences, which present a kaleidoscopic diversity and cultural 'buzz' only on the surface. Thus, for example, the hundred-mile continuous sprawl that is the city-region of Los Angeles is designated by Charles Jencks a *heteropolis* that contains eight million citizens, 18 urban village cores, 140 incorporated cities, 13 major ethnic groups and 86 languages (1996).

However, comprehensive ethnic mapping of Los Angeles and its districts carried out in the late 1990s emphasizes the fragmentation underpinning this heteropolis (for example, Waldinger and Bozorgmehr, 1996, Allen and Turner, 1997) and its intense polarizations of race, ethnicity and gender. For example, 88 per cent of all lawyers in Los Angeles are white and male. One in five of all private household servants come from one, small, Latin American country (El Salvador), while another third are black women. Fifty per cent of all factory assembly workers are Mexican women. Not surprisingly, the average earning power of different groups in Los Angeles also varies enormously. In 1990 an average worker from a Salvadorean or Guatemalan background earned about $22,000, while a Japanese earned $46,000 and a Russian earned over $50,000. Both of the latter two groups earned more than the average Anglo (that is, white English-speaking) immigrant (quoted from Soja, 2000: 288). This very sharply defined segregation of professional and economic roles along ethnic lines is referred to as 'niching' (Soja, 2000: 289). More tellingly perhaps, this economic and professional 'niching' in Los Angeles is replicated in its urban space. Some 54 per cent of whites, 40 per cent of African Americans, and 37 per cent of Latinos living in Los Angeles County in 1990 resided in areas dominated by their ethnic group (that is, in areas where that group represented 80 per cent of the population). This suggests that the surface diversity of Los Angeles masks a situation in which most ethnic groups are to some degree entrenched within ethnic enclaves. On the other hand, only 17 per cent of Asians lived in areas with 80 per cent or more of their ethnic group, making them the most dispersed section of the population in terms of urban geography, indicating relative success in dispersing away from ghettoized spaces and generating increased wealth.

The inequalities of income and quality of life generated within the Network City cited in the late 1980s and early 1990s, and perpetuated by fragmentation into distinct zones, continue to have an exacerbating effect in the twenty-first century. In their concept of the Splintered City, Graham and Marvin (2001) emphasize the power of physical and virtual infrastructure to increase polarization and subvert attempts at creating a more egalitarian urban society. For example:

> Whilst enormous investment is going into new optic fibre 'pipes' for the Internet, exponential increases in demand continually fill up any new space, creating Internet connection logjams. In response, companies like Cisco, which make the 'smart' routers and switches that organize flows on the Internet, are now devising ways of 'sifting' the most valued and important 'packets' of information from those that are deemed less important. The idea is that, in times of Internet congestion, the most valued 'packets' from the most profitable customers will be allowed to pass unhindered while the rest are blocked. Thus, beneath the rhetoric that the Internet is some egalitarian and democratic space, profound inequalities are being subtly and invisibly integrated into the very protocols that make it function.
>
> (2001: 4)

Conclusions

We have observed that the main themes associated with the Network City are those of hypermobility, flows and fragmentation. As cities strive to become more connected to the global network of investment, information and knowledge in order to become influential nodes or hubs of that network, they demand a flexibility and hypermobility of both goods and people to move to those parts of the network that are more productive. This is true of both managers and workers who follow investment trajectories around the globe. As cities become more embedded in the network, so it is necessary that cheap air travel and swift rail networks facilitate opportunities for synergetic meetings between cities. Castells memorably refers to these collective trajectories as 'space as flows', which in his opinion is gaining dominance over the traditional idea of urban space as a 'local place' that acts as a boundary of significance for human identity and activity. However, within the drastic restructuring required for cities to be globally competitive along the lines identified by Sassen and Graham and Marvin, it is being suggested that the internal networks within cities are also becoming splintered and fractured, thus reinforcing inequality along multiple socio-economic axes. Thus the Network City is also the Fractal City (see Soja, 2000: 265).

The significance of the Network City for the issue of hybridity is that it is the main driver behind the rapid and increased diversification of urban societies, producing Jencks's heteropolis. Some have questioned, however, the extent to which the increased plurality and diversity have been allowed to co-mingle, or whether it has stratified and fragmented urban society further.

The Mongrel City

In this section we shall be focusing on the writing of Leonie Sandercock, an Australian postmodern planner who has written extensively about the impact of global immigration on cities, and its implications for the cultural, social and political life of what she defines as the post-colonial society (2003: 5). Her two key books on these issues are *Towards Cosmopolis* (1998) and *Cosmopolis II: Mongrel Cities of the 21st Century* (2003).

In the first book, she attempts to redefine the purposes of the planning tradition by contrasting the paternalistic top-down methodology of planning through most of the twentieth century with a more fluid and partnership-based approach better suited to the postmodern city. In the modernist traditions, the planner was the 'expert', squeezing every citizen into housing schemes or homogenized urban spaces in the name of the common good (often expressing consciously or unconsciously a form of cultural imperialism – see Sandercock, 1998: 184; see also Young, 1995). In the postmodern, post-colonial city the role of the planner is, in Sandercock's view, to acknowledge and listen to the plurality of voices that now exist. She must then use her expertise as a tool at the disposal of processes that will lead to local civic cultures based on the recognition of difference within a framework of coalition politics to ensure basic norms of social justice. Part of the commitment to this 'politics of difference' (1998: 184) is a radical realignment of ideas about what is important about the city. It is not merely a capital-generating machine within a globally connected market. Rather, it is 'the city of memory, of desire, of spirit; the unruly city as opposed to the planners' dream of the rational city – a dream that came out of the social sciences with its social and spatial technologies of control' (1998: 207).

This is the basis of Sandercock's utopian vision of the post-colonial city as *cosmopolis*, the urban society that literally includes the world in all its ethnic and cultural diversity, and which is committed to recognizing that diversity within a pluralistic democracy, including the creation of public spaces where all feel safe and affirmed in their identity. The crucial difference between Sandercock's utopia and those physical, technocratic utopias envisaged by modernist planners is that Sandercock realizes that her perfect society will never be achieved. It can only ever be in the making. Cosmopolis is instead a commitment to an inclusive style of politics, and an educational process; an attitude of mind that is prepared to accept the existence of difference and the emergence of hybridity as a consequence of allowing the Other (that is, the global migrant) to share the same urban space. Sandercock describes her cosmopolis as 'my imagined Utopia, a construction site of the mind, a city/region in which there is a genuine connection with, and respect and space for, the cultural Other, and the possibility of working together on matters of common destiny, a recognition of intertwined fates' (1998: 125).

As its title suggests, *Cosmopolis II: Mongrel Cities of the 21st Century*, is a conscious sequel to the earlier book. In her introduction, Sandercock implies that the book has been written as a response to the events of 9/11, and the global fear of the Other or 'stranger in our midst' that has been stoked by responses to that event.

Recent visits to European cities have alerted her to 'rising levels of anxiety about immigration. Questions of tolerance and peaceful co-existence seem ever more urgent in what I am calling "the mongrel cities of the twenty-first century".' She explains her use of this startling adjective:

> I have appropriated 'mongrel' from Salman Rushdie (1991) and use it in same spirit as he does: as both provocation and term of approbation for the kinds of changes that are happening in cities the world over, as they become more multi-ethnic and multi-cultural. This book is a manifesto of sorts: a radical manifesto for twenty-first century cities.
>
> (2003: xiii)

She focuses, as a consequence, on practical issues of how cities face the 'operational challenges' of meeting this rising tide of fear, and what she sees as the pastoral imperative of how 'we stroppy strangers might live together in these cities without doing each other too much violence'. She also steps up her critique of the concepts of 'multiculturalism' and 'community' by asking whether they are part of the problem being faced by 'globalized localities', rather than the solution. She recounts case studies from a variety of global cities that she considers show good practice in this regard. For example, in Birmingham in the UK, the local city authority has created participatory networks of consultation on the future role of its multicultural communities, many of whom are still experiencing economic marginalization and rising gun crime. Part of the consultation involved a 'public confession' on the part of the local authority that its economic package in the 1980s had not 'provided a culturally inclusive representation of the city, which left many of its communities feeling invisible and resentful' (2003: 18). Other strategies she details include overhauling the planning system to weed out some of its discriminatory assumptions, supporting market and planning mechanisms that promote indigenous business, and initiating intercultural dialogues that address fears and anxieties as well as social needs and material conflicts (2003: 133).

A main concern of Sandercock's two books is therefore to address directly the 'backlash' created by the shifts in cities away from fixed and homogeneous identities to increasingly diverse and hybrid ones. Some of the case studies she offers are more convincing than others. However, one of the strengths of her first book is the way she describes the experiences of being hybrid citizens. These new hybrid identities emerge from the 'voices from the borderlands' – namely those who have been 'marginalized, displaced, oppressed or dominated' (1998: 110), and who provide an alternative way of reading the social and cultural processes of the city, especially when it comes to identity and difference. Sandercock chooses writers like bell hooks, Gloria Anzaldúa, Cornel West and Guillermo Gómez-Peña, whom she says 'choose to celebrate, rather than lament their position on the margin or the borderlands – a part-physical, part-metaphorical territory' (1998: 111).

For example, Gloria Anzaldúa is a Mexican-American woman of Indian descent who died in her early sixties in 2004. She was a poet, storyteller, children's author and academic who explored what she described as a new *mestiza* consciousness that is 'shaped by cultural collision, forged out of mental and emotional states of perplexity and confusion' (Sandercock, 1998: 113). She defined herself as a woman who constantly crossed borders not only in the geographical sense (as when she visited her family in the impoverished Mexican communities living just across the border in the United States) but also in the sense of class, race, sexuality and culture as a lesbian woman of colour.

Crucially she described herself as developing a 'tolerance for ambiguity' that was willing and able to transcend duality by working with the tensions within all these different elements, even though some of the memories of racism and systemic prejudice she carried were very painful, not least the way 'the white teachers used to punish us for being Mexican' (quoted Sandercock, 1998: 113). At great personal cost, she saw her role as not walking away from the ongoing racism and sexism bred by ignorance or wilful prejudice that she encountered daily and which others within the feminist movement experienced as intolerable. She coined the idea of herself as a *nepantlera* (from the Nahuatl word *nepantla*, meaning 'at the margin' or 'between two worlds'), a new kind of visionary cultural worker whose role is to move within and among multiple worlds, and in using this movement, to transform them. Her methodology was, according to a posthumous biographer, 'to listen carefully to all parties and revealing the flaws in all forms of group-thinking, she ... attempted to create broader, more inclusive communities' (Keating, 2004). Key to resisting all forms of rigid labels and categories was the political task of developing new alliances and identities based on affinity, which she called, just before her death, the 'new tribalism'.

Another Mexican-American writer and performance artist, Guillermo Gómez-Peña, similarly refers to the weariness of constantly travelling across dual histories, languages and cultural identities, but is he also committed to creating 'alternative cartographies' based on experimental, multifocal and hybrid visions and realities (see Sandercock, 1998: 114). The following extract from a performance at a theatre in Berlin featured Gómez-Peña in the following theatrical guise:

> Gómez-Peña, 'El Mad Mex', wore a costume that was a mixture of an exaggerated version of an Aztec warrior and various symbols of global pop culture; one arm was encased in a plastic brace covered with the icons of the Power Rangers. At one point he put on boxing gloves, one fist adorned with the American flag, the other with the Mexican flag, and proceeded to land blows from each side against his head repeatedly.
>
> (Shapins, 2003)

Sandercock's 'voices from the borderlands' concept, with its emphasis on the role of the immigrant as the bearer of new experimental and hybrid identities, has echoes in the work of Papastergiadis (2000) on the varying responses of diasporic communities as they adapt to living in host countries.

Sandercock's writing therefore emphasizes the growth of hybrid cities, and starkly states that in her opinion there is no turning back, or hiding, from this trend (2003: 127). As we have seen, she considerably toughens her rhetoric on the growth of fear in wider society, and mistrust of the Other. But arguably, her cosmopolis still works powerfully as an activating concept rather than a practical guide. Critics of her work accuse her of occasional whimsy and somewhat naive theorizing. A depressing feature of her case studies of practical experiments in multiracial and multi-ethnic coalitions is that they are almost all short lived, a fact she herself acknowledges (1998: 157). However, her vision of the hybrid (or mongrel) city emerging from the collapsing colonial order at least acknowledges the importance and possibility of change into new cultural identities and political processes (particularly at community level) that involve creative working between different sectors of the urban tapestry, and across disciplines.

The New Bohemian City

This complex of ideas about the nature of the postmodern, post-industrial city is closely related to those theories concerning the Network City. It refers to the way that many of the industrial cities of the nineteenth and twentieth centuries in the West have had to reinvent themselves in order to capture a market share of the new global market now dealing primarily in knowledge, information and investment. But it also involves a massive rebranding exercise based not just on traditional boosterism and marketing, but a whole strategy that revolves around cultural and architectural plans designed to send out a message that the city in question is a tolerant, convenient, but also exciting and pleasantly countercultural environment in which to live, work and play. The main market for this rebranding is not only global tourism (an increasingly important dividend to be gathered), but the young professional researchers, designers and managers (identified by Richard Florida [2002] as the *new bohos*, or bohemians) that a city needs to boast as a resource to attract the right kind of investment. The profile of these people is typically newly graduated or qualified; for example, there is the *super-creative core* made up of those engaged in computers, mathematics, architecture, engineering, social sciences, arts, design, entertainment, sport and media, and a *creative class* made up of the managers of business and financial operations, legal, healthcare and high-end sales (Florida, 2002: 328). These types of people will typically delay starting families until their late twenties or early thirties in order to be flexible enough to move where the market dictates. The reward for this flexibility is a high disposable income, which will be spent accessing the new urban lifestyle in the postmodern city, revolving around retailing, entertainment and culture – aspects that in some quarters are considered to define the *city of liveability*. The combination of these factors is perceived by some to run the danger of producing a synthetic city; a cultural and entertainment playground primarily for the new urban elite that offers a standardized and sanitized version of what cities should be. This has been called the *city lite* – 'lite' being the advertising moniker for something that approximates to an original product (for example, beer or mayonnaise) but with the unhealthy bits taken out (see Bender, 1996). The implication is that smart, busy people with active lifestyles will buy these products because of the need to present themselves as slim and in control (and therefore employable and desirable) citizens.

We will now unpack some of the wider significance of boosterism, the city of liveability, and city lite for understandings of hybridity, before finishing with a neo-imperialistic critique that questions some of the assumptions contained within these clusters of ideas about the nature of post-industrial urban society.

Boosterism is not a new concept. The term was first popularized in the satirical novels of Sinclair Lewis, which revolve around the delusions of grandeur held by local politicians within small Mid-Western towns, as epitomized in books such as *Main Street* (1920) and *Babbitt* (1922) – though the activity, if not the word, dates back to the later decades of the nineteenth century. It gained a new lease of life in the United States in the land development speculation that drove the massive expansion of cities such as Los Angeles in the post-war boom of the 1950s. However, the concept of boosterism emerged again during the 1980s and 1990s, when it became allied to a new form of local municipal governance that has consciously sought to work in partnership with private business in order to provide the right cultural, housing and tax environments by which to attract global and regional inward investment for the physical regeneration of declining city environments (for instance, see Peck and Ward, 2002). David Harvey wrote a seminal account of these processes in an article entitled 'From Managerialism to Entrepreneurialism: The Transformation in Urban Governance in Late Capitalism' in 1989. He describes how the 'managerial' approach of city authorities in the 1960s gave way to 'entrepreneurial' forms in the 1970s and 1980s in both the UK and the United States. By managerialism in a UK perspective, he refers to the role played by the local authority in implementing central government directives on regional development designed to secure full employment in the manufacturing sector. These included inducements in the form of grants, free loans and publicly subsidized infrastructure such as industrial estates. Harvey, from his neo-Marxist perspective, refers to this as a Fordist-Keynesian regime of capital accumulation (1989: 8).

However, key economic and political events in the 1970s forced local municipal authorities to rethink radically this rather passive strategy. These events included 'deindustrialization, widespread and seemingly structural unemployment, fiscal austerity at both the national and local levels'. But what is more significant is the economic pressure for local authorities to shift to a more entrepreneurial model, regardless of their own political persuasion. According to Harvey, 'The greater emphasis on local action to combat these ills also seems to have something to do with the declining powers of the nation state to control multi-national money flows, so that investment increasingly takes the form of a negotiation between international finance capital and local powers doing the best they can to maximize the attractiveness of the local site as a *lure* for capitalist development' (1989: 10, emphasis mine). What he is describing is the symbiotic economic relationship between the local geographical space (that is, a city and its region) and the flow of the global market (to return to Castells's theory).

Harvey goes on to describe four ways in which local municipal authorities have entered into economic partnership with global business. First is in the form of public and private investments in physical and social infrastructures that strengthen the economic base of the city region as an exporter of goods and services. This will be facilitated by the usual local subsidies, including tax breaks, cheap credit and procurement of sites. It will also be backed up by the qualities, quantities and costs of the local labour supply. As well as a large pool of qualified professionals, international firms are also looking for low-cost services to support their employees. As Harvey ominously suggests, 'Local costs can most easily be controlled when local replaces national collective bargaining and when local governments and other large institutions, like hospitals and universities, lead the way with reductions in real wages and benefits' (1989:12).

A second way to attract global investment is to boost the consumer potential of a city region, which becomes a much more complex task than simply building more shopping malls. Greater incentives for consumption by the discerning citizen with disposable income to burn is increasingly seen as dependent on a much larger package that focuses on the 'quality of life'. Harvey gives a long list that is worth quoting in full because of its implications for the New Boho City of Liveability, which we will explore in a moment:

> Gentrification, cultural innovation and physical upgrading of the urban environment (including the turn to postmodernist styles of architecture and urban design), consumer attractions (sports stadia, convention and shopping centres, marinas, exotic eating places) and entertainment (the organization of urban spectacles on a temporary or permanent basis), have all become much more prominent facets of strategies for urban regeneration. *Above all, the city has to appear as an innovative, exciting, creative and safe place to live or to visit, to play and consume in.*
> (Harvey, 1989: 14, emphasis mine)

Third, cities now have to provide the right infrastructure for high finance, government, and information gathering and processing (including the media). This will entail providing an efficient global communication system (including access to an international airport), sufficient office space, efficient internal and external distribution systems, and sufficient qualified support staff (for example, universities, but especially scientific research with strong commercial potential, business and law schools and media skills).

Finally, city regions still have a national or government-based redistribution role with regard to important contracts such as defence, health or education. The disciplines introduced by partnerships with private business can help make city regions more competitive and attractive to big government contracts through techniques relating to marketing strategies and business plans.

By way of illustration of the impact of these dynamics of municipal entrepreneurialism, Harvey describes the 'transformation' of his home town of Baltimore, which in the early 1970s was commonly described as 'the armpit of the east coast' (1989: 5). By the mid 1980s, however, Baltimore was appearing on the front cover of *Time* magazine under the title of 'renaissance city'. According to the article, it had shed its image of dreariness and impoverishment in favour of one reflecting a 'dynamic, go-getting city' (1989: 6). The *Sunday Times* in 1987, described the transformation in similarly glowing terms:

Baltimore, despite soaring unemployment, boldly turned its derelict harbour into a playground. Tourists meant shopping, catering and transport, this is turn meant construction, distribution and manufacturing – leading to more jobs, more residents, more activity. The decay of Baltimore slowed, halted then turned back. The harbour area is now among America's top tourist draws and urban unemployment is falling fast.

(quoted in Harvey, 1989: 8)

Harvey also credits this swift transformation with providing a stronger sense of place and local identity, and politically consolidating the power and influence of the local public-private partnership that brought the project into being.

However, there have been high costs to this transformation. It is the public sector that has absorbed much of the risk of the private capital investment, with the result that local services to the poor have often been cut back. This is reinforced by the fact that this major urban investment has failed to shift local unequal income distribution in any progressive way, since the majority of employment opportunities are low-skill, low-pay and insecure service-sector jobs. Manchester has undergone as dramatic a shift as Baltimore since the late 1980s in transforming itself from a declining *cottonopolis* (a city based on textiles and other heavy manufacturing industries) to an *ideopolis* (a city region whose capital is now predicated on the ability to create new knowledge, ideas and information; see Atherton, Baker and Graham in Graham and Rowlands, 2005: 69–74). We shall return to Manchester's urban renaissance in a moment, but some latest statistics from Manchester make sober reading and support Harvey's thesis on the social costs of the transformation. According to the Greater Manchester Low Pay Unit research summary for 2004, nearly one-third of all jobs advertised in the conurbation were connected with catering, cleaning, care work and shop work; jobs predominantly associated with female employment and low pay. Over 90 per cent of part-time jobs paid less than a couple with two children would receive in Income Support. More than 40 per cent of part-time jobs also paid insufficient to cover access to statutory sick and maternity pay, and did not entitle the worker to a state pension in older age. More than a third of all jobs in Manchester (full-time and well as part-time) paid less than £5.15 per hour. Equally poor quality-of-life indicators reinforce these poor economic indicators. For example, men still have an average life expectancy below 70 in the Manchester urban area, more than five-and-a-half years younger than the average for England and Wales. The infant mortality rate is nearly double the national average, death rates from heart disease and strokes are 90 per cent higher than national averages, and suicide rates are 60 per cent higher.

Harvey further points out that since all regional cities adopted this economic growth model during the 1980s, any competitive advantage has been nullified. This has led to catastrophic oversupply of consumer- and culture-led infrastructure in the United States, which one suspects will be followed in the UK, especially in northern English cities that are still struggling to negate the disproportionate 'global' pull of London and the South-east of England in terms of graduate recruitment and other forms of brain drain. As Harvey anticipated nearly twenty years ago, 'How many successful convention centres, sports stadia, Disney-worlds, harbour places and spectacular shopping malls can there be?' (1989: 57) These are high-risk projects that can easily fall on hard times, but as ever it will be local communities that disproportionately bear the economic and social cost. Thus Harvey, for one, is under no illusion that, behind the glittering façade of regenerated city-regions, plenty of rot lies, including increased impoverishment and social deterioration.

This analysis of the birth of Harvey's 'entrepreneurial' city allows us to move on to briefly describing the concepts of the new boho ideopolis and the city lite. The first nametag is a joining together of two concepts. The new bohemians (also known as the creative class) refers to a socio-economic category of new urban dwellers first identified by Richard Florida (see above). These dwellers are likely to be single or in childless partnerships, and will contain a high percentage of the gay and lesbian community. The significance of the creative class Florida has 'discovered' as an influential global subset is confirmed by Castells's work on the restructuring of employment hierarchies in the networked phase of late capitalism. Castells expands the classic Marxist formula based on those who control the means of production (bourgeoisie) and those whose labour is sold as a commodity (namely the workers or the proletariat). Within the post-industrial (or post-Fordist) city, these categories have been redefined, but are no less hierarchically ordered. Now at the top of the economic chain Castells identifies the *commanders* (those who decide and implement the strategic decision-making and planning) followed by the *researchers* (who provide the innovation in products and processes). Next come the *designers* (who adapt, package and target the innovation) and then the *integrators* (the middle management tier who manage the relationships between the decision, innovation, design and execution of the product). At the bottom of the hierarchy are the *operators* (those who are allowed to execute tasks under their own initiative and understanding) and the *operated* (those 'human robots' whose function it is to execute ancillary, preprogrammed tasks that have not been or cannot be automated) (1996: 259). Florida's concept of the creative class can probably be assumed to encompass the first three groups of Castells's scheme.

Having established this creative class as the new global elite, Florida then extrapolates the type of city it would like to live and work in. He creates a boho city index with which to measure a city's suitability for the new bohemian. The index includes such criteria of desirability as the number of patent applications per head of city population, the percentage of residents who are not categorized as 'white British', and the number of services provided to the gay and lesbian community in the city. Although his methodology contains some unexamined assumptions for which the empirical evidence is questionable, such as the apparent assumption that gays and lesbians are more likely to be creative than straight people, the clear implication of Florida's research is that if a city wants to be prominent in the league of global cities and thus have a competitive edge over similar cities in diverting inward investment, then it has to attract a critical mass of these significant global citizens.

The concept of the ideopolis is, as we have already seen, key to describing the shift from heavy manufacturing (the role of many regional cities and smaller towns in the UK for most of the nineteenth and twentieth centuries) to the production and consumption of knowledge and ideas at the turn of the twenty-first century. Ideopolis is an American concept based on an updated version of the Italian renaissance city-state (Westwood and Nathan 2002) which, in modern terms, could be described as sixteenth-century urban spaces of cutting-edge culture (especially art and architecture), ideas, inventions and economic growth fostered by global trade links. Ideopolis thinking stresses the importance of human capital in generating the necessary economic conditions to remain globally competitive, especially in terms of ideas, creativity, research and design. However, there are key infrastructures that need to be provided in order to encourage this human capital and to create a city 'where people want to live, to learn, to generate and exchange ideas and do business'. The following list was developed by the 'Core Cities Group' (a network of eight former industrialized English cities outside London) as a response to the concept of the ideopolis:

- effective communications and transport infrastructure, including international airport and IT connections
- a distinctive city centre, including strong architectural heritage and iconic new physical development
- nationally and internationally recognized facilities
- facilities for research, development and innovation involving good links between higher education and the commercial sector
- large numbers of highly skilled professionals and a well-educated work force
- an inclusive and diverse population
- a reputation for excellence in arts and culture, with supporting service sector
- good local governance and policy/political autonomy
- commitment to environmental responsibility and investment
- a good stock of high-quality residential options.

It so happened that when Richard Florida tested out his boho city index on cities in the UK in 2002, the city that had the highest ratio of research patents to head of gay population was Manchester; the implication he drew was that a large gay population was an indicator of a tolerant and liberal community, which made it more likely to attract the kind of creative people responsible for patent applications. One major reason for Manchester's pre-eminence on this index is its highly visible gay and lesbian quarter of pubs and clubs in a previously run-down area next to an industrial canal. This very small area (basically a pedestrianized street some 300 metres long) has acquired national recognition through being the setting of several TV dramas, which together with a highly successful annual Gay Pride week epitomizes this conflation of the new boho and the ideopolis. Manchester's current transformation from cottonopolis to ideopolis includes other classic ingredients first outlined by Harvey nearly twenty years ago and which he observed in his home city of Baltimore. I attempt to capture these shifts in an article written with other Manchester-based theologians:

[Ideopolis] means bidding farewell to the old industrial Manchester of factories and mills – a city built on manufacturing and production – and ushering in the brave new world of café-bars, nightclubs, huge retailing hubs, cultural and heritage industries, urban lifestyle apartments, university mergers attracting 74,000 fulltime students, cutting-edged research and small-business incubators. This is a city making its living through the thriving 'knowledge industries' and a 24/7 party culture, and representing a decisive shift from production to consumption. The attempt to create a city of 'liveability' based on cultural diversity, leisure and high-quality architecture and design thus reflects significant economic and urban shifts. 11 per cent of all jobs in Manchester are now retailing-based, with thousands more employed in bars, restaurants, hotels, cultural industries and fitness clubs. Sankey's Soap factory in Ancoats (once Manchester's industrial heartland) is now a state-of-the art dance club ... former factories are now desirable apartment blocks for young single professionals, named after that 1960s movie epitomizing urban chic, *La Dolce Vita*.

(Atherton, Baker and Graham, 2005: 72)

However, as we have seen, all that glisters is not gold, and significant sections of the Manchester community struggle to participate or reap any benefit from the new Manchester evolving from the developers' dust.

Nevertheless, the above description of the new bohemian/ideopolis does resonate with the last concept I want to explore in this section; that of the city lite. We have already briefly discussed the concept of lite as applied to food and drink products. Thomas Bender, a New York social historian, applies this brand indicator to cities, emphasizing the way the historic and cultural identities of cities (which helped define a unique sensibility and sense of polis) are now 'repackaged' as consumerist items offering an *ahistorical* experience based on safety, convenience and standardized elements for individuals to partake of. In a 1996 article for the *Los Angles Times* he traces the relationship of cities and their citizens throughout the last millennium and up to the present age, which he sees as radically discontinuous from what has gone on before:

For a millennium, cities have carried history and sustained our cultural traditions through their universities, museums and libraries and in their physical fabric, with its traces of social succession. 'In a city,' Lewis Mumford has written, 'time becomes visible.' The complexity of that history, like the social and physical complexity of the city more generally, nourishes the human spirit, even as it tries it. Life in the Lite City reveals no passage of time, no history. The City Lite does not age; it is consumed and replaced. It is any time and any place – it no longer holds culture nor provides an orientation to past and present for its residents.

(Bender, 1996, quoted in Soja: 2000, 247)

Despite a possible charge of elitism, and an overly nostalgic view of twentieth-century American cities, Bender's analogy is nevertheless a powerful critique that goes to the heart of the restructured city. In relation to our present emphasis on hybridity, it asks searching questions about the depth to which difference and hybridity are truly tolerated. Is the postcolonial city representing a genuine breaking of binary stereotypes into new and liberating identities, or is it merely a tourist package that conforms to the need to rebrand for the sake of global competitiveness? With that question hanging for the moment, I now turn to my last urban concept.

The Locally Liveable City

By way of contrast to some of the 'helicopter' views of the hybrid city offered in the above section, I want to focus on some important thinking from a UK context about the nature and purpose of the hybridity/multicultural agenda. This will focus on the work of Ash Amin from Durham University, who has reflected on the impact of the 'race riots' that occurred in some northern English UK towns in 2001, and the subsequent policy by the UK government to pursue a programme of 'social cohesion'. Amin is dismissive of this agenda, seeing within it some of the utopian elements within multiculturalism that claim it is possible to 'build' geographically local neighbourhoods based on discovering shared values and a shared sense of place (Amin, 2002). This is because the post-riot government report *Building Cohesive Communities* (2001) makes no reference to the impact of colonialism and globalization, both of which means that locally affective ties for immigrants will be problematic. Instead, the report calls for the creation of public spaces and mixed-tenure housing policies that will create a place-based urban civic culture that, in the words of Sandercock, will supposedly promote 'the freedom and pleasure of lingering, the serendipity of the chance encounter and the public awareness that these are shared spaces' (2003: 94).

However, what Amin characterizes as fear of change within disenfranchized white working-class communities too poor to move, and white flight by upwardly mobile working-class citizens into existing middle-class areas who are antagonistic to the presence of upwardly mobile ethnic-minority communities, also make it difficult for 'host' communities to sign up to socially cohesive local neighbourhoods (Amin, 2002: 2).

What Amin proposes instead is a more 'organic' approach to hybridity that not only prefers minimal government interference but has minimal expectations of the need to produce 'social cohesion' in the first place. He bases these radical thoughts on previous research undertaken by Martin Albrow in the south London borough of Tooting, which exemplified a 'situation of minimum levels of tolerable coexistence' between citizens of different religio-ethnic backgrounds. Rather than sharing a common sense of local space, people who happened to live and work in this borough simply went about their day-to-day lives, which, because of the highly globalized nature of this local space, often involved emotional and financial transactions across continents and generations. Albrow describes some of the fluid complexity he discovered in Tooting:

> Individuals with very different lifestyles and social networks can live in close proximity without untoward interference with each other. There is an old community for some, for others here is a new site for community which draws its

culture from India. For some, Tooting is a setting for a peer group leisure activity, for others it provides a place to sleep and access to London. It can be a spectacle for some, for others, the anticipation of a better, more multi-cultural community.

(Albrow, 1997: 51)

For Amin, an important difference between Tooting and Bradford (one of the cities caught up in the 2001 riots) is that the former is, on the whole, economically comfortable, without the 'dog-eat-dog' economic competition within ethnic communities for scraps of economic activity (such as taxi driving or fast food outlets) that occurs in deindustrialized towns like Bradford. The relative affluence of Tooting (so Albrow implies) allows its various citizens to consciously choose 'civil inattention and avoidance strategies' that at least set out to avoid friction rather than seek it. It is a much-diluted concept of social capital that goes directly against government assumptions and policy. Yet Amin can see the application of some of Tooting's experience to more economically marginalized multi-ethnic communities. He calls for an enhanced awareness of the significance of what he calls 'micro-publics', spaces of compulsory dialogue and prosaic negotiation where, in a sense, people have no option but to engage with citizens from different backgrounds.

He defines such 'sites' as the workplace, schools, colleges, youth centres, sports clubs, community centres, neighbourhood houses – and possibly spaces such as community gardens, childcare facilities, and neighbourhood watch schemes. This awareness of micro-publics needs to be fed into what Sandercock calls 'organizational and discursive strategies' at both community and national levels, since these sites will not automatically become sites of social inclusion. She offers some case studies from Birmingham and Vancouver to support Amin's thesis. But the thinking behind these examples is that, over time, these 'sites' acquire an everyday character that 'overcomes feelings of strangeness in the simple process of sharing tasks and comparing ways of doing things' (2003: 94). She supports Amin's call for a radical rethinking of those government-based social cohesion initiatives based on urban design and housing policy. Rather, the language of community cohesion needs to be reframed within understandings of 'local accommodation to difference' (2003: 96), and located in what Amin would call 'the city's micro-publics of banal multi-cultures' (2002: 13); in other words, building on what is already there, rather than trying to create something that may never exist.

Conclusion

Throughout the course of this chapter I have attempted to highlight different theories about the way cities have evolved and the way these theories have impinged on understandings of hybridity. Two of our clusters of theories have focused on economic globalization (the Network City) and its impact on social and cultural space (the New Bohemian City). We have suggested that despite the large increases in ethnic and cultural diversity brought to cities in recent times, the impact of these changes to move urban societies from monocultures to hybrid ones has been largely limited. The heteropolis (at least on US experience) is in fact a fragmented mosaic, with most diasporic communities living in neighbourhoods where those of the same ethnic, religious and cultural group are in the majority. Citizens also tend to work in professions sharply segregated along ethnic lines, referred to as 'niching'.

Meanwhile the New Bohemian City creates vibrant cultural quarters based on an apparent tolerance of difference and openness to new cultural forms. Thus Manchester has its gay and lesbian quarter, its Chinatown, its 'Curry Mile'. However, if the function of these areas is primarily economic and cultural, how deep does this celebration of diversity and difference go? Do these shifts represent a genuine hybridization of urban space, or are they simply part of a rebranding exercise – a product that enhances the global profile of the city in question and its attractiveness to a new urban elite.

The other two clusters of theories (the Mongrel City and the Locally Liveable City) attempt to represent a more street-level and unglamorous understanding of the role of hybridity in the 'mongrel' city, with its lack of pedigree and ethnic purity. Writers like Sandercock and Amin prefer to wrestle with the formidable but necessary practical steps that one needs to take in order to reduce fear and misunderstanding of the Other and allow a peaceful coexistence. This coexistence allows citizens to use the city in peace, and prosper according to their potential, which is the dream of all migrants and helps fuel the city's dynamism and creativity (Sandercock, 1998: 211). Using case studies, we have seen that a number of creative solutions are rehearsed, ranging from deliberately strategic coalitions (that is, local-authority driven) to more spontaneous ones. Almost all, however, are short lived or else are still at a fragile, experimental stage. The implication of Sandercock's cosmopolis reinforces this provisionality by stressing that, in seeking a perfect society, tolerance of ambiguity and a creative respect for difference is in fact an approach to life, not a physical place; 'it is only ever in the making.' Amin's thesis differs from Sandercock's work in that he seems to be arguing for an understanding of an emergence of hybridity on almost a daily, incremental basis. He wants to argue against the quick-fix, government-sponsored initiative in favour of something more sustainable and long term that has very the modest aims of demythologizing difference on the basis of normal interaction as a prerequisite for any deeper engagement between the different communities who share the same 'globalized locality'.

We can thus see that the business of understanding and negotiating difference in cities is complex and ambiguous. For me, it is beautifully summed up in a case study used by Jane Jacobs in her book *Edge of Empire* (1996). As her title suggests, Jacobs is interested in what she perceives to be the ongoing colonializing tendencies in the so-called post-colonial city; processes she refers to as neo-imperialism. One of the places she observes this process occurring is in the regentrification of Spitalfields in the East End of London. This has been brought about by the physical expansion of the City of London (London's global financial hub) and will require this area, which when she wrote was largely inhabited by Bengali businesses and street traders, to be transformed into 'Banglatown', a redeveloped quarter of smart Asian restaurants and fashion stores that nevertheless, via the use of heritage sites, tells the 'story' of the one of London's most historic market areas, stretching back to the Middle Ages.

The set of relationships involved in the creation of this new hybrid space are complex. The concept of Banglatown has not been foisted on an unwilling and impoverished diasporic community. Rather, the existing Bengali business network understood the inevitable nature of the transformation of their area and took the strategic decision to develop the Banglatown concept as a 'package' to put to the developers, thus ensuring that they had some control both financially and culturally over the way their community space developed in the future. As Jacobs reports, they 'actively engaged in elaborating essentialist constructions of identity through commodified systems in an attempt to wrest control of power and space' (1996: 71).

However, the key to their relationship with the City of London lies in the word 'essentialist'. In offering a 'tourist' version of their own culture that will not confront the visitor with any political or historical complexity about the Bengali diaspora and its colonial relationship with British culture, or the racism experienced by Bengalis in East London, the Bengali business community may have bought an important financial stake in the future, but at what cost? It could be an example of an entrepreneurial diasporic community deliberately readapting itself in a fully conscious relationship with the developers. Jacobs simply raises the question of whether this domesticated version of their culture represents a form of neo-imperialism; that is, the commodification of one culture by a dominant economic other. She offers another interpretation of what she calls 'the politics of place' that is unfolding in Spitalfields. 'Here a multiculturalism of convenience emerged based on a properly placed (that is, spatially segregated) Bengali community. Ordered and domesticated, the Bengali residents of Spitalfields could become a safe, present-day supplement to the narrative construction of Spitalfields as the emblematic place of an embracing, tolerant Englishness.' (1996: 71)

Since the time of Jacobs's analysis, the electoral ward of Spitalfields has been officially renamed 'Spitalfields and Banglatown', and at the 2001 census 68 per cent of the population were of Bangladeshi origin. The Baikashi Mela festival was established in 1998 to celebrate the Bangladeshi New Year, and is now London's biggest such event, bringing in large revenues to the community. Indeed, such is the wealth generated by such events that the money sent back to Sylhet, from which many British-based or -born families originate, has made it one of the richest cities in Bangladesh, with new shopping centres and other building projects funded by 'Londoni' money. The incorporation of Banglatown into the ward name, the wealth generated by vibrant tourism for both expatriate and native Bangladeshis, and the close ties it has developed between continents are all perhaps evidence that Jacobs's predictions ten years ago have been partially met. Bangladeshi identity has been integrated both spatially and politically into a part of England already suffused with countless other identities, to the apparent benefit of most who are engaged in it.

This example, and Jacobs's interpretation of it, reminds me of two contrasting theories of hybridity. One is the *bricolage* theory, which suggests that an artificially constructed hybridity has been based on the conscious selection of disparate cultures for some hoped-for artistic or political effect. It reflects, so its critics say, a consumerist approach to culture that often results in meaningless cultural overload. An example of this is John Hutnyk's critique of the regular World of Music and

Dance (WOMAD) festival, where he sees its focus on world music as an example of 'commercial aural-travel consumption' and its collections of 'representative musicians' assembled from the corners of the world as a late-twentieth-century version of the Great Exhibitions of the nineteenth century (Hutnyk, 2000).

This somewhat artificial concept of hybridity is also conveyed in Jacobs's phrase 'the multiculturalism of convenience' and the implication of her phrase is that this bricolage type of hybridity does not address the fundamental power equation located in that part of East London. The 'hybridity' that she observes is probably more likely to be a form of neo-colonialism whereby the Other is given a limited amount of expression, but is still ultimately defined by the host (or dominant) culture.

A more authentic form of hybridity is what Mikhail Bakhtin defines as 'organic hybridity' (1981: 360). Bakhtin locates his interpretation of organic hybridity within an historical understanding of the evolution of languages. The way language evolves proves that no culture is free of outside influence; all are the by-product of the cultural cross-fertilization that has accompanied all movements of people. While organic hybridity does not disrupt the sense and order of community in the same way as more intentional forms do (such as we saw in Chapter 1 with Beckford's work on Dread Pentecostalism) it is nevertheless an important 'creative storeroom' of images, words and ideas. Bakhtin calls these 'unconscious hybrids', saying that they are 'pregnant with potential' to create more authentic hybrid forms. For example, ten years after Jane Jacobs's survey of Banglatown, a more organic but far-reaching hybridization is beginning to emerge. This is the evolution of a form of English among young British Bangladeshis that is heavily influenced by Bengali, with elements of vocabulary rapidly moving into mainstream English across the country as well (for example, *nang*, meaning good, *creps*, meaning training shoes, and *skets*, meaning slippers).

It is perhaps too early to detect the real significance of this example of hybrid idiom. However, its importance to the post-7/7 landscape of multicultural Britain should not be underestimated. Some elements within the popular media are trying to polarize opinion about the identity of Islam and Muslims within Britain, in particular by portraying their religious identity as a reactionary and therefore dangerous force. The involuntary entering of Bengali vocabulary into mainstream English (albeit at the moment within media and youth culture) could be interpreted as a sign of growing confidence within the Bangladeshi diaspora that is both recognized and affirmed by elements of the 'host' culture. It also suggests that the Bangladeshi community is here to stay; they are a permanent diaspora whose presence is finally and irrevocably moving British culture into a more pluralized identity.

Chapter 3

Hybrid Civil Society and Hybrid Governance

My aim in this chapter is to explore further some of the implications of the urban shifts that we have observed in the previous chapter. We will now look at the way people relate to one another (sociology) and how diverse cities and societies should be governed (political philosophy and governance policies) in relation to understandings of hybridity.

The Language of Civil Society and Social Capital

Profound economic and political shifts that radically alter the way societies are structured have always produced deep questioning about the nature of human belonging and identity. The unparalleled changes to Western society wrought over a fifty-year period (roughly 1830–80) by the Industrial Revolution and the consequent birth of the industrial city gave birth to sociology and the social sciences. The observations of the impact of the change from an agrarian to an industrial society still hold tremendous resonance (as we shall see shortly). Now, as we enter into a new stage of human social reordering in the West (namely, the shift from an industrial to a post-industrial and increasingly globalized society) it is hardly surprising that there is renewed and intense speculation as to the way human beings relate to another at the local as well as global levels.

Much of this renewed discourse about human relationship in post-industrial, globalized communities is being couched in terms of civil society and social capital, so we should briefly look at some definitions. A common understanding of civil society is that it is another kind of Third Space – a space of human interaction that is not directly influenced by the state or the market. As Douglass and Friedmann express it, 'It is the society of households, family networks, civic and religious organizations and communities that are bound to each other primarily by shared histories, collective memories and cultural norms of reciprocity.' (1996: 2) This emphasis on 'shared histories, collective memories and cultural norms of reciprocity' is an often-cited and therefore influential definition. It is also possibly a conservative one, which stresses a view of community that is quite static, locally based and with strong moral overtones. One also wonders if there is a strong aspirational, even nostalgic element to it (this is how we think communities once were, and should be again). More recent commentators, such as David Halpern in the UK, prefer the term 'associational life' perhaps because of the more nuanced and fluid way it allows observers of human

47

social life to simply reflect on the contexts in which human beings come together to express a sense of sharing and solidarity. For example, longitudinal research in the United States (Putnam, 2000) suggests that traditional forms of civil society based on the physical association of membership for the mutual advancement of members or volunteering within structured activities (for example, Parent-Teacher Associations, Federation of Women's Clubs and the Rotary Club) are in sharp decline. This decline is to some extent countered by the continued popularity of reading groups and the rise in encounter and self-help groups such as Alcoholics Anonymous, though as Halpern points out, 'almost by definition, their scope and focus are relatively narrow' (2005: 202). We shall look more closely at different 'types' of civil society, and where the areas of growth and decline appear to be, later on in this chapter.

If the concept of *civil society* is an attempt to define the purpose of why human beings connect to one another outside the activities of the state and the market, then *social capital* tries to understand the nature and significance of those connections, and how they either build up or diminish civil society. Its usefulness as a concept lies in the way in which researchers believe one can measure its impact (or outputs) on individuals and wider society, just as one can with economic capital. A civil society with high stocks of social capital has generally been proved to be one that is healthier, more crime free and with higher levels of both economic and educational achievement.

There are numerous definitions of social capital, but they tend to cluster around the simple idea that 'relationships matter'. As John Field says in his summary:

> By making connections with one another, and keeping them going over time, people are able to work together to achieve things that they either could not achieve by themselves, or could only achieve with great difficulty. People connect through a series of networks and they tend to share common values ... To the extent that these networks constitute a resource, they can be seen as forming a kind of capital.
>
> (2003: 1)

Halpern summarizes nine overlapping ways in which understandings of social capital are expressed. There are three *components* to social capital: networks, norms and sanctions. These concepts stress the levels of trust required for networks to function. There are three levels of *analysis* at which one can measure the impact of social capital: the individual (micro-level), the group and neighbourhood (meso-level), and the national and global level (macro-level). And there are three *types* or *functions* of social capital: bonding, bridging and linking. Because we shall be referring to the last set of definitions later in this chapter, we need to briefly explore these three functions further now.

Bonding social capital refers to an inward-looking series of relationships that reinforce exclusive identities and homogeneous groups based, for example, on family, ethnicity, class or gender. The ties within this type of group are strong.

Bridging social capital refers to outward-looking relationships that create bridges with other groups of different cultural, social, economic and political status. Putnam's examples of this type of social capital are 'civil rights movements, youth service groups and ecumenical religious organizations' (2000: 2–3). Putnam also offers a memorable image for understanding the different functions of bonding and bridging capital: 'Bonding social capital provides a kind of sociological superglue whereas bridging social capital provides a sociological WD 40' (Putnam, 2000: 3).

Linking social capital refers to extent to which an individual's or a community's networks are capable of linking up to other networks in order to address the inevitable asymmetrical nature of power and resources. Halpern describes it as 'a special form of bridging social capital that specifically concerns power' (2005: 25).

Having established some of the basic concepts behind civil society and social capital, I will now move on to locate the origin of these concepts within sociology.

Most commentators (for example Field, 2003, Halpern 2005, Putnam, 2000) agree that the current political interest in social capital can be traced back to the early 1830s and the work of the French commentator, Alexis De Tocqueville, who undertook a tour of America to observe the outworking of democracy in what would later emerge as an economic powerhouse. Coming from the European tradition, with its strong belief in class-based hierarchies as the guarantor of social cohesion, he was initially troubled by the concept that all American citizens were formally equal in the eyes of the law. He expected to find a highly atomized society with an inbuilt propensity for future despotism. Instead he found a vigorous form of political economy, at the heart of which was America's associational life based around a strong civil and religious core. This core was a product of the way American pioneer society structured itself around the emergence of individual settlements, which grew into villages and towns, but managed to retain their sense of individuality within a common set of values inherited from the Puritan tradition. The cornerstone of this tradition was a concept of mutual accountability before God and one another, with decisions about the future growth of the community often based on consensus following a majority vote. The 1787 constitution had allowed this 'localism' to continue to flourish while at the same time ensuring some level of recognition for and commitment to a federal notion of governance that was designed to prevent these communities falling into insular isolationism. De Tocqueville himself commented on this dual system of local/federal political economy: 'The one fulfilling the ordinary duties and responding to the daily and infinite calls of community, the other circumscribed within certain limits and exercising an exceptional authority over the general interests of the country' (quoted in Bender, 1978: 85)

This ability to preserve a vigorous associationalism within the context of rapid economic growth and national identity was, for de Tocqueville, the genius of American society.

In their political associations, the Americans, of all conditions, minds and ages, daily acquire a general taste for association and grow accustomed to the use of it. There they meet together in large numbers, they converse, they listen to one another and they are mutually stimulated to all sorts of undertakings. They afterwards transfer to civil life the notions that they have thus acquired and make them subservient to a thousand purposes.

(Book 2, Chapter 7)

In other words, a high level of civil engagement was teaching people how to cooperate across civil life, and as such was nurturing the skills and values necessary for a new, non-European form of democratic society, which Field describes as a 'relatively open, clearly post-aristocratic system' (2003: 30). De Tocqueville is thus a key source for those such as Putnam who are keen to stress the importance of civil engagement and social capital for a vigorous democracy.

De Tocqueville was less impressed by the levels of civil engagement and democracy he saw emerging within the rapidly urbanizing context of Europe (at a time when American society was still largely agrarian). On a visit to Manchester in the late 1830s, he saw vigorous economic growth and wealth-creating potential, but only for the minority. For the majority, the experience of engagement in the industrial processes and urban living was brutal and dehumanizing. In what is now a famous quotation, he wrote: 'From this foul drain the greatest stream of human industry flows out to fertilize the whole world. From this filthy sewer pure gold flows. Here humanity attains its most complete development and its most brutish; here civilization works its miracles, and civilized man is turned back into a savage.' (1958: 108)

His observations were echoed by many, most famously by Friedrich Engels, whose experience of Manchester as a trainee manager for one of his father's factories in the 1830s helped him to create the first systematic urban theory of the industrial capitalist city (Engels, 1969).

These political analyses, raising serious questions about the moral and economic implications of industrial capitalist society, where picked up later in the nineteenth century by sociologists who reflected on the wider *social implications.* Key exponents of emerging sociological categorizations of different types of society were Ferdinand Tönnies and Emile Durkheim.

In 1887, Tönnies reflected on the transition from an agrarian society, based on the village as the basis for social organization, to an industrial society predicated on the town or city as the foundation for social organization. The former society he called *Gemeinschaft* (roughly translated as 'community') which was based around localized networks of family, wider kinship groups (that is, the extended family), friends and neighbourhood; patterns of group solidarity characterized by 'intimate, private and exclusive living together' (quoted in Bender, 1978: 17). The emerging urban society he called *Gesellschaft* (roughly translated as 'society'), which was based on competition and impersonality and is 'an artificial construction of an aggregate of human beings' (quoted in Bender, 1978: 17) The essential difference between pre-urban and urban societies was that in the former, 'people remain essentially united in spite of all separating factors', whereas in the latter 'people are essentially separated in spite of all uniting factors'. A later commentator on Tönnies's thinking summed up the transition from community to society as a process that is 'replacing living tissues with structures held together by rivets and screws' (Ross, 1969: 432).

Durkheim chose to heighten the question of embeddedness within the wider networks raised by Tönnies's typology. However, instead of using the language of community and society he discussed the coexistence of societies based on *mechanical* vs. *organic solidarity.* Mechanical societies were those based on commonly understood norms and values transmitted through face-to-face interaction and reinforced by traditional rituals. Organic solidarity is that which is constructed between individuals on the basis of mutual interdependence rather than the obligation of social ties. This mutual interdependence had to be negotiated across social differences and increasingly specialized occupations. His thesis was that those living in societies based on organic solidarity were more prone to social isolation and cultural alienation, a condition he called *anomie*. He substantiated his thesis with meticulous research on the occurrence of suicide, which fell into distinct social patterns despite its intensely personal character. He found much lower rates of suicide among the widowed than the divorced; in summer months than winter; in Catholic nations than Protestant ones; in larger families than smaller ones; and in rural areas than urban ones. The common factor behind these differences in suicide rates was that the higher rates were associated with conditions of 'excessive individualism'. As an antidote to this perception of social fragmentation Durkheim also observed that the suicide rate tended to drop during times of war, reflecting the increased bonding of a nation when threatened by a common enemy. His conclusion was that 'suicide varies inversely with the degree of integration of the social groups of which the individual forms a part' (1951: 74).

One key aspect of this early sociological thinking is that it seems to articulate the tension between belonging, on one hand, to locally spaced networks, and on the other, to the more anonymously based networks – predicated on global flows – that we observed in the previous chapter. Durkheim's work appeared to suggest that more modern social forms, based on smaller social units that are more isolated and rely on self-selecting criteria, were more likely to lead to mental distress. Meanwhile, sociological thinking in the post-war period attempted to crystallize the momentum of Tönnies's original dichotomy between community and society into a developmental theory called *modernization theory*, which stressed that a more complex and (by implication) more advanced form of social life based on urban living would emerge. For example, Talcott Parsons developed four dichotomies of social formation based on urban theories of that period. They are designed to reflect the 'choices' open to any citizen (or 'actor' in Parsons's terminology) that are appropriate in any encounter with another:

- affectivity vs. affective neutrality
- particularism vs. universalism
- ascription (quality) vs. achievement (performance)
- diffuseness vs. specificity.

The first dichotomy reflects, for example, the difference between greeting a long-lost relative or close friend and that of an encounter with a civil servant or other bureaucratic agent. The third represents the choice between whether to accept someone's familial or ethnic status as being most significant, or their professional role. The fourth is the choice between responding to another as a whole person, or just that part of them that is expressed through a specialized functional role. What subsequent theorists did was to ascribe historical values to each column so that the left-hand term of each pair was associated with 'traditional' social forms, and the right-hand one with 'modern' ones (Bender, 1978: 22). This closely follows Louis Wirth's classic formulation contrasting the rural-folk society that he saw being superseded by the urban-industrial one (Wirth, 1938).

However, postmodern sociologists currently reflecting on the emergence of social forms within globalized communities are tending to resist this notion of historical evolution. This is no doubt due to the general rejection of modernist metanarratives that, as we have observed in Chapter 1, tend to reinforce simple binaries (in this case, traditional vs. modern social forms). Amin and Thrift, for example, identify six forms of postmodern urban sociology that express the importance of belonging both locally and globally. These include traditional notions of living in planned communities and close-knit diasporic communities that also thrive over global distances by interacting through technological media in ways that do not subordinate them to the global community but suggest reciprocity and solidarity. They then add ideas about 'light sociality', which include friends ('the families that we choose'), bunds (community-building done of the basis of mutual interest and sentiment, such as that conducted over the internet) and sympathy for others encouraged by modern media's coverage of global tragedies (Amin and Thrift, 2004: 46).

To this list could also be added John Reader's notion of 'enclaves of interim intimacy', which he derives from his experience of working in rural communities in Worcestershire that are increasingly being used as commuter hubs for workers in Birmingham and beyond. He writes from that increasingly significant hybrid space within the UK that has been dubbed the *ex-urb*; the commuter suburb that, for reasons of perceived safety and quality of life, lies beyond the suburban peripheries of towns and cities and is located within the countryside itself. Reader defines his 'enclave of interim community' as a 'substitute' for former structures of community life (in this case fashioned on notions of rural *gemeinschaft*) that rely on 'close but fragile relationships'. The motivation for seeking these enclaves by new ex-urban dwellers is driven by 'increased social mobility, enhanced working pressures and subsequent uncertainty and distance from family support networks, each created or exacerbated by the forces of the global economy'. Reader observes: 'Local churches and community groups readily collude in constructing (these enclaves) without … recognizing that they are "for the time being only" and may potentially undermine the older "community values" of reciprocity and commitment to locality' (Reader, 2005: 137) Reader is suggesting that globalized workers who can afford to live the ex-urban lifestyle are hollowing out (my term) existing forms of local community for their own needs. This is a classic example of what I am suggesting is a hybrid notion of belonging and identity; one that is locally based but predicated on choice and mobility and influenced by global patterns of economic wealth creation.

If we take a long-term view of how notions of belonging and identity have emerged since the nineteenth century, we can see a trajectory that suggests that local and kinship-based networks of space have been superseded by associational flows based on urban forms that stress individualism and mobility. We have seen how 'modernization' theory has strongly suggested (as its name would imply) that urban-industrial forms in an either/or form were replacing rural-folklore patterns of social ordering. However, postmodern sociology (along with postmodern urban theory) suggests that despite the pervasiveness of Castells's theory of 'space as place' being replaced by one of 'space as flows', local spaces based on family and kinship ties remain significant, especially for those uprooted by global capitalism. It is therefore more accurate to propose that human social forms, for increasing numbers of citizens, are in fact hybrid expressions of local, associational, global and virtual 'forms' of community.

This sociological complexity based on hybrid forms of belonging and identity is reflected in current notions of political governance. We now return to the discussion of civil society and social capital, but with the specific purpose of exploring the emerging understandings of political governance in globalized localities.

Liquid vs. Solid Civil Society

In Douglass and Friedmann's definition of civil society at the beginning of this chapter, I referred to 'a society of households, family networks, civic and religious organizations and communities that are bound to each other primarily by shared histories, collective memories and cultural norms of reciprocity'. I implied that this might be considered a conservative and nostalgic definition. It also seems quite a static definition in *where* it chooses to locate civil society. As we have briefly seen in relation to Putnam's US-based work, institutions such as family, civic and religious organizations are precisely those in apparent sharp decline. For example, membership of trades unions in the United States has declined from 32 per cent in the 1950s to 14 per cent by the beginning of the new century. Church membership has fallen by 10 per cent in 40 years and attendance by 20 per cent. The trend buckers in this respect are a cluster of Christian fundamentalist and other evangelical groups, although controversy does surround their membership figures (see Halpern, 2005: 203). Meanwhile, the average family size is declining; the current level in the UK is 1.7 children per woman (down from a peak of 2.95 in the mid-1960s) while in the United States, the current figure is 1.8. There is also solid statistical evidence to show that the time spent engaging in social capital at a family level is also on the decline. For example, the proportion of UK families reporting sitting down for family dinners has fallen 32 per cent since the 1960s (Halpern, 2005: 206).

Putnam's evidence of the decline in these 'traditional' areas of civil society is offset by apparent growth in non-traditional forms of social capital. Halpern defines these in his own summary of Putnam's work as the rise in self-help groups, social movements and religious fundamentalist groups. In terms of political activity, the proportion of the US population that has taken part in political protests has slightly risen. In terms of informal socializing, all indicators are down except for going to the gym, watching and playing sports – though as individuals rather than in teams – and perhaps speaking to distant friends and relatives. Volunteering has increased, but mainly from the over-60s; that is, the pre-baby boomers whom Putnam defines as the 'conscientious volunteering generation' (Halpern, 2005: 210).

Recent surveys of British civil society confirm some of these US trends, but uses different terminology. The CENTRIS (Centre for Research and Innovation in Social

Policy and Practice) 2003 report, entitled *Unravelling the Maze: A Survey of Civil Society in the UK*, divides UK civil society into four typologies. These are:

1) Associations: voluntary organizations and charities outside the family that are not primarily to do with paid employment.
2) Labour and professional organizations: trades unions, employers associations, chambers of commerce.
3) Communities, faith communities and families: communities in the local, geographic sense as well as those united by belief or kinship.
4) New tendencies and movements (also called non-institutional civil society): groupings that coalesce around a single issue, such as the *Stop the War* campaign.

According to CENTRIS's audit, Sectors 2 and 3 are essentially stagnant or in decline. Sector 1 is in decline except for those parts that are becoming more professionalized and presenting themselves as public-service providers, in line with government policy on the Third Sector. As this sector becomes more professionalized so it loses touch with local communities, and those who have traditionally enjoyed volunteering for its own sake (including faith communities). It is Sector 4 that is showing the most obvious growth, and we need to briefly define its emerging characteristics:

- They are often without form, structure or permanent locus, and comprise networks and 'loose congeries of groups and individuals' (therefore hard to assess).
- Shifting coalitions of groups with different general purposes, but with some specific aims in common, means that there is overlap between non-institutional and some parts of the formally constituted civil society.
- They are marked by use of the internet and electronic communications, enabling campaigns to be orchestrated and groups to form without formal structure and officers (bureaucracy).
- They often form around a single issue and use direct action (campaigns since 1997 that have had a national impact include animal welfare, anti-capitalization and globalization, environment and transport, farming and the use of the countryside; racial discrimination, social policy and welfare, vigilantism, weapons of mass destruction).
- They attract large numbers of young people.
- Their general tenor is anti-materialistic, and of opposition to the establishment.
- They display great fluidity, their components 'forming, dissolving and reforming according to their commitment on this or that issue'.

(CENTRIS, 2003: 46).

This broad-brush picture of civil society is largely substantiated by other, more detailed work within the UK. Membership of associations is in broad decline in some sectors (for example, Women's Institute membership is down by 46 per cent from 1972 to 2002, trades union membership fell by 41 per cent from 1979 to 2000, while the rate of infant baptisms in the Church of England has declined from 70 per cent of the population in 1950 to 23 per cent of the population in 2000). However, associations with a strong environmental emphasis, such as the National Trust and the RSPB, have shown significant rises in the period since 1970 (see Halpern, 2005: 212–13). Volunteering is up among the over-65s and the over-50s. Statistics based on surveys of political activity from 1986 to 2000 show that the proportion of members of Sector 4 organizations (New Tendencies and Movements) who say they would go on a demonstration rose from 6 to 10 per cent (although this figure does not include recent high-profile political campaigns that attracted large numbers of protesters such as those against the Iraq war and the ban on hunting with dogs, and for fair trade. This increase in what CENTRIS calls *non-institutional* civil society appears to be a response to the decline of institutional civil society, especially that associated with political activity, such as the steady decline in representative voting; for example, the turnout at the 2001 general election was 59 per cent, compared to a peak of 79 per cent in the 1959 election. The reason for this decline is generally held to be a weakening in trust and/or confidence in the mechanisms of institutional government (see Halpern, 2005: 215, Field, 2003: 94).

The significant point to make from this raft of data on civil society and levels of social capital (and what I have reproduced here is the merest tip of the iceberg) is not only to note where its increases and decreases are recorded, but also the terminology used to describe its different typologies. Putnam, for example, tends to use the typology of *traditional* vs. *alternative.* CENTRIS uses the typology of *institutional* vs. *non-institutional.* Halpern, in his global overview of increases and declines in social capital, stresses that the one major trend that is discernible across the various countries he studied is the shift from *collective* forms of social capital to *individual* forms (2005: 222), to the extent that, even in societies where social capital is increasing, citizens are participating according to their own individual choices and value systems rather than being influenced by membership of or solidarity with any recognizable collective. Thus the term 'moral entrepreneur' has been coined to describe how people mix and match values and value systems to fashion their own particular viewpoints and strategies for action, rather than drawing them from some overarching, systemic view of the world. In Sweden, a society typically high in social capital indicators, the concept of 'solidaristic individualism' has been devised (Rothstein, 2001: 219).

I myself will be exploring the concept of *solid* and *liquid* in relation to social institutions, including churches and faith groups. One could argue that the traditional typologies of civil society in general decline identified by the CENTRIS audit are 'solid' forms of civil society. They have traditionally required paid-up membership, paid or voluntary officers who are usually voted for, and accountable financial and legal frameworks, including written constitutions. Larger organizations will also have substantial physical infrastructures such as buildings, many paid staff, and regional and local branches, and will probably be formally linked with other organizations engaged in similar work. 'Liquid' civil society, as we have seen, requires few if any of these things to function, relying instead on electronic communication, publicity and a few key volunteers to co-ordinate events. However, it is worth remarking that large-scale demonstrations such as the Make Poverty History march in Edinburgh, held in July 2005 and attended by 250,000 people (to coincide with the G8 summit on African debt and climate change) was a hybrid event that deployed both solid and liquid forms of civil society. Although open to anyone simply to turn up on the day, detailed negotiations had nevertheless taken place beforehand between large non-governmental organizations (NGOs) such as Christian Aid and Oxfam, and the city authorities such as the police and local government, to maximize the safety of those taking part and minimize the potential for public disturbance. The event was stewarded by volunteers from a wide range of public civil-society institutions such as trades unions and faith groups.

Political philosophy and sociology is thus recognizing that there is increasingly a 'mixed economy' of engagement that is reflecting a hybrid methodology and sense of affiliation by which individuals are participating in governance. A key concept used within political philosophy to describe these trends, which we can add to those already mentioned above, is the spectrum of political participation between *representative* and *participatory* democracy.

Put simply, *representative* democracy is where an individual citizen within a parliamentary or local authority system votes for an elected representative to represent their views on their behalf in that arena. *Participatory* democracy is a form of politics where an individual citizen bypasses any parliamentary system and expresses their voice directly via some form of individual or collective action that directly addresses the issue they are concerned about and attempts to provoke a change in specific policy or wider civic opinion. Representative democracy typically relies on 'solid' structures associated with the Weberian model, namely, political parties to select party leaders, regular national and local elections and a civil-service bureaucracy to provide 'expert' advice and deliver public resources paid for by central government. It also relies on 'tight' hierarchical and command-and-control structures, including – at central government level – the close physical proximity of ministry buildings (Stoker, 2004: 24).

Participatory democracy is more 'liquid' in its expression, as we have already seen, and has its roots in the radical social movements of the late 1960s and 1970s. From that era comes the principle of expressing one's own 'voice' and not allowing someone else to express it for you – or even worse, ignore or silence it. Albert Hirschman defined 'voice' as 'any attempt to change … an objectionable state of affairs, whether through individual or collective petition to the management directly in charge, through appeal to a higher authority with the intention of forcing a change in management, or through various types of action and protests, including those that are meant to mobilize public opinion' (Hirschman, 1970, quoted in Stoker, 2004: 25). Participatory politics is also 'looser' in its structure, relying more on networks of communication than on hierarchies of control.

New Labour and the Growth of 'Multi-level' Governance

'Governance has become important due to changes in society … and the new governance is a strategy to link the contemporary state to the contemporary society' (Pierre and Peters, quoted in Stoker, 2004: 10).

According to Gerry Stoker (2004), the history of institutional government in Britain in the post-war era has gone through three distinct phases. The first, immediate post-war phase witnessed the setting up and delivery of public services by local authorities within a national welfare state. The public sector had the monopoly on decision-making, expertise and delivery. The 1970s and 1980s, primarily under the influence of Conservative administrations both locally and nationally, saw the shift to a new public management system which forced public services to become more responsive to the needs of local customers and adapt to more competitive management practices borrowed from the private sector, including cost-cutting and the use of competitive tendering. The third phase has been emerging since the mid 1990s, with an increased emphasis on the concept of localism: 'namely that the key task for local government is to meet the needs of its community either directly or indirectly' (Stoker, 2004: 14). The focus is moving away from simply being a question of the most efficient way of delivering services towards being a search for a variety of solutions – favourable to the wishes of the local community – to a variety of issues. This in reality means a networked rather than tight structure of governance, and involves working within a complex set of relationships at different levels of civil society. At local government level, these relationships include central government, public service providers and quangos such as police and health services, local business and the local community and voluntary sector, as well as direct communication with residents and other 'service users'. Within this form of governance, 'managerialism' is not equated with pure economic efficiency, but with taking on the challenge of working across boundaries and aiming for 'the goal of holistic working' (Stoker, 2004: 14).

New Labour and the Third Way

This shift towards a hybrid from of governance that works interactively with all three sectors of civil society (local government, private business and the community and voluntary sector) and via a variety of different methods (for example, target-setting, arms-length bodies, market mechanisms, local partnerships), needs to be seen in a wider philosophical and political context, which can be summed as the Third Way. The philosophy of the Third Way presented the UK's Labour Party (unofficially branded 'New Labour' by Tony Blair following his election to the party leadership in 1994) with the broad principles and rhetoric with which to present itself as a progressive, modernizing party from the centre-left that would appeal to the majority of voters and allow it to be voted into power for the first time in 18 years. Those years in opposition (1979–97) had also sharpened its desire not only to win one election but to remain in power long enough to be seen as a 'natural party of government' for the twenty-first century. This meant reaching out and appealing to a much wider core than its traditional urban working-class support base. The origin of Third Way philosophy in the UK is probably most closely associated with the thought of the sociologist Anthony Giddens, an acknowledged influence on Tony Blair's thinking and the evolution of New Labour (*The Third Way*, 1998). As long ago as the early 1990s, he posited the theory of the 'reflexive project of the self' (see Giddens, 1991) as an inescapable fact of late (or post) modernity and therefore the new basis of social life and social policy. The notion of the self is no longer something 'fixed' that we inherit. Rather, according to Giddens, it is a narrative or biography we constantly update about ourselves, which is capable of being explained to other people and integrating events that take place in the external world. The construction of the self is also closely related to choices of lifestyle that are offered by the modern media.

Therefore, any model of government that doesn't take into account the significance of individual choice and the individual's right to fulfilled potential is doomed to electoral failure. However, as a left-of-centre party, New Labour wanted to expand this notion of the individual beyond a merely neoliberal market model of economic man or woman into something that allowed the self-fulfilling individual to express their identity and choice within the wider context of civil society. One New Labour strategist in 1997 reflected that the language of social capital allowed the possibility of squaring the circle of 'building solidarity in a secular society' while at the same time being 'exposed to the full rigours of a global market and committed to the principle of individual choice' (Leadbeter, 1997: 35).

The political hallmarks of the Third Way can be summarized thus:

- the belief that there is no alternative to the market economy
- a celebration of the contribution of civil society
- a commitment to a continuing, if different role of the state

(Stoker, 2004: 50–52).

This agenda, according to Stoker, has shaped New Labour social policy in three key areas. First, as part of maintaining a sustained electoral base, but also being seen as a modernizing force, New Labour has set out a new form of political management that has involved experiments in devolution and establishing progressive coalitions and partnerships.

Second has been the cluster of policies more closely associated with Gordon Brown and the Treasury and centring on the concept of 'entrepreneurial welfarism'. This has allowed New Labour to distance itself from the welfarism of Old Labour, which is criticized for having created a dependency culture rather than providing citizens with the means to take responsibility for their own lives. This means an emphasis on redistribution not simply of income (for those in the strata of society ranging from the lower-middle class to the unemployed working class) but more significantly, life chances and opportunities. Any income distribution is therefore linked to incentives to take up education or training schemes that will improve employability and business skills and overall human potential.

However, under the entrepreneurial welfare system, these new opportunities also carry the responsibility of being active citizens. This means ultimately having to take a large measure of individual responsibility for providing the necessary safety nets once provided by the state. For example, workers ensuring they have adequate pension provision, or students taking out government loans for their university tuition that they must repay once they have secured postgraduate employment. It also means having to take responsibility for wider civil society in the form of an obligation to our fellow citizens. The spectrum of thinking on the extent to which the state has a right to extract these obligations in return for opportunities is mixed, ranging from liberal to communitarian outlooks (Stoker, 2004: 52). However, an early consensual position on personal responsibilities is defined by Stuart White, namely: 'the responsibility to work (in return for a share of the social product) and to make an effort to acquire relevant skills for work; the responsibility to be a good parent ... the responsibility to pay a fair share of taxes; the responsibility to respect the environment' (1998: 26). This broad contract has recently been hardened on the government's side by controversial legislation aimed at enforcing good behaviour from adults as well as children through such mechanisms as obligatory parenting classes, enforced via parenting orders. The Anti-Social Behaviour Act 2003 allows Local Educational Authorities (LEAs) to impose fines ranging from £100 to £1,000. These potential sanctions are used mainly to address children's truancy from school or antisocial behaviour while in school.

The third element of the Third Way social policy is restoring the capacity of the state to deliver a more responsive and quick service to its citizens via the use of new information technologies and partnerships. Part of the wide use of partnerships is driven by the need to search for 'joined-up solutions to complex problems', which will result in pragmatic outputs (Stoker, 2004: 52). This final element is closely connected to what Stoker calls New Labour's 'fatalistic outlook' on government (Stoker, 2004: 82), namely, the absence of trust it perceives to exist between the centre and the local. In response to this perception, much of New Labour's social policy is designed to build up the processes of trust through the impression of handing over real autonomy to local authorities and communities, and creating networks where accountability and decision-making can be shared horizontally rather than vertically. This 'new localism' thus acknowledges the changed social and political landscape we have referred to earlier – the decline of 'modernist' government based on representative democracy and an expert bureaucracy, and the rise instead of the individual citizen as consumer who is naturally sceptical of any authority, and whose political engagement has to be 'bought' with a complex system of incentives and responsibilities that give the impression of choice and local control. This element of voluntary coercion has to be supported by extensive use of media presentation and high-quality marketing (known by its more derogatory title of 'spin').

However, the strong managerial element that New Labour inherited from the Conservatives, whereby central government maintains control of funding streams and sets timetables and targets for reform, ensures that a competitive, market-driven approach is maintained. Those organizations or partnerships that most successfully meet the government's target criteria often receive preferential options for future funding. Stoker and others liken this 'centrally incentivized' performance to a 'lottery in which a complex variety of prizes have been offered to successful reformers but where the selection of winners reflects a complex mix of their capacity and chance' (2004: 69). If this sense of participation in new localism is truly perceived as taking part in a 'lottery', then this will counteract genuine attempts at building up a sense of trust within political networks. There is also the potential for tension within a system of governance that proclaims a rhetoric of local control and autonomy (namely a horizontal approach) while applying a framework of central managerial control (a vertical approach). How does this hybrid, Third Way approach to governance work in reality? We will take as a case study the New Deal for Communities programme.

The New Deal for Communities Programme

The New Deal for Communities (NDC) programme was established under the Government's strategy (announced in 2000 as the National Strategy for Neighbourhood Renewal) for dealing with community and physical regeneration in Britain's poorest communities. It involved giving a grant of £50 million, paid out over a ten-year period, to each of 39 such areas with populations ranging from 4,000 to 11,000. Taken together, these 39 areas represent the poorest one per cent of the population of England and Wales.

The purpose of the £50 million grant was to encourage each local community to establish long-term strategies for the regeneration of their neighbourhoods in partnership with key agencies such as local authorities, businesses, statutory providers and other partners in the voluntary sector. The NDC money would be controlled by a local board comprising members of all the key stakeholder groups, but with a majority made up of local residents. The first task of all NDCs was to agree a community development plan on how this money was to be spent over the ten-year period. The NDC boards are charged with meeting local targets under five headings set by central government: health, education, environment, transport and housing. Local authorities provided much of the capability infrastructure via the use of seconded employees. The performance of the NDCs and their progress in attaining the government targets is monitored and evaluated on behalf of the government by a consortium headed by the Centre for Regional Economic and Social Research (CRESR) and Sheffield Hallam University.

According to annual reports produced at first by the Office of the Deputy Prime Minister (ODPM – the minister whose remit at the time included local government), and since 2006 by the Department for Communities and Local Government (DCLG) the 'success rates' of the various NDCS programmes have been variable. Several have experienced difficulty in establishing processes of accountability, communication and trust within the tight timetables demanded for establishing community development plans and spending the money. The demands of handling large budgets, learning and understanding technical jargon, and working across different disciplines and cultures also put strains on the participants who often did not have sufficient training and experience before they undertook the roles demanded by the NDC programme. The fact that top advertised posts were remunerated according to civil service pay scales in excess of £50,000 a year for those outside the communities, while those within the communities who spent several hours a week managing the programmes received no more than reimbursed expenses, was also a source of considerable resentment.

Some NDC programmes have, however, been successful in creating workable structures of communication and delivery. One that is held up as an example of good practice is the East Manchester NDC. Those residents directly engaged in the process have learnt important skills of political negotiation and have worked closely with a broadly sympathetic and flexible local authority team. One success area has been the creation of a resident-led initiative to provide new housing for rent as well as development, via the creation of a new housing association. A steering group of local residents worked hard to get existing Manchester City council tenants to agree to a stock transfer to allow the new not-for-profit housing company, called Eastlands, to come into being. They brought with them £20 million from the NDC budget as a start-up dowry for the new company, after which it would have to borrow on the financial markets.

A new board was set up to run Eastlands and handle the business concerns. Under the rules set by the National Housing Federation (a government quango), the proportion of units rented at market rates is limited to 30 per cent – though given that 100 per cent of the units used to be rented at affordable rates, this is nevertheless felt to be a high proportion, especially given the way housing prices are set to rise following the arrival of prestigious city-living schemes such as the New Islington development, whose aim is to make East Manchester the 'Venice of the North'. The 30 per cent of local residents left on the new board will also change from being tenant representatives to company directors. This means they have to put the interests of the company first, which might well conflict with their ability to be accountable to their fellow tenants, and to fight for their needs. This conflict of interest proved too much for some of the original pioneers, who felt they had to leave the board in order to remain part of the community.

Reflecting on the East Manchester experience, local commentator Hilary Wainwright outlines some of the difficulties encountered in trying to implement the 'new localism'. She observes that where local political initiatives gain momentum under government initiatives, it is severely compromised by the different sets of rules being operated by national quangos (such as the National Housing Federation). Likewise, the participatory way of decision-making pioneered in one small sector of a city like Manchester has no way of 'breaking through' and influencing practice across a whole city or region. Nor is there a strategy for thinking through the impact of how the infrastructure gained through the NDC programme by one local community (for example, a youth centre or swimming pool) affects the provision in other areas that are not members of the programme. As Wainwright says:

> There are two issues here. One is that of subsidiarity: What decisions can best be taken locally without damaging consequences for people elsewhere, or losing any benefits from being part of a city-wide strategy? The other is of participation: How

can the diverse and sometimes conflicting views of people in different localities
feed into the wider strategic decision-making.

(2003: 105)

We have seen how New Labour's hybrid or multi-level governance approach is giving
mixed messages that are not inspiring great levels of trust. This is mainly because the
full impacts of new localism have not been fully assessed. Does the experience of
the NDC programme imply, for example, that new localism's benefits in community
empowerment can only be locked within that small community, thus affecting the life
chances of very small numbers of people? On a more general level, the unresolved
dynamics between the centre and the local appear to be causing a breakdown in
intended trust and communication. Research in local Manchester communities
undergoing regeneration shows high levels of cynicism, weariness and mistrust at
repeated attempts at partnership and consultation, because they perceive that some of
the managerial rhetoric and practice emanating from the centre undercuts apparent
power given to local contexts (see Baker and Skinner, 2005).

Faith Communities and Civil Society

I will end this chapter with a summary of the role of faith communities within this new
era of governance. The amount of government-sponsored literature in this area is
increasing, including two substantial documents (within the space of three years)
providing detailed guidance to local authorities, setting out policy objective held in
common with faith groups and how best to achieve them (LGA, 2002; Home Office,
2004).

Perhaps the first question we need to ask is 'Why?' Why this growing interest in
deploying faith communities within the context of developing civil society and social
capital, beyond the general reasons already discussed in relation to the Third Sector as
a whole.

There are perhaps three reasons. The first concerns the specifically religious
framework within which New Labour operates; in particular the strong influence
Christian faith has traditionally played from the earliest inception of the Labour Party
and the way it influences the policy framework of the two main architects of New
Labour, Tony Blair and Gordon Brown (Dale, 2001). Mark Chapman, in *Blair's
Britain* (2005), details the key influence that religious figures such as the Scottish
Quaker moral philosopher John MacMurray had on the young Blair during his days at
Oxford University (2005: 16), and how they communicated to him the importance of
a society constructed on moral responsibility. An overt appeal to the ethical traditions
contained within global religions has allowed Blair to do what hadn't really been done
in Britain since the era of Archbishop William Temple in the 1940s – to bring the
element of morality into politics. This does not equate with the US experience, in
which certain evangelical forms of Christianity have united with the neoconservative
agenda at the highest level (including an overtly born-again-Christian president in
the White House) to influence social policy at the federal level at the expense of

'liberal' state legislation allowing (for example) legal marriage for homosexual couples or more liberal abortion laws. Rather, Tony Blair uses faith as reinforcing mood music by making occasional and uncontroversial references to his own religious convictions, but also by making sure that when he addresses any religious-based conference, he uses the occasion to reinforce the government's message about the positive effects that faith communities bring in terms of their functions and values. Thus for example, at a Christian Socialist Conference in 2001, he referred to faith groups as:

> ... playing a fundamental role in supporting and propagating values which bind us together as a nation ... looking outwards to the needs of others, beyond your own immediate members, is a prime expression of your beliefs and values ... In carrying out this mission you have developed some of the most effective voluntary and community organizations in the country.
>
> (Blair, 2001)

This expresses a wholly positive view of faith-based communities that, in terms of the social capital theory we covered earlier, is predicated on 'bridging' social capital (looking beyond their own members to the needs of others). He also acknowledges the long history of community care and development within British society traditionally carried out by churches and other faith communities.

These examples of Tony Blair's religious rhetoric reinforce the second reason why faith groups are playing an increasingly significant part within the social capital/governance agenda. It is the wide range of functions that they are perceived by wider civil society to perform. At a speech to the Faithworks conference (a national network of mainly Evangelical churches), which coincided with the run-up to the 2005 election, Tony Blair commended the organization for its work in the following areas of society: homeless people, young people and their parents, managing three academy schools (secondary-level education), and involvement in running campaigns against international poverty and injustice. The speech concluded with Blair saying: 'I would like to see you play a bigger, not lesser role in the future. I say this because of the visible, tangible difference you are making for the better in our society for so many people. That is the proof of your faith in action in the service of others' (Blair, 2005).

We can notice from the list that much of the social capital carried out by faith groups is of a skilled and subtle kind, working with those at the farthest edges of society as well as within mainstream social provision. A further dimension to the understanding of faith-based contributions to social-capital outcomes emerges from the English North-west. An economic impact survey carried out by the Northwest Development Agency estimated that the amount of work offered by faith communities in both statutory and voluntary capacities contributed the equivalent of £94 million each year to the regional economy of north-west England (NWDA, 2005).

The third reason for government interest in the contributions of faith communities can arguably be put down to the post-9/11 effect, which in the UK had been amplified by serious race riots in some English northern towns and cities during the summer of 2001 (see Baker, 2005). Subsequent government reports on the causes of these riots stressed the parallel nature of lives lived by many members of ethnic communities in many of Britain's smaller towns and cities (for example, Home Office, 2001). Physical zoning of communities is exacerbated by social zoning, whereby different communities use separate schools, and support separate cultural and religious practices. In the opinion of these reports, separated communities produce poor social cohesion because they never encounter one another and therefore have perspectives of the Other that are easily distorted. This can produce a social atmosphere that leads to generally fearful and suspicious communities – the complete antithesis of the trust that is supposed to be the basis of social capital. Because of the deeper penetration of faiths in British society through the processes of globalized migration (see Chapter 1) local breakdowns in civil society based on religious or ethnic fault lines can both reflect and influence global patterns of conflict in ways that become mutually reinforcing. This means that faith groups are no longer seen as tame allies in a government-constructed agenda about multiculturalism and bridging social capital. Rather, they can be sources of negative bonding capital that establish divisive relationships between themselves and the wider civil society, and ally themselves with global networks that they perceive to be more sympathetic to their identity than local ones. Thus the government is concerned to pursue closer ties with what they perceive to be the mainstream traditions of faiths in the UK, in the hope of being able to exercise some control over the more radical elements.

Thus 9/11 and subsequent bombings in European capitals during 2004–05 by Islamist terrorist cells has sharpened the debate about the role and identity of faiths in civil society. There was already a discernable shift to a more critical perspective on faith-based engagement from a series of reports that not only reminded government of the spectrum of faith positions in relation to engagement with civil society, but also suggested that government's views of faiths and community was far too 'functionalist' and 'conservative' (see Furbey and Macey, 2005). That is to say, government appears to be interested only in what faiths can deliver to its agenda, irrespective of the values and beliefs they also bring – some of which will be compatible with mainstream and liberal political thinking, but some of which will be profoundly dissonant.

PART 2
PUBLIC THEOLOGY IN THE
THIRD SPACE

Chapter 4

'Mainstream' Christian Realism: The Foundation for a Third Space Social Ethics

In Part 1 I have attempted to construct the basis of an argument identifying the concept of Third Space hybridity as a central theme of the last twenty years or so. We have seen how the philosophical theories of Bhabha and Lévinas concerning the fundamental instability of culture and identity, especially when it is brought into contact with the Other, have been converted into a theory of post-colonial politics and culture by Bhabha and others. I then attempted to show how the concept of hybridity is expressed at the levels of popular culture, urban development and local politics in ways that directly impact and affect the way people construct identities for themselves and the communities in which they live.

I ended Part 1 with a brief overview of the way that churches and other faith communities are being deliberately invited by New Labour to enter into an increasingly multi-levelled and hybrid political discourse about UK social policy. This represents the bridge into Part 2, in which we will focus on three elements by which I believe the churches can engage with the Third Space in order to better connect with postmodern, post-industrial and post-colonial society, but also by which to evaluate their existing praxis. This we will do by looking at the three aspects of what I would call a performative public theology for the twenty-first century: a Third Space social ethics, a Third Space ecclesiology and a Third Space theology.

The purpose of this chapter is to prepare the ground for a description of a Third Space Christian social ethics, and discuss how it might operate. I will argue that the central component of a Third Space social ethics is a radical reformulation of the Christian Realism tradition. In order to do that, this chapter will focus on the existing tradition of Christian Realism (which I am calling the mainstream tradition) and describe how its origins and thinking make it accessible as an existing source within Christian social ethics for translation into the plurality and ambiguity of postmodern life.

The terms *social ethics* and *public theology* will be used in a fairly interchangeable fashion. One definition of social ethics I am working with is that which seeks to engage the Christian community explicitly with urban, economic and political processes. This is done in the hope that debate and praxis (practical action that is reflected on theologically) will be generated within the churches on issues of marginalization and injustice, but also emerge from dialogue with other agencies and communities whose agenda of creating just and sustainable spaces is the same. In this sense, this definition of social ethics is compatible with a public theology – that is, the sharing of insights, concerns and good practice in the social and political spaces that remain within postmodern society, for the sake of public (or common) goods.

I shall also be using the term Third Space throughout these chapters as a shorthand term to describe how new patterns of Christian praxis and theology emerge when you allow the processes of hybridity to occur. As we have seen in Part 1 of this book, the Third Space is both a literal and metaphoric area where traditional assumptions based on either/or definitions or top-down methodologies collapse under the need to engage with a multiplicity of influences that now compete with each other on equal terms. These influences are mainly linked to the mobility and fluidity of postmodern living caused by the demands of the global market, which have produced rapid diversification but also growing polarization within swiftly expanding urban and social spaces. They are also linked to the epistemological crisis of modernity, which has seen the collapse of metanarratives and trust in authority structures, in favour of individual choice and the expression of identity.

The following two chapters need to be seen in terms of a single narrative. In this chapter, I will argue for the need for a 'reformulation' of traditional ideas within the postmodern world we now find ourselves in. I will offer a definition of Christian Realism, and why it is already well placed to engage in the complexity of postmodern society. I will then trace some of the ideas and themes of what I am calling 'mainstream' Christian Realism by looking at some key thinkers within that tradition, and show the usefulness, but also the limitations of their ideas for the task that is now needed.

In Chapter 5 I will offer a proposal for a reformulated and 'radical' Christian Realism, woven from some current writers engaging with the Christian Realism tradition, which will contain within it what I believe will be the key components of a Third Space social ethics. This will be an ethical approach that will combine realism with flexibility when it comes to harnessing the creative potential of the hybridized world in which we now live, while simultaneously directing it towards just and sustainable outcomes for both local and global communities. A *radical* Christian Realism will be compared with Liberation Theology to show the points of connection with that tradition, but also how the former is better suited to engage with the complexity of some of the ethical challenges raised by a plural and complex postmodernity. This is because Liberation Theology, with its epistemological viewpoint of the poor, tends to fall into the trap of binary analysis (in this case, a rich vs. poor dualism), which can stifle the emergence of hybrid solutions to complex problems.

The Need to 'Reformulate'

One of the imperatives for a radical reformulation of Christian social ethics has previously been referred to in Chapter 2 – that is, the pastoral problematic presented by the fear and suspicion of the Other, which is eroding the possibility of a creative response to the evolution of more just cities and just civil societies.

Another imperative is the growing economic polarization that is occurring at both global and local levels, and threatening the sustainability of both human and non-human ecologies.

The third imperative derives from what has been identified as a situation of 'cultural and epistemological crisis', whereby the homogeneity of modernity – in terms of a liberal Enlightenment Western model – has been fragmented into competing and disconnected discourses. This is the thesis put forward by Alasdair MacIntyre in his influential book, *After Virtue* (1981). In this book he describes the failure of the Enlightenment project to find universal and rational bases for human behaviour by which an outcome or *telos* to human behaviour could be conceived. Traditionally, the telos has been to make the transition from 'man-as-he-happens-to-be' to 'man-as-he-could-be-if-he-realized-his-essential-nature' (MacIntyre, 1981: 52). Ethics (whether sanctioned by divine or human authority) was traditionally 'the science which is to enable men how to make the transition from the former state to the latter' (52). What MacIntyre has done is to show how so-called universal precepts, such as justice (from Aristotle onwards), were all culturally conditioned by context and tradition, and that each context and tradition was intimately linked to the community in which they were formulated.

Thus the liberal-based consensus that one could construct a single common good, based on Western assumptions of economics, political democracy, planning, justice and social policy, has been truly dismantled. The ability of theological authority to control or even guide human behaviour via revealed principles has also been radically called into question, and the lack of moral clarity about what constitutes human behaviour has produced a number of responses. Some have withdrawn into a religiously sealed hermeneutic based on divine revelation (that is, beyond human revelation) from where they attempt to out-narrate other narratives (for example, Milbank 1997, Hauerwas 1981).

MacIntyre's advice for those experiencing an epistemological crisis, during which they realize that 'their previous schema of interpretation has broken down irredeemably in certain highly specific ways' (1981: 143), involves a two-stage process of resolution. First, there is a need to examine, in all conscience and good faith, how and where the now dysfunctional world view was misleading. Second, to use this reflection as a basis for 'reformulating' the previous ideas into a new and expanded narrative that both has some continuity with the previous metanarratives while also enabling fresh and authentic engagement with the present context. The reformulation proposed in the next chapter is therefore not the attempt to exchange one metanarrative epistemology with another. Rather it will seek to move some existing elements of the Christian Realism tradition from an over-dependence on rational and empirical bases to a more *narrative* one, thus preserving a hybrid form somewhere between theory and narrative-based epistemologies. Out of this, I am hoping something recognizably new will emerge that takes the debate about Christian engagement with postmodern spaces further on.

There are three points of potential engagement between the Christian Realism tradition and Third Space hybridity. First, there is within Christian Realism a tradition of interdisciplinary engagement (especially with economics and politics).

Interdisciplinarity is an important methodology within postmodern debates concerning the nature of cities and civil society, and will be an important tool in helping to articulate a 'hybrid' ecclesiology.

Second, it has an epistemological bias towards seeing human history as a potential locus of salvation and transformation on the basis of human endeavour, albeit from a perspective of 'realism'. This makes it potentially well disposed to engaging with the complexity of postmodern plurality, rather than seeking to escape or ignore it.

Third, and connected to the second, it has an inbuilt bias towards creating spaces of hope, justice and inclusivity based on redistribution of scarce resources and the empowerment of human processes, a tradition that chimes in well with the postcolonial and postmodern planning discourses identified in Chapter 1.

The Definition and Origin of Christian Realism

The definition of Christian Realism contained in the *Christian Dictionary of Ethics* takes Reinhold Niebuhr's formulation as normative. Realism, he writes, 'denotes the disposition to take *all factors* in a social and political situation which offer resistance to established norms into account, particularly the factors of self-interest and power' (emphasis mine). Niebuhr attempted to hold in dialectical tension the God-given freedom to exercise human conscience and responsibility in choosing moral paths (often 'the lesser of two evils', as in the case of war), with the belief that the ideal of love revealed by Jesus in its divine perfection lay beyond human endeavour and was thus a source of hope and inspiration to human attempts to create just societies as well as a source of judgement. This approach was to attempt to steer a path between cynicism and nihilism on the one hand, and false utopianism on the other.

The Social Gospel and the Origins of Christian Utopianism

Normunds Kamergrauzis, in his recent overview of the history of Christian Realism (Kamergrauzis, 2001) traces its origins to the emergence of the Social Gospel in the 1870s in the United States. The United States was emerging from the Civil War and during the following decades a new and vigorous form of capitalism emerged that laid the foundations for a new industrial and urban identity. This rapid industrialization and urbanization led quickly to the same processes of social and economic polarization that had occurred sixty years earlier in Europe. National wealth increased enormously, but those who owned the means of capital and production benefited disproportionately compared to the majority of the population, who were paid subsistence wages for their labour.

Existing ecclesiological and theological structures were unable to respond adequately to the deep structural changes taking place at the social and political level, especially with regard to the inequalities and immiseration of the urban poor that was being produced on a vast scale. Kamergrauzis sums up the prevailing theological climate at the time:

The traditional orthodoxy of nineteenth century American Protestantism was dominated by a profound individualism that resulted in a preoccupation with individual salvation ... Biblical fundamentalism, an otherworldly pietism and conservative orthodoxy ... that were capable neither of dealing with social changes or giving satisfactory responses to the circumstances of the time.

(2001: 34–5)

The Social Gospel thus emerged as a reaction to this static and conservative response to rapid urban and industrial changes sweeping the United States. The inequality foisted upon urban workers was denounced as contradictory to the will of God and the development of a wholly human life. The Social Gospel rejected the prevailing theological belief that all present social structures were ordained by the will of God, and unchangeable. It challenged both laissez-faire capitalism and Protestant individualism with a reformulation of Christian faith that stressed the doctrine of God's immanence, via the Incarnation of Christ, in the human suffering of the world – an immanence that entailed a radical connection, not disjunction, between human history and the will of God. The ethical teachings and gospel accounts of Jesus' life and Passion were reinterpreted to stress the political and social dimensions to his proclamation of the Kingdom of God with regard to the commitment to practise justice at all levels of human society, but especially to the poor and marginalized.

As well as the doctrines of God's immanence (as Father of all creation), the nature of being human and the Kingdom of God also became distinctive theological underpinnings of the Social Gospel. There was a willingness to engage with the insights and methodologies of the emerging social sciences, such as sociology, and biocentric notions of progression and evolution. There was a recognition that theology alone was an inadequate tool to reflect on the rapid processes of change epitomized by urbanization and industrialization, because of its isolation from the radically changed circumstances of peoples' lives. The desire to affirm the presence of God working within the world rendered necessary the use and interpretation of context and empirical study. This interaction between sociology and theology led, over time, to an essentially liberal reading of the ambiguities between a dynamic process of urbanization and industrialization on the one hand, and the challenges of creating just and fair working conditions on the other. During the 25 years up to World War I there was a sense of social optimism derived from beliefs in evolution and progress. Darwinian notions of evolution were linked inextricably, in this thinking, to theological concepts of the Kingdom of God, suggesting that humans could progress in terms of moral understanding, social awakening and technological achievement towards the perfect society envisaged by the Kingdom.

A key exponent of Social Christianity was Walter Rauschenbusch, a New York Lutheran-Baptist minister who ministered in the Hell's Kitchen area of the city in the 1880s and 1890s. His utopian vision involved the Christianization of the whole social order in line with the ethical convictions of Jesus. This included the economic sphere, and the structure of capitalism, whereby evolutionary change towards the moral standards of the gospel would, he believed, eventually turn all people towards good. He believed that the environmental contexts in which people found themselves strongly influenced their moral behaviour. Sin was thus largely structural rather than personal, in that the un-Christianized social structures contain 'the superpersonal forces of evil … thus encouraging the predilection towards individualism, pride and selfishness which go against the solidaristic view of society proclaimed by the Gospel and epitomized by Jesus in his mission and ministry' (quoted Kamergrauzis, 2001: 41). With regard to capitalism, for example, he argued that its unbalanced polarization of rich and poor went against the values and norms of a Christianized social order, and thus against the equality and intrinsic dignity inherent in the notion that every human is a child of God. If God is 'Father' to all, then all humans are 'brothers' and it was the fulfilment of the common good, rather than the individual good, that was to be pursued.

The outbreak of World War I prompted a radical reappraisal of the liberal and scientific utopianism of the Social Gospel, on two fronts. First was the belief that humans could exercise their capabilities in choosing the right political and individual path (in line with wider currents of liberal theology). Second was the belief that a radical overhauling of political economy and society (in line with Christian principles) would inevitably lead to an overhauling of human nature for the better. It was this disregard for the ambivalence of human nature, and the superficial optimism within Social Gospel thought, that the Christian Realists came to challenge as they emerged during the post-war period in both Europe and North America.

Karl Barth, Crisis Theology and the Origins of Christian Pessimism

In this section I want to outline some of the theological objections of the Social Gospel raised by the theology that emerged in Europe after World War I. While not directly identified as Christian Realists, the thinking of such theologians as Karl Barth, Emil Brunner and Dietrich Bonhoeffer are highly influential on subsequent Christian Realist thinking.

Following the destructive upheaval in Europe after the 1914–18 war, Barth formulated what he called a *theology of crisis*. This crisis reclaimed theology from a divine rather than a human perspective, for which rigorous exposition of the Bible, in its capacity as the inerrant Word of God, was required.

Within liberal theology, the 'given-ness' of Christianity (its fixed and dogmatic components) had been minimized in favour of human experience, and it was believed that Christian faith and tradition could be deployed to serve quite specific economic and political demands. The proper place of Christian revelation had been usurped by the category of human experience as a source of ethical revelation. Robin Lovin reminds us that under liberal epistemology, 'Both Christian dogmas and social values were viewed as imperfect, changing, historical realities' (1984: 7) .

The 'crisis theology' of Barth had a cultural as much as a theological impetus. In the aftermath of World War I, the European vision of social and religious progress, running in parallel towards an approximation of the Kingdom of God on earth, was seen as thoroughly discredited. Barth and others were keen that European Protestant theology should distance itself from the liberal Enlightenment project, for fear that faith itself might become a casualty of the post-war crisis. Thus the first theological task after the war was to identify the Christian message so that it might address with renewed clarity the problem of collapsing social order and theological integrity.

Notions that the Kingdom of God could in some way be established on earth were replaced by what Niebuhr described as 'the emphasis of orthodox Christianity upon the perennial sinfulness of the world and the need for salvation which transcended the whole sphere of socio-ethical relationships' (Niebuhr: 1934, quoted in Kamergrauzis, 2001: 44). Two implications for the development of Christian Realism flow from this crisis theology of divine revelation.

The first is a suspicion of natural law (that is, a moral strategy based on observable principles within the laws of nature and the universe). In a rejection of Kantian ethics and the subsequent tradition of German idealism, Barth maintains the unbridgeable gap between the absolute transcendence of God and the sinfulness of human beings. This viewpoint is also is designed to do proper justice to the once-and-for-all transformation of nature by the redemptive act of Christ on the cross, and his subsequent resurrection. Thus, it was not just post-war European culture that was to be found wanting from the perspective of God's sovereignty, but all cultures at all times. The Kingdom of God no longer becomes a participatory project, whereby divine and human efforts at creating a perfect society are conjoined. Rather, it becomes a judgement on human history, since it is God who inaugurates its coming and sets the terms for its advance.

The second implication is identifying where the location for moral discourse and engagement is. If the role of humankind is to hear and become obedient to the word of God as revealed in Christ through a proclamatory reading of the Bible (what one might call a 'proclamatory hermeneutic'), then the place where it will be best heard and acted upon will be the church community. As Lovin says, 'The church as the community of those attentive to the Word of God and mindful of their history as God's covenant people becomes the important locus for moral discernment' (Lovin, 1984: 9).

On this basis, any attempts within the wider community to discern general moral principles are seen as flawed. Within such discourses, Christians may offer important guidance to society, but that guidance will be achieved by witnessing to what they know in conscience before God, rather than from their own resources (Lovin, 1984: 12–13).

The uncompromising nature of this stance does have to be seen in the context of the role of the German church during Hitler's accession and rule in the 1920s and 1930s. Barth's theological position allowed the church to distance itself, as a Confessing Church, from any calls to cultural or national identity that Hitler lay before it, and to retain a sense of its own integrity, while at the same time critiquing the excessive leadership claims of Hitler himself.

However, a question needed to be asked of the Church's ability to carry out this task with sufficient rigour and consistency, being mindful of its own propensity for structural sinfulness in the past. Barth hints at the churches' provisionality within this area by explaining what he saw as the role of conscience in defining an obedient response to the Word of God, a feature of human life sanctioned by God as a way of 'already' knowing God's will but only fully realized eschatologically (that is, within the context of God's final reign). For Barth, here is a tension between what is 'already given about the world and our knowledge of it', and what is 'not yet' in terms of complete perfection and understanding. The church is therefore caught within this *already/not yet* theological and temporal landscape; it is 'between-times', and from Barth's perspective, should be much more oriented towards the 'not yet' than the 'already'. It's fair to say that other theologians who were in conversation with Barth were more open to a dialogue between Christian revelation and wider culture and society. Emil Brunner and Dietrich Bonhoeffer also responded to the crisis in European culture and theology during the interwar period, but it's through their more dialogical approach that we begin to see the emergence of Christian Realism.

Emil Brunner and Dietrich Bonhoeffer: A More Hopeful Analysis

Both Brunner and Bonhoeffer share Barth's insistence that the sovereignty of God's command is the starting point for Christian ethics, but both saw workable parallels between that command and the stable structures of human life such as family, government, economic life and the church. These structures and patterns of authority are observable by all and provide the basis for a common action between Christians and other sectors of society in ensuring that these structures of human life are maintained. Brunner calls them the 'orders of creation', which means that a compassionate parent, a skilled technician or an able governor are, in a real sense, doing God's will when they perform these functions well. This human responsiveness is, for Brunner, part of a Christian vocation, or calling. He argues that it is part of our vocation to make our response to the human situation a form of obedience to the divine command. Brunner, in his concept of *Wortmächtigkeit* ('word power') also endorses, to a limited extent, the power of human rationality that we can use as a means of communicating with and understanding each other. Not only is this a creative gift between humans, but more importantly is essential for experiencing and understanding the unique human relationship with God.

Human reason therefore does not give us the content of revelation, but it does enable us to recognize and understand it. It is the point of contact between God's initiative and human responsiveness.

However, Brunner has been criticized for his conservative perception of the nature and role of these 'orders of creation'. Because he chooses to locate a main focus of God's revelation not in the church alone, but in these other orders of creation as well, he invests a great deal in ensuring that they should not change. Too much mutability would rob them of the inherent stability required to serve the purpose of clear and long-term guidance for human ethical behaviour. A basic position of Brunner's is that if an order of creation (such as a form of political democracy, or the institution of marriage) works tolerably well, then it should be not altered for fear of revolutionary instability. Lovin summarizes Bruner's position thus:

The primacy of preservation does not oblige us to accept evil just because it exists, but it forbids us to risk the good that does exist for the sake of a possible improvement ... Appreciation for the achievements of the prevailing order induces one not to take risks and makes it difficult to understand those who see so little hope for their own future that they would risk everything on the chance of total social change.

(1984: 54)

Bonhoeffer shared Barth's stress for the need of a radical, church-based critique of absolute power, and in the earlier years of his theological and ministerial career in the 1930s he was a teacher and leader in the Confessing Church. However, by the time Bonhoeffer is working on his own *Ethics* he is, like Brunner, keen to respond to the idea of the 'natural' being a source of ethical guidance – although in his view, it does have only a *penultimate* value. The ultimate epistemological base for Bonhoeffer is the world reconciled by God in Jesus Christ, through his Incarnation and suffering. For Bonhoeffer, reality is relational. Jesus Christ is the centre of all reality because he is the *Man for Others*. 'His personhood is expressed in being there – in being there in three ways: being there for men, being there for history and being there for nature' (quoted in De Gruchy, 1999: 216)

The art of 'being there with and for' is constitutive of the world being reconciled to God. Christ therefore exists as community, and this is the ultimate basis for reality. Because everything is in relationship to everything else, it is possible to devise universal moral claims and duties that support the notion of community. Since one of the main ways open to human beings of expressing community is through our bodies, Bonhoeffer is concerned to enshrine in the area of universal law the idea of *human rights*: the right not to experience torture, the deprivation of liberty, rape and so on.

The status of these universal rights and duties is 'penultimate', but important in that they point towards the ultimate, and are of the one and same reality as the ultimate. This is where his concept of 'mandates' emerges. Mandates, for Bonhoeffer, help form human behaviour in their role as examples of 'structured moral responsibility within this overall relational reality' (quoted in De Gruchy, 1999: 217). Examples of mandates would read very similarly to those 'orders of creation' identified by Brunner: family, economic life, citizenship and the state, the church, circles of friendship. They push us towards the 'being-with-and-for-others' that Bonhoeffer defines as the ultimate expression of divine reality; a lifetime 'filled with the obligations, opportunities and responsibilities that reflect the requirements of life together' (quoted in De Gruchy, 1999: 221). It is through living out these requirements that we learn to exercise responsibility, and to accept the natural limitations that will protect us from the totalitarian impulses to control and dominate, which sinful human nature is prone to. These human mandates, although occurring naturally at the level of family and community, can also be the basis for public documents in the form of legislation that impose limits on the activities of the state. These universal constraints however are not based on reason or logic alone, but are discovered from the experience of human history. Bonhoeffer believed that Christian ethics therefore needed to be committed to 'an open investigation of the resources that are available to determine what actions we can take that respect the natural limits of our existence and that avoid claims to a power over our lives we do not, in fact, possess' (quoted Lovin, 1984: 172).

Bonhoeffer thus suggests, in his *Ethics*, an open but realistic partnership on the part of Christian ethics in response to mandates given by God. Within this penultimate ontological space, based on partnership, Bonhoeffer creates an area where considerable human theological creativity can occur, mingled with a sense of moral responsibility. It is part of the essence of God's relationship with his creation that humankind is given a free responsibility for shaping how the word of God can speak to each generation, a task that is held within the context of God's ultimate forgiveness (De Gruchy, 1999: 223). The human response in respect of this free responsibility is obedience, and the life of discipleship. Part of this discipleship is a careful, prayerful but hopeful analysis as to how Christ is to be revealed, the form of Christ that will best speak to the present age. A key recurring question Bonhoeffer was always asking was: 'Who is Christ for us today?'

Part of a contextual analysis that Bonhoeffer offered concerning his own age was the apparent triumph of secular modernity, created by the evolution of human autonomy, a process he traces back to the thirteenth century. When he surveys the advances in the fields of science, politics and culture, he concludes that the world has now reached a stage of self-confidence where ' "God" is being pushed more and more out of life, losing more and more ground'(quoted in Selby, 1999: 233). In one of his most famous quotations on this subject, written from his prison cell on 8 June 1944, he declared, 'man has learnt to deal with himself in all questions of importance without recourse to the "working hypothesis" called God' (quoted in Selby, 1999: 233). This required a radical reinterpretation of the role of Christianity in a world now come of age (*Mündigkeit*). Bonhoeffer sees Christianity moving away from a childlike dependency on the comforts of a clericalized and cultural religion, and its conservative ideologies supporting the dying social order that had been swept so powerfully away by the counter-revolution of Nazism (Müller, 1967: 203–04). Indeed, he believes that this move to adulthood is desired by God as part of the liberation of human beings to understand true autonomy and responsibility within a world where God is not a *deus ex machina*, waiting in the wings to restore the world in a final act of transcendent finality, but where God is 'truly a suffering participant in the life of the world' (Selby, 1999: 235).

Christianity needs to be liberated from its own Christian past if it is to engage in a future world *etsi deus non daretur* (as if there were no God). In practice, a 'religionless' Christianity returns to the person of Jesus Christ, not the Western, liberally enlightened but culturally conservative institution that bears his name. In the person of Jesus Christ, and especially in his Passion and crucifixion, Bonhoeffer finds God's most radical and complete identification with the historical development of the world in its joys and sufferings. This identification liberates human beings from child-like dependency on cultural/ideological institutions and outmoded myths to a proper, adult and free engagement through discipleship within a secularized world where to all intents and purposes God is absent. In his Man-for-Others epithet, Jesus shows us not a God who 'removes our history from us in order to make it himself ... but who himself becomes a man in our history and this-worldly life' (Müller, 1967: 212).

However, this stress on discipleship to the crucified and powerless Jesus/Man for Others is not a nihilistic and pessimistic identification with suffering for its own sake. The responsibility of recognizing the complexity and pain of the world is offset by the freedom gained in applying the full range of human creativity and compassion to its structural injustices, an exercise that is essentially hopeful rather than hopeless. If the church exists at all, it exists 'only when it exists for others' (Selby, 1999: 241), and it is from this perspective of *relational epistemology* – working from the underside of history rather than the perspective of privilege – that the church and theology should, according to Bonhoeffer, 'come to look with new eyes at matters great and small ... that our perception of generosity, humanity and justice and mercy should become clearer, freer, less corruptible' (quoted Selby, 1999: 242).

From this broad-brush analysis, the roots of Christian Realism in the Social Gospel, and incorporating the strong influences of the three writers identified above, begin to be uncovered. They are:

- a critique of the social consequences of neoliberal laissez-faire capitalism and a desire to rediscover the prophetic voice of the church in relation to abuses of political and economic power
- a belief in God's immanence, principally through the Incarnation, the cross and Passion of Jesus Christ, and historic interpretations of the Kingdom of God as both a process within history as well as an outcome of history
- a commitment to interdisciplinary methods of analysis whereby theology and the church work in conjunction with social sciences (particularly economics and sociology and other systems theories)
- a stress on the ethics of Jesus as a response to structural as well as individual sin, and as the basis for the exercising of human autonomy and responsibility
- a view of the Church as *semper reformanda*, and while it may be the preferred locus of moral reflection is by no means the only and perfect source
- a belief that the structures of the world and human rationality are a valid source as the basis for moral intervention in wider community, but are penultimate rather than ultimate sources of knowledge.

Christian Realism: Holding the Tension between Utopianism and Pessimism

Having uncovered the contours of the emerging Christian Realist tradition, I will now turn to the work of theologians who are explicitly linked with that tradition. In doing so, we will explore the three specific aspects of Christian Realism identified at the beginning of the chapter, which directly engage with the emerging literature of Third Space hybridity (see page 67).

1) Commitment to the Interdisciplinary Analysis of Political and Economic Power

Christian Realism has traditionally engaged with both socialist and Marxist analysis to develop a distinctive Christian ethical approach to the workings of the market economy and the role of the state. In more recent years the argument has moved on to examining the dynamics of the global economy and the role of governance at local and global levels, including the growing significance of civil society and social capital.

The tradition of middle axioms in christian realism: from William Temple to Ronald Preston   The concept of middle axioms (or the middle level) within Christian Realism emerged during the 1930s and 1940s, and represented attempts to link the ethical demands of the Christian gospel to concrete situations within any given historical context. Traditionally they have been expressed in church statements and reports on social responsibility, which seek to define broad areas of response to economic, social or political situations as a means of guiding individual Christian response without undermining the moral responsibility of the individual to act according to conscience and choice. According to Joseph Oldham's classic definition, prepared for 1937 Oxford Ecumenical Conference, middle axioms are '… attempts to define the directions in which, in a particular state of society, Christian faith must express itself. They are not binding for all time, but are provisional definitions of the type of behaviour required of Christians at a given period in given circumstances' (quoted in Visser 't Hooft and Oldham, 1937: 209).

William Temple provides a classic expression of middle axioms in his book *Christianity and Social Order*, written in the early 1940s. Temple, as Bishop of Manchester in the 1920s and as Archbishop of both York and then Canterbury in the 1930s and 1940s, witnessed at first hand the diminishing of human life caused by mass unemployment, poor education and derelict housing. The crisis prompted by these turbulent decades prompted him to proclaim a bold vision of a reconstituted society where the innate, God-given dignity of humankind, created in the image of God and redeemed to life in all its fullness by the Incarnation of Jesus Christ, required the production of decent spaces for people to live and work in, be educated and cared for, irrespective of their status or ability to pay. His six famous middle axioms included the following (abridged) objectives:

- every child should find itself a member of a family housed with decency and dignity so that it may grow up as a member of that basic community in a happy fellowship
- every child should have the opportunity of an education till the years of maturity, so planned as to allow for his peculiar aptitudes and make possible their full development
- every citizen to be in secure possession of such income as will enable him to maintain a home and bring up children in the conditions described above
- every citizen to have a voice in the conduct of their business or industry … and the satisfaction of knowing his labour is directed to the well-being of the community

- every citizen should have sufficient daily leisure with two days of rest in seven and ... an annual holiday with pay
- every citizen should have assured liberty in the forms of freedom of worship, of speech, of assembly and of association for special purposes.

(Temple, 1976: 96–97)

These middle axioms were offered by Temple within the context of a quasi-Keynesian economy whereby the pragmatic dynamics of consumption and profit are not seen in isolation (that is, as an end in themselves), but are held within a cultural, moral and political duty to ensure that these goals are bound within a legislative framework. The state would have (for example) the right to determine through the tax and rating system the amount of profit any homeowner or builder is allowed to make from their enterprise (Temple, 1976: 112–13).

The power of Temple's manifesto is largely due to the moral authority of his office (the Church of England of his day was still a unifying symbol within a reasonably stable and homogeneous society based around church and state) and to his enormous popularity as a charismatic and forward-thinking wartime archbishop.

Temple's thinking was updated in the 1970s by Ronald Preston, writing in the context of the transition in Britain from a mixed economy to the neoliberal market following the massive deindustrialization of the British economy and the attendant social problems of unemployment and poverty. He stressed the need for the rigorous assessment of empirical evidence, while at the same time acknowledging the partiality and provisionality of much empirical data. Two key ideas emerge from Preston's development of the middle axioms. First is the *dialogic* nature of the encounter between empirically based research and the Christian viewpoint, so that the middle axiom emerges from an interdisciplinary process. Secondly, this concept of a dialogic relationship, rather than a traditionally hierarchical one (with Christian revelation being given a priori dominance over empirical research), reveals a growing perception of the *ambiguous nature of the world*, and of ethical reflection itself. As he wrote in the early 1980s:

> No one can be sure of the correctness of an analysis of a current situation; no one can be certain of the consequences of encouraging some trends and discouraging others; no one can foresee what will be the effect of unexpected innovations. In matters of ethics as well as doctrine our pilgrimage is by faith not by sight.
>
> (Preston 1983: 154)

Preston's development of thinking about the nature of middle axioms also acknowledges the declining influence of the Church of England as a national entity in British life, which raises the question for him of how best to express theology within the public sphere. It leads to two further elements of the Christian Realism tradition that it is important to identify at this point. First is the discipline of trust involved when walking in a world of growing ambiguity and plurality; Christian social ethics is 'a pilgrimage by faith, not by sight'. Secondly, the commitment to discerning a common good remains a pastoral and theological priority, despite the growing fragmentation of social and cultural norms. The role of the Church is vital in this, as the vehicle by which a social ethic for making the world a better place, based on gospel values, is shared and transmitted. Thus the Church exists for the sake of others, rather than for itself. It offers guidance to the wider world rather than being in itself the social ethic by which the wider world is judged.

Ronald Preston and the search for the common good   Preston supported Temple's notion of the common good as the overriding criteria by which to measure ethically the role and impact of the market economy. This Preston defined as a minimum level of income, health care, social services and education. However, for him, the concept of the common good was also deeply related to a view of the connected nature of human society, which meant that all members of human society are mutually responsible for satisfying the basic needs of each other, without taking into consideration either personal merit or the extent of their disadvantage. In other words, those who are marginalized through poverty or lack of a democratic mandate were not excluded on the basis of personalized deficiency such as a lack of 'effort, ability and luck' (quoted Kamergrauzis, 2001: 160). Rather, they find themselves in this position due to the structures that exist within wider society – what Preston calls the 'status quo' of political and economic power that Christian social ethics needs to challenge. In particular, it needs to confront the way the market produces inequalities in purchasing power, thus favouring those with existing wealth who can attract the economic resources to pay for luxuries while the poor often cannot pay for necessities. Preston is thus supportive of the concept of the preferential option for the poor, by which they have the right to basic material and social facilities.

This preferential option for the poor, Preston argues, is redolent of the way God's grace operates (that is, bestowed on all regardless of human merit) and in particular the way Jesus' consistent concern for the poor and the suffering is presented in the gospel narratives as a special metaphor for the divine grace. However, Preston is also committed to giving the marginalized a voice by which their perspectives can be heard, and thus creating 'a forum where those affected can speak for themselves about the discrimination and oppression against them' (quoted in Kamergrauzis, 2001: 160).

This commitment to a forum is an example of where Preston expands Temple's middle axioms, by developing the theme of citizenship, which Temple mentions but doesn't properly define. This means reassessing the traditional outputs that an economic system should deliver for all citizens (such as decent housing, employment, health care and so on). While these are important, they are not the only criteria by which to measure the moral integrity of a government's economic or political policy. An equally important benchmark is the way in which government policies either hinder or facilitate participation in processes of empowerment and self-development. This moves the theological debate more into the current expansion of the concept of poverty as an aspect of social exclusion (see, for example, Townsend, 1979; and Hills, Le Grand and Piachaud, 2002). Perhaps the greatest criticism of the welfare state – the new incarnation of the state that was at the heart of Temple's Christian-based social order – was the dependency culture it created. What is being expressed in

Preston's understanding of citizenship is a more proactive and partnership-based engagement in decision-making processes directly affecting the lives of those excluded from wealth and power. As Kamergrauzis summarizes: 'Participation within social structures is also seen as a necessity for the full realization of human potential in relationships with others' (Kamergrauzis, 2001: 161).

Preston develops this notion of citizenship with the idea that in order to further enhance a proactive sense of participation, democratic processes need to promote the concept of the 'responsibilities' of citizenship as well as the concept of rights. The responsibility in this case is to participate in public processes of democracy and decision-making for the sake of the common good. The political economy that he considers best at delivering the right conditions for human wellbeing to flourish, while at the same time respecting the inner dynamic of the market economy, is the Democratic Socialist Economy.

The Democratic Socialist Economy   The Democratic Socialist Economy is not a return to the Christian Socialist critique of capitalism that allowed for only the limited working of the profit and competition motives in favour of public ownership of the means of production. Preston argues instead for the proper role of competition in the market on the basis that it prevents stagnation of the economy, recognizes the proper place of diversity within human life in relation to capacities and aptitudes, and rewards individual growth and responsible stewardship of scarce resources. This view represents a fairly traditional Protestant understanding that wealth-creation is a God-given human potential, but also that the freedom and responsibility to decide how best to manage that wealth-creation for the sake of the common good is equally a God-given gift.

Unlike the economic philosophy of the New Right that emerged in Britain from the late 1970s through to the mid 1990s, Preston does advocate a boundary on the extent to which the market should be allowed to develop. Economic efficiency and the elegance of its theories are not means in themselves, nor the only criteria by which the market economy should be judged. Any evaluation of the market has to reflect its impact on wider society, and that broader evaluation should have pre-eminence over the neoliberal axiomatic belief that society is made up of a collection of wealth-creating individuals. 'Society is greater than the sum of individuals who compose it. Society is prior to the individual' (Preston, 1991: 178). Preston personally sees 'some form of social welfare economy as the least bad way of running the economy' (Preston, 1983: 63). This will mean a combination of 'voluntary codes of ethics and of good practice alongside some forms of government legislation' to create appropriate boundaries for the operation of the market (Preston, 1991: 75).

The Third Economic Way   Preston's thinking represents the Christian Realist understanding of the Third Economic Way, a consciously middle or hybrid way that seeks to steer a path between a number of different economic, political and theological issues. It is a way that seeks to avoid the polarity of either too much faith in economics (the neoliberal mantra of the New Right) or too much faith in politics (the state control of the economy favoured by the Old Left). It seeks to enhance the dynamics of the market in terms of providing individual choice, growth and opportunities for expression and development, while at the same time advocating some legislative and regulatory mechanisms to ensure that the wealth generated works to the benefit of the whole of society.

However, Preston's theological realism prevents him from sanctifying the perspective of the poor, on the understanding that once in power, the poor often succumb to the human temptation to wield power for its own sake. There is also the theological realism that Preston deploys in his understanding of the tension between human self-interest and the Christian command to love your neighbour as yourself. While it may be good to hope for occasional glimpses of self-sacrifice from individuals, he argues that it is more prudent and predictable to allow the market to function in such a way that the needs of neighbours are met through the provision of economic goods and services available to all citizens.

Later Christian Realism: John Atherton and the mainstreaming of the global economy   Later writers in the Christian Realist tradition consider the Democratic Socialist Economy too static a model to engage effectively in a pluralistic and partnership-based world. For example, John Atherton focuses on global scarcity and marginalization, and in his 2003 book, *Marginalization*, holds up a series of 'wild facts' about the nature of global marginalization. For example, 1.3 billion people are compelled to live on less than US$1 a day, 3 billion (nearly half the world's population) have not enough to eat, and 60 million people a year die of hunger and hunger-related diseases. Like Preston, Atherton is committed to keeping a *relational* dimension to his critique of the workings of the market. For him, the writings of the economist and moral philosopher Amartya Sen are pivotal, with their emphasis on people-centred analysis and his commitment, through use of the United Nations Human Development reports, to promoting the aim of developing human capabilities as the objective of global political economy. Sen's definition of human capability is 'having the freedom, and therefore the capability, to be and to do, to pursue one's self-chosen purposes' (quoted in Atherton, 2003: 66). The capability to pursue self-chosen purposes is the main criterion by which to measure progress against the forces of marginalization, a perspective that moves beyond the Rawlsian concept of a just distribution of primary goods. In other words, it is not simply the resources for human functioning that are required, but the freedom these economic commodities bring in order to promote self-development and freedom for all in a sustainable and mutually enhancing way.

For Sen, the basic building blocks required for creating conditions by which self-development and self-determination can occur are decent environmental conditions, good governance, decent healthcare and education facilities, and basic human rights.

The question for Atherton, arising from Sen's building blocks, is to what extent the purposes of the global economic market can be developed along the lines of delivering what he sees as the priority of 'pro-poor, pro-environmental economic growth' (Atherton, 2003: 158).

Despite the enormity of the marginalization problem facing humanity, Atherton is clear that economic growth remains essential for delivering the resources required for the proper functioning of human capabilities, not least in the human fulfilment provided by participating in an active economic life. This is particularly true when a variety of factors coalesce to produce a *virtuous* cycle of growth (such as the presence of good governance, educational and research structures, the technological infrastructure to improve communications, and the positive encouragement of women in the market and in education). In this way virtuous cycles of growth continue to have significant roles to play in the reduction of marginalization, and Atherton cites the examples of India and South Korea as countries that are benefiting from such processes, with increasing rates of literacy and GDP.

However, Atherton is also aware of the counter-forces inherent within the global capitalist economy, linked with the processes of modernization, that keep many countries and regions of the world within a *vicious* economic cycle. These include an inability of the market to prioritize different types of utility, the treatment of land as a factor of production rather than a force of nature, the invasion of market forces into all aspects of human life, the paradox whereby labour-saving technology also produces systems of exploitation, and the growing separation of the rich from the poor, whereby the rich can choose to inhabit spatial zones completely divorced from any reference to local space or communities (Atherton, 2003: 86–7).

A Reformulated Christian Political Economy

Atherton's proposed solution to marginalization is a reformulated Christian Political Economy that features a number of different elements. The main purpose of Atherton's reformulation is similar to that expressed by Preston's Third Way: an attempt to bring together, within a hybrid space, two disparate elements within the economic debate. For Atherton, these disparate elements are summarized in terms of *ethical* vs. *engineering economics*. These are Sen's terms and refer to justice-based questions about the kind of economic system one wants (the ethical component) versus the supposedly value-free approach to economics favoured by neoclassical economists (the engineering component). The latter approach is favoured by those wishing to reduce the political dimension of economics (the role of the state in regulating the market). They stress the scientific and efficiency criteria upon which the market is based; for example, the supposedly consistent variable of customer preference satisfaction. What Atherton's Christian Political Economy seeks to do is create a dialogue whereby engineering economics can re-engage with an ethical base, and it does this via a variety of different methods (Atherton, 2003: 151–2).

It begins from an anthropological base, with an ethical reformulation of the neoclassical theory of human behaviour as *Homo Economicus*, which in J.S. Mill's definition is 'A being who invariably does that by which he may obtain the greatest amount of necessaries, conveniences and luxuries, with the smallest quantity of labour and physical self-denial ...' (quoted in Atherton, 2003: 152). A reformulation of this definition would involve, for example, retracing the moral components within Adam Smith's work that included the 'broader motivations of humanity, generosity and public spirit' in order for the distribution of goods to be established. It would also involve tracing, as Sen does, the elements of trust and goodwill that all good business practice requires for its proper functioning (and which is most readily apparent in the economic dynamics of South East Asia or Japan, for example), as well as the principle of justice often enshrined within taxation and welfare systems aimed at enhancing the efficiency of what the market distributes.

Atherton's reformulated political economy would then move onto a valuing of the different ways in which efficiency in the market is enhanced by the valorization of components other than production and price mechanisms. For example, a lack of investment in education provision or tackling gender inequality exacerbates a situation of inefficiency because of the inequality it produces. Better-educated, more gender-integrated economies have higher repositories of knowledge and skills and possess, therefore, higher levels of productivity, thus reinforcing the trend whereby societies with higher growth rates are also those that are more egalitarian.

Atherton would then add to a reformulated Christian Political Economy the interdisciplinary thinking of current political philosophy, which seeks the best ways to promote inclusive societies within regions, cities and communities that are not only experiencing economic polarization but also increased ethnic diversity through immigration. Thus, for example, he endorses Iris Young's concept of *differentiated solidarity*, which allows marginalized groups to participate in decision-making processes through positive discrimination strategies and widening use of communication techniques based on narrative and rhetoric rather than purely reasoned argument.

To this would be added the development of measurement systems by which to gauge progress in reducing marginalization, in line with the systems developed by the UNHD reports (such as the HDI – Human Development Index – and GDI – Gender-related Development Index) and utilized by Sen to develop his arguments. The continued and developed use of measurement systems is important for Atherton because it represents 'an exercise in applied ethics and theology as performative discipline' (Atherton, 2003: 161).

Atherton then adds to the mix the insights of the growing resurgence in religious-based economics from the Judaeo-Christian-Islamic traditions, all of which have a 'bias to inclusivity' towards the proper care and inclusion of the poorest sections of society (Atherton, 2003: 167). Specifically, from within the Christian tradition, there has emerged the Jubilee 2000 debt-relief campaign, which brought to the fore the moral issue of how to deal with unpayable debt on the part of the poorest nations. From the Muslim tradition there has re-emerged the practice of interest-free banking, rejecting as it does the concept of usury in financial transactions, a practice that lies at the heart of the market economy. Instead of the usual practice of charging interest on a loan (often at exorbitant rates, and with the highest rates going to the poorest borrowers), both the bank in which the money is deposited, and the borrower, share in either the profits or the loss of the business, thus making it in the interests of both parties that viable businesses are produced. The system also allows for the provision of loans in kind (for example, cattle), thus enabling those from poorer Islamic societies in the South to participate.

Finally, there is what Atherton refers to as the *Christian heteroclitical tradition*, which provides the important sources of 'heretical' thinking that challenge the assumptions of mainstream economies and economics. This tradition stretches back to the eighteenth-century Romantic tradition and continues through to the present day in the writings of David Jenkins and the Radical Orthodoxy movement. The main significance of this tradition is the multilayered texture of critical engagement it represents with mainstream economics, and the way it enacts a methodology that Christian public theology will need to engage in if it is to reconnect with a problematic as complex as marginalization. It also warns the mainstream of its constant need to adapt if it is to survive. For better or worse, this constant mutation is what late capitalism has managed to achieve. 'Capitalism and mainstream economics have endured because of their willingness and ability to reformulate their traditions in the light of greatly changing contexts' (Atherton, 2003: 177).

All of the above elements proposed by Atherton as part of his Christian Political Economy reflect a growing sophistication and interdisciplinarity. He takes this strand of Christian Realism substantially towards the domain of Third Space hybridity in advocating the desirability of listening to narrative and experience alongside data measurement. Listening to narrative and experience would have been something of an anathema to Preston, for whom empirical data was the pre-eminently trustworthy source of interdisciplinary working. Such use of narrative within Christian Realism has also been developed recently by Duncan Forrester (2001) and among feminist theologians and economists such as Karen Lebacqz and Ann-Cathrin Jarl, who are also deployed by Atherton in the service of his reconstructed Christian Political Economy. For example, Jarl calls for an economic system that allows the greater participation of people in meaningful, non-oppressive and non-alienating ways, and in doing so calls attention to an alternative to Mills's *Homo Economicus*. For feminist economists such as her, the *Imperfectly Rational Somewhat Economical Person* is a type far more likely to be found in the structures and relationships of the real world, and is thus the basis for a deeper ethical reformulation of the impact of economic policies.

In Atherton we have seen the beginnings of a discussion about the need to incorporate different 'voices' within a performative understanding of Christian Political Economy that allows a more narrative type of experience to shape the delivery of a pro-poor, pro-environmental strategy. Atherton's scheme is increasingly influenced by interfaith and feminist perspectives, thus chiming in well with the epistemological base of Third Space hybridity, which takes as its starting point the post-colonial perspectives of women and diasporic global communities.

We now explore the second area of overlap between Christian Realism and Third Space hybridity identified at the start of this chapter: the epistemological bias towards seeing human history as a locus of salvation. We have already explored this in relation to the thinking of Bonhoeffer, but we will now explore it with a closer look at the output of Reinhold Niebuhr.

2) Human History as a Locus of Salvation

Niebuhr, writing in the United States from the 1920s to the 1960s, experienced throughout his life various swings between confidence in, and distrust of, political attempts to create a better society. He attempted a consistent approach by using a three-way triangulation between Liberalism, Marxism and Christianity. A brief study of the way he uses these three points of reference will show that they are well suited to a Third Space hybridity methodology – namely, one that is interdisciplinary, pragmatic, flexible and symbolic. We will look at each one of these three reference points in turn.

Liberalism Niebuhr engaged in a fluctuating relationship with Liberalism throughout his life. In his early career he was highly dismissive of the historical optimism underpinned by Liberalism, which was the predominant tradition within the 1920s American Protestant scene from which he emerged. According to Kenneth Cauthen, the main tenets of this theological Liberalism were: 1) an emphasis upon the authority of experience; 2) an emphasis on ethics; 3) a recognition of human social environment; 4) a confidence in reason; 5) the devaluation of the authority of Scripture; 6) acceptance of historical investigation into the Christian faith; 7) a dynamic view of history; 8) an emphasis on the humanity of Jesus; 9) a recognition of the importance of toleration (quoted in Stone; 1972: 35–6).

For Niebuhr, the destructive experience of World War I, and his reluctant support for it despite his pacifist instincts, led him to question radically the role of religion in the 'comfortable' support of notions of progress and evolution. He wanted to endorse a form of Christian religion that could be a source of hope but not facile optimism for a nation experiencing urbanization, poverty and racism. He looked for a religious expression that preserved a wider sense of hope, while at the same time acknowledging the seriousness of the moral struggle. Religion could best serve the purpose of humankind, he believed, by taking the struggle between good and evil seriously without resorting to simplistic dualism. It was in the moral struggle between good and evil that human beings developed their sense of personality and identity. Key to this struggle was the growing importance attached to the pastoral tension between the *real* and the *ideal*. The vision and impetus provided by religion to build a society of justice and 'brotherhood' was, in his view, hopelessly compromised by the squalid, polarized and violent communities we manage to build on earth. It is therefore the tension that exists within the eschatological horizon of the Reign (or Kingdom) of God. Human history since biblical times, theologically speaking, is in this view the interim period between the inauguration of the Kingdom of God by Jesus at the start of his ministry (Luke 4) and its final completion on the Day of Judgement. The perspective of ultimate divine judgement is therefore always present, as the corrective to any overweening belief that humans are self-sufficient in their access to grace, perfection and salvation. What exists within human history, from the perspective of divine perfection, is the radical sinfulness that lies at the heart of the human will.

However, the inauguration of God's kingdom within human history does infuse it with the constant possibility of transformation, which in its best moments embodies and anticipates God's perfect justice and restoration (as envisaged, for example, in the vision of the heavenly city in Chapter 21 of the Book of Revelation). Examples from the Judaeo-Christian tradition, which Niebuhr sees as holding a workable tension between the real and the ideal, are the Old Testament prophets and the person of Jesus Christ. The Hebrew prophets drew much of their religious genius from their sense of struggle between the ideal and the real. They operated within the interim zone of Yahweh's command to practise peace, justice and obedience, and the reality of political compromise and oppression that characterized Hebrew urban society, centred on the cultic base at Jerusalem. The prophets exploited that dynamic to bring about reform and transformation of some aspects of Hebrew religio-political structures, and indeed the consciousness of the Hebrew people, particularly in times of exile.

Meanwhile the cross of Christ is symbolic, particularly within Niebuhr's early thought, of the 'perfect type of moral beauty that lies at the very heart of reality'. It represents the 'ideal of love that sets its objectives so high that they can never be attained' (quoted in Stone, 1972: 48). This ideal, enacted in the events of the crucifixion, is at one level powerless against the powers of the real world, and thus represents the general powerlessness of the 'ideal' in the real world.

Thus the 'ideal' notions of progress and evolution towards human enlightenment embodied in modernity and liberal theology were, to Niebuhr, theologically naive and overoptimistic. He was in his earlier writing highly critical of Liberal assumptions, and uses both Marxist and Christian sources to critique them. We have already elaborated some Christian-based critiques of Liberalism, and we now look at some of his Marxist-based critiques.

Niebuhr's Marxist analysis tends to reflect his most pessimistic belief about the positive outcomes of human history. His strongest Marxist phase was in the late 1920s and early 1930s, when he most despaired of the possibility of structured political reform to deal with the continuing inequalities of post-war America, and the rise of fascism in Europe. The allure of Marxism for him was its political 'realism', which uncovered the severity and extent to which the use and abuse of power undermines any 'liberal' aspirations concerning the possibility that change might be brought about without sacrifice and conflict. He agreed with the Marxist analysis of class power, whereby the privileged class would resist all efforts to improve the competitive position of the underprivileged class until the pressure of events brought about by the inner contradictions of capitalism (namely its concentration of power in the hands of a small elite) triggered the crisis of history and the collapse of not only capitalism, but also Western civilization (of which Liberalism was one of the main expressions). Marxism's dialectic view of history, namely the emergence of a new world order born out of the conflict of the class struggle between the proletariat and the ruling elite (in dialectic terms, the *thesis* and the *antithesis*), fitted in better with Niebuhr's Christian understanding of human history as constituting a struggle between the forces of good and evil.

However, Niebuhr's embracing of Marxism was never unequivocal, and his critique of it grew with increasing unease at the political abuses of Stalinism in the Soviet Union. The failure of Marxism to provide a workable alternative to the economic and political crises of the 1930s and 1940s, culminating in World War II, forced Niebuhr to re-evaluate his original criticisms of Liberalism. This also was driven by a growing respect for the achievements of Franklin D. Roosevelt's administration in forging the post-war structures of global civil society, such as the United Nations and the Marshall Plan.

One aspect of political Liberalism that never left Niebuhr, even when critical of its utopianism, was its roots in the sixteenth and seventeenth centuries as the first signs of democratic protest against feudal society. 'The ideas at the heart of the liberal faith ... are ideas about freedom and also ideas about the conditions, political and social of making freedom secure' (Plamenatz, 1963: 89). The notions of individual freedom inspired by Locke envisaged the natural rights of human beings flourishing within a circumscribed form of government that both protects and defines them. In Niebuhr's opinion, this was the basis of mature and pluralistic understandings of democracy and civil society. Thus, in the 1950s and 1960s, he appeared to appreciate anew the commodity of democracy as the only workable bulwark (however flawed) against the extremes of either fascism or communism, and to recognize the roots of democratic thinking and practice within the ongoing legacy of western Liberalism. At its best, it defends the individual against the totalitarianism of the state, and also against the totalitarianism of other individuals. Niebuhr sums it up in one of his well-known aphorisms: 'Man's capacity for justice makes democracy possible; but man's inclination to injustice makes democracy necessary' (quoted in Stone, 1972: 112). Democracy achieves this by its developed system of checks and balances, elections and separated bureaucracies, whose aim is to protect citizens from misuses of power.

As well as the 'gift' of democracy, Niebuhr sees within political Liberalism an innate pragmatism that emerges as a strongly explicit dimension to Christian Realism in his later output. This pragmatism is related to Niebuhr's dynamic understanding of history as ultimately being beyond the rules of either logic or organic development. Although trends and patterns do move towards a significant future, their ambiguities will not be uncovered by some inner logic within history itself, as thought by both classic and modern philosophies (see Niebuhr, 1949). Rather, the progression of history can only be interpreted from resources that stand beyond it, namely the mysteries of creation and providence and the revelation of the life and death of Christ that symbolically reveal clues about the meaning of the rest of history. According to Fitch's analysis of Niebuhr's theology of history, 'History has unity by faith, but not by sight' (quoted in Kegley and Bretall, 1956: 293).

This relativized view of human history from the perspective of the divine means that Niebuhr is sceptical of any neat theories of history. Previous attempts to implement political programmes on the basis of divine, natural or rational grounds have been undermined by the relativizing forces of history. Therefore every government institution can only be evaluated on its usefulness in providing the basis for the flourishing of the common good. As Stone remarks, 'Niebuhr judged political ideas in terms of their results. The verification of political theory in terms of its products revealed his deep pragmatism ... he often introduced such judgements with the words of one of his favourite texts, "By their fruits ye shall know them"' (Stone, 1972: 158).

This pragmatism means that a government's political programmes and institutions will regularly become outdated and require modification. However, these modifications are not to be done in the complete absence of guiding principles or moral givens. According to Stone, the given parameters of Niebuhr's Christian pragmatism were 'a recognition of the complexity of the issues of economics and politics, a commitment to justice, and an acceptance of a sense of responsibility for political life' (Stone 1972: 156). We shall explore the theological bases for these parameters in the concluding chapter.

Niebuhr's return to liberal pragmatism has been construed by some as an unhealthy lurch towards conservative social ethics that lost touch with his earlier, radical thought. Beverley Harrison, for example, traces this back to Niebuhr's 'idealist' reading of Marxism, which undermined the role of Marxist social analysis within subsequent Christian social ethics (Harrison, 1985: 60–62).

The point I am making is that the emergence of a political pragmatism (within the confines of attempting to discern the common good and a commitment to justice within an interdisciplinary context) is one potential link that can be developed between the Christian Realist Tradition and Third Space hybridity.

Marxism   We have already identified the importance of Marxist political realism for Niebuhr's critique of liberal utopianism. We have seen how in his rediscovery of pragmatic (rather than utopian) Liberalism, Niebuhr largely disowned Marxist social analysis and was highly critical of Communism as an expression of an alternative to Western democracy. However, Marxism did provide him with the basis for a healthy realism concerning the potentially exploitative and dangerously utopian tendencies within Christianity.

At the height of his Marxist 'phase', Niebuhr had become convinced that the logic of the Marxist view of history moving towards crisis was irresistible, and he attempted to forge a compromise at a mythic level between Marxism and Christianity, since he saw in Marxism a more 'moral' interpretation of the upheavals within history than that supplied by orthodox Christianity. As he explored the mythical basis of Marxism, particularly in relation to its confident predictions of the outcome of human history and its belief in empirical social analysis, he became increasingly mistrustful of its totalizing claims, and the ways it functioned as a quasi-religion. The specifically religious aspects of Marxism and Communism identified by Niebuhr included:

- the dogmatic belief in the doctrine of progress, and the utopian nature of society once the catastrophe of historical conflict had been enacted
- the uncritical 'messianic' symbolism attached to the dispossessed classes
- its 'oversimplification of morals' (Niebuhr, 1931: 462) by which the principles of equality and loyalty towards the proletarian class are absolutized in an unbalanced way
- its preservation of itself from critical or relativizing discourses in ways that closely mirror many religious systems in the West.

Niebuhr summarized his critique of Communism thus: 'Marx is its Bible and the writings of Lenin have achieved a dogmatic significance for it comparable to that which the thought of Thomas Aquinas had for the medieval church' (quoted in Stone, 1972: 66).

He observed that the utopian aspects of Marxism, and its promise of salvation through the epistemological bases of scientific theory and materialism, blinded its adherents to the tyrannical abuses of the systems it propagated. This was also a key critique of his understanding of the tendencies towards religious perfectionism within the neo-orthodoxy of Barth, which he considered too uncritical of political tyranny.

Christianity The main focus of this section will be Niebuhr's Christian anthropology and his treatment of the concept of justice, because both are central to the Christian Realist tradition.

Niebuhr's anthropology is crucial because it is closely linked with his Kingdom-of-God metaphysics, which is concerned to express the dynamic interplay that emerges within human history from both the potential for good and the potential for sin; the hopefulness of the already inaugurated kingdom against the judgement of the divine end-time (*eschaton*).

At the centre of Niebuhr's anthropology is the notion of freedom, which carries with it the inextricable ability to commit evil and thus the need for human redemption. This is a highly ambiguous position, but is designed to critique the facile optimism of liberal utopianism and theological Pelagianism, as well as counteract the pessimism of secular existentialists and theological Augustinianism.

Humankind for Niebuhr is a creature of nature, bound to a particular time and place and to specific historical contexts that shape its destiny. But humankind is also a spiritual creature that has the ability to understand something of the nature of its boundedness by reference to a universal, whole perspective. However, humankind, because of its bounded nature, can never have a dispassionate view of the universal, or a neutral perspective on the common good. The particular or local perspective will always colour the global one.

Niebuhr draws on the thinking of Martin Heidegger and Søren Kierkegaard (Stone, 1972: 96, Veldhuis, 1975: 30) to reflect on how this ambiguity produces an existential anxiety within human beings, and thus a constant striving to overcome it. This anxiety is both creative – in the spur it provides for human achievement – and destructive – in the frustration and anger it produces by the imprecise knowledge of where the limits of human freedom actually lie. This imprecision is traced by Niebuhr to a pre-existing state of evil that shows some ongoing influence of Augustine's category of original sin. Within Niebuhr's symbolic and existential reading of the Genesis myths, the alternative to sin (which is a mixture of error and conscious rebellion against the finitude of the human condition) is acceptance of insecurities by trusting that 'the insecurities of history, the abyss of meaninglessness and death will be overcome by God' (Stone, 1972: 98).

The pervasiveness of anxiety provokes two strands of sinfulness: self-deification (that is, excessive pride) and idolatry/fetishism (the projection of god-like status onto a person, object or ideology), both of which are designed to produce feelings of security. Niebuhr is most concerned at the human capacity for the will-to-power, which always threatens to snuff out the potential for free self-determination, both within ourselves, but also within others. This will-to-power needs to be seen as a catastrophic consequence of the inability of humans to trust the divine word of love expressed in the Incarnation and Passion of Jesus Christ.

By contrast to the human will-to-power, the ethic of Jesus is the ultimate standard by which to judge human endeavours in the areas of justice and democracy, because of its rejection of power. Jesus' transcendent and uncompromising ethic of love is based on fulfilment as self-sacrifice for the sake of another person or cause. Theologically expressed, the *agape* love of Jesus (based on non-reciprocal, sacrificial love poured out for the sake of the Other) is the context in which the *eros* love of humankind (which can stretch its meaning from sexual libido to mutual friendship, but even at this point is motivated by selfishness because it needs something in return) is contained. Within this moral universe, all egoism is rejected as expressing sinfulness, and the role of ethics is to reduce egoism. Jesus bears testimony to an ideal that is powerless in the world. The crucifixion is the ultimate symbol of love's fate in the world, and the resurrection is a symbol of its fulfilment, but it stands outside the possibilities and mechanisms of history. It is an ahistorical event, and as such is problematic if it is to influence social ethics and discussions about justice. Niebuhr attempted to reconcile its usefulness to ethics by claiming that although Jesus' ethic of love could not be realized in human history, it was relevant because it relativized other standards and lifted other norms to new heights; it provides 'the pull of obligation' for human behaviour whereby humankind seeks to 'realize in history what we conceive to be already the truest reality – that is, its final essence' (quoted in Stone, 1972: 81). Elsewhere, Niebuhr characterizes this tension between the ideal of love and human attempts to fulfil it within history as the paradox of 'impossible possibility', whereby 'the Kingdom of God is always a possibility in history, because its heights of pure love are organically related to the experience of love in all human life, but it is also an impossibility in history and always beyond every historical achievement' (Niebuhr, 1935: 42).

There were similar problems with the role of justice within Niebuhr's ethics. He regarded the principles of equal justice as a similar expression of the law of love that also belonged to the 'world of transcendent perfection' (quoted in Stone: 1972: 83). While justice itself as a simple principle does not provide political solutions, 'rules of justice' can be formulated to meet the needs of specific occasions, though Niebuhr stresses their very provisional nature. These rules of justice can be formulated from '... the fruit of a rational survey of the whole field of human interests'. However, they also 'embody too many contingent elements and are subject to such inevitable distortion by interest and passion that they cannot be placed in the same category with the logical propositions of mathematics or the analytic proportions of science. They are the product of social wisdom and unwisdom' (Niebuhr, 1949: 193). Nevertheless, despite the contingency of these rules, Niebuhr did believe that one could define an ascending scale of moral possibilities, emanating from the core principle of justice that is based on *agape* (selfless love). These ascending scales of moral possibilities are later developed into 'regulative principles', which are not dissimilar in function to the development of middle axioms within the mid-20th century British context already discussed.

We now move onto our third and final area of overlap between Third Space hybridity and Christian Realism.

3) The Bias towards Creating Spaces of Hope, Justice and Inclusivity

The Post-Niebuhr Political Tradition of Christian Realism   Niebuhr was criticized by many (including his own brother Richard – see Fox, 1985: 144–5) for having an ethical stance too predicated on the concepts of perfection contained within his understanding of Jesus' absolute law of love. This understanding of perfection was reinforced with an over-pessimistic anthropology that stressed the endemic nature of original sin. Preston, for example, argues that the Augustinian doctrine of original sin, while essential for a 'realistic' understanding of human nature and its inability to create just structures in which to live, should not be seen as the dominant force in human capabilities. Of equal consideration is the existence and role of *original righteousness*, which emerges from the theological strand that sees humankind as being created in *imago dei*. From this perspective emerges our potential to exercise a conscience, a capacity to engage in moral discernment, and a capability to understand the importance of moral values and principles such as freedom, equality and fellowship and to a limited extent act upon them. The doctrine of creation, in Preston's view, allows these things to emerge independently of the revelation of Christ, thus reflecting a less pessimistic view about human capability to act in ways that can be for the common good, and to exhibit 'the capacity for concern of others' in tension with 'the tendency to selfishness' (quoted in Kamergrauzis, 2001: 67).

What emerges more strongly for Preston than for Niebuhr is the role of the church community as the 'framework' in which ethical decisions are made. Through the mutuality of relationships shaped by public worship (including the dimensions of praise and confession) and private prayer, the ability of Christians for moral discernment and just action within the wider community is deepened. This form of 'character formation' is the distinctive role the church can play in its engagement with the wider world. However, this ideal of the church needs to be set in the context of the reality of the church community, which throughout all generations is capable of acting in rigid, inward-looking and oppressive ways (see for example the Christian and post-Christian feminist critiques of Beverley Harrison, Sharon Welch, Mary Daly and Daphne Hampson).

Atherton and the Age of Partnership and Reconciliation   Atherton identifies the emergence of the 'Age of Partnership and Reconciliation' during the transitional upheavals of the late 1970s up to the present day – a period that has seen Britain move from an industrial to a post-industrial society, the increased emphasis on consumption rather than production, the rediscovery of the market, and the impact of globalization, which has brought wealth and mobility but also acute poverty to all parts of the globe. It follows on from what he characterizes as the Age of Voluntarism and Atonement (in the nineteenth century) and the Age of the State and Incarnation (the post-war consensus from 1945 to the mid 1970s). The present era has also (partly as a response to the 'take over' of the local by the global) paradoxically seen the resurgence of 'furious' religion, nationalism, regionalism and local civil society. The retreat of the power of the state, the fragmentation of local communities and the family, the rise to prominence of other faiths and spiritualities in the UK, and the growth of consumerism and mobility, have left the church seriously weakened at an institutional level (Atherton, 2000: 83–5).

It is also the age in which no 'grand' or metanarrative can emerge that will give direction to an overriding analysis of what is occurring, nor is it an age in which growing marginalization and threats to environmental sustainability can be met by the resources of any single sector, be it the state, the market or civil society. Rather, what is emerging is the need for a partnership-based approach to the analysis and tackling of major ethical and justice issues (at both local and global levels) in which the faith communities have an increasingly significant role to play (see Baker, 2005). 'It is as though the new age is requiring increasingly our ability to construct connections between perspectives and with others. It is about finding ways of holding together often profound differences for our own self-sufficiency and for future living on earth. It is about an emerging age of partnership and reconciliation' (Atherton, 2000: 84).

As part of the preparation for these processes of partnership, Atherton believes that the church should not only engage in interdisciplinary analysis and practice, but also reflect more critically on its own processes. This is the only viable methodology for a church to adopt within a pluriform world, and it marks a movement from an overt teleological perspective of the churches' mission and identity to one that is more oriented towards concepts of *process*, *movement* and *ongoing critical interaction*. Atherton quotes Eduard Bernstein in relation to the once-held belief in the inauguration of a socialist utopia:

> I have extraordinarily little feeling for, or interest in, what is usually termed 'the final goal of socialism'. This goal, whatever it may be, is nothing to me, the movement is everything. And by movement I mean both the general movement of society, that is social progress, and the political and economic agitation and organization to bring about this progress.
>
> (quoted in Atherton, 2000: 85)

Atherton also brings in Hans Küng and Duncan Forrester to support his thesis that in this age of partnership and reconciliation, the task of social ethics is primarily one devoted to *praxis* – that is, reflecting on lived experience. This praxis is:

> A distillation and reformulation of existing trends in society and the world, in the light of a faith that has journeyed through detailed interactions of atonement and voluntarism, incarnation and state. It is about a major change in our thinking and practice as a response to continuing change, in order to effect change.
>
> (Atherton, 2000: 84)

This emphasis on praxis represents a decisive move away from liberal assumptions about the efficacy of preordained strategies, or 'catalogues of policy recommendations' (Küng, 1997: 82). Rather, Atherton conjectures, this is a definitive move into post-liberal territory (both theologically and politically) where the need to engage in partnership with a wide variety of partners, including those who operate from a perspective of hard-line positivism – be they Christians, Muslims, Hindus or secularists – is paramount.

However, Atherton is also clear that within what might be defined a post-liberal, post-evangelical age (see, for example, Tomlinson, 1995), some clear rearticulation of Christology is essential if Christian theology is to engage publicly in the debates concerning the future of our planet. This is because of the proven importance of having a distinctive identity within partnerships. For him, the essential elements of a post-liberal Christology focus on the praxis of reconciliation, which returns once again to the cross, not in the Niebuhrian sense of the self-sacrificing ideal of love, but in the sense of 'a multi-dimensional practice of reconciliation between people and God, people with each other and the whole created order' (Atherton, 2000: 17). The cross stands as a symbol of reconciliation in both the present and future. The far side of the cross points towards the ultimate reconciliation of everything in the perfect love of God. For those of us in the interim period of history, living in the shadow of this side of the cross, 'the fragments' of the final reconciliation from the far side sustain us. The emphasis on reconciliation and partnership is shaped by the pastoral emergency of how social ethics and the Christian faith as a whole engages in the collective task of saving our planet from the quadruple impacts of:

- environmental despoliation and species annihilation
- disease pandemics (such as HIV/Aids in Africa and Asia)
- growing practice of ethnic cleansing and acts of terrorism
- the immiserating instability caused by growing polarities of wealth and access to the resources for a dignified life.

Atherton quotes Boyle to stark effect. 'There is one world and it is not endless, and we have to work out among ourselves how we are to live in it together or we shall die in it separately' (quoted in Atherton, 2000: 84). The overall *telos* of a Christian social ethics of reconciliation and partnerships is thus the production of 'a reformed and reconstructed person in community' (Atherton, 2000: 17).

Chapter 5

Radical Christian Realism: The Springboard for a Third Space Social Ethics

Towards the end of the last chapter we were beginning to identify some of the key ways in which mainstream Christian Realism was beginning to fragment into interesting new directions following the collapse of the Liberal/Enlightenment consensus and the main economic and political foundations on which it was built. We identified some the outcomes of these foundations: ideals of a common good, the welfare state, macroeconomic policy, representative democracy and top-down planning, as well universalizing metanarratives associated with progress, justice, science and technology, multiculturalism. According to Atherton's typology of 'ages', we have since the late 1960s been moving ever faster into a Post-liberal Age, characterized by the need to promote reconciliation by working in creative partnerships with a wide variety of other partners. The 'reconciliation' envisaged by Atherton is not a grand project with a single identifiable outcome (like the 'common' good). Rather, it is a more akin to a process, which is flexible but focused enough to deal in a multidisciplinary way with multi-causal problems associated with global capitalism, urbanization and ever-increasing issues of sustainability. Thus, for example, his reformulated Christian Political Economy is a dynamic, interdisciplinary process involving the interplay of at least six different elements, ranging from the empirical to the narrative, the heretical to the mainstream. The purpose of this chapter is to continue the momentum generated by Atherton's thinking to push further and bring in other key elements which, I argue, will be required for the transition from a mainstream to a radical Christian Realism.

Normunds Kamergrauzis and the Possibility of a Reformulated Christian Realism

Normunds Kamergrauzis, in his book *The Persistence of Christian Realism*, uses a doctoral thesis on the work of Ronald Preston as the framework to define some criteria by which to discern an ongoing tradition of Christian Realism. The epistemological crisis identified by MacIntyre following the collapse of the Western Liberal Enlightenment project since the 1960s, and the emergence of counter-narratives of contextualized thinking, is the starting place for Kamergrauzis's thought. He accepts the given-ness of the postmodern situation of plural contexts and competing truth claims as the epistemological and cultural backdrop against which Christian social ethics needs to emerge. The overall aim of Christian social ethics from this perspective is to maintain a distinctive identity while being open to relationships of reciprocity with other insights, disciplines and partners. There is more to be said about this in our final chapter, but for now a summary of Kamergrauzis's position will suffice. The distinctive identity for Christian social ethics emerges from the theological categories of creation, Christology and eschatology. Christology and eschatology we have briefly looked at in the previous chapter.

The category of creation is deployed by Kamergrauzis in two ways. The first is the traditional one already described, and which can be traced back to the Social Gospel and William Temple – that is, a recognition of the fundamental and inalienable human dignity of every person on the basis of being created in the image of God, the *imago dei*.

The second is the way he develops a sub-theme of creation, namely *stewardship*, whereby humankind partakes in 'the exercise of social responsibility in engagement with the economic and political sphere within the context of plurality as part of the creative activity of God in the world' (Kamergrauzis, 2001: 244). Part of expressing 'stewardship' is the concept of *solidarity*, which locates social ethics away from the universalizing principles of justice as formulated by Rawls towards the specific response to concrete situations wherein people find themselves most disempowered and curtailed by fear. This idea has similarities to Bonhoeffer's 'Man for Others' Christology whereby the Christian disciple stands in solidarity with the Other, not for any motive of furthering one's self-interest but as a 'work of love' alongside the worst off. The basis for this solidarity is the difference which belief in God makes, and 'represents the intimate relationship between God and human, expressed in the mystery of faith' (Kamergrauzis, 2001: 246). The advantage of a rekindled ethics of solidarity, expressed in this way, is that it allows for meaningful engagement within a pluralistic context, emerging as it does from a consciously Christological position (but also one that non-Christians can share), while being open to other perspectives and contexts, including operating outside one's own framework of belief. Kamergrauzis summarizes his thinking thus:

> So understood, solidarity as shaping the way of being emerges as the basis for a model of Christian engagement with the public sphere. Indeed this kind of solidarity that goes beyond one's own social context and tradition has resources within itself to relate to and engage with 'the solidarity of the shaken'; that is with those who are excluded from participation in the interpretation of justice and the distribution of power.
>
> (Kamergrauzis, 2001 : 245)

Kamergrauzis develops this thinking with reference to Andrew Shanks's work on 'the solidarity of the shaken' (a concept developed by Jan Patocka from the struggle of the Czech movement for democracy that led to Charter 77). This 'trans-boundaried engagement' or solidarity with the experience of being shaken can lead to the rethinking of one's own life story in the light of shakenness, in the sense of being shaken out of complacency and what Shanks calls 'mental anaesthesia' (quoted in Kamergrauzis, 2001: 246). Thus, an ethics of solidarity not only takes one physically beyond one's 'comfort zone' in terms of an openness within public solidarity. It also 'promotes a learning process from encounters with other traditions' (Kamergrauzis, 2001: 246).

Our study of Kamergrauzis' description of possible future directions for Christian Realism, in the light of postmodern plurality, shows him moving decisively away from 'the presupposition of a broad moral consensus' in order to step out 'in faith' to engage in an interaction with its 'own distinctive resources and the plural nature of the moral world via a commitment to solidarity with those who are disempowered' (Kamergrauzis, 2001: 248). In the course of this process, each person's own narrative (hitherto greeted with some suspicion within Christian Realism) becomes reflectively shaped in order to engage 'beyond one's social context and tradition'. Unfortunately, Kamergrauzis does not elaborate on what that this might mean in practice, but he does offer a decisive shift in the epistemological framework of Christian Realism.

A Feminist Ethical Critique of the Christian Realist Tradition

We now examine some of the general principles arising from feminist ethics that are applicable to this debate, before looking at some specific critiques offered by feminist ethicists in relation to the Christian Realist tradition. This will be done in order to better define some of the contours of a reformulated Christian Realism based upon solidarity and stepping outside one's own boundaries in order to engage with other traditions in a pluralistic context.

Elaine Graham, in her introductory essay to a recent overview of feminist ethics (2003), outlines three key differences from the prevailing, male-dominated norms of social ethics.

First, is a *renewed moral anthropology* that rejects the crude dualisms perpetuated by patriarchal social ethics. As we have already seen, Niebuhr in particular based his anthropology on the idea of humankind being caught in the tension of limitless possibilities while being bounded to a particular time and space. This tension is the product of a deep anxiety caused by humanity's lack of control over its fate, and is a major cause of human sin. A dualism emerges within Niebuhr's thought between recognizing the possibilities of limited individual regeneration (through reflection on the example of Christ's self-sacrifice) counterbalanced by pessimism that groups such as nations only function to acquire power over others. Feminist ethics rejects this anthropology based on the need for humankind to transcend limits and the need to control or achieve autonomy from others. This reflects a 'male' agenda for autonomous personal identity based on a crude Freudian analysis of the need for the male child to separate himself in early childhood from the mother, thus identifying masculinity in relation to 'a denial of everything associated with nature or femininity' (Graham, 2003: 21). In contrast, girls from an early age are 'socialized' on the basis of the 'self-giving love' of the mother, and through this learn to experience and value interdependency, sensitivity to the needs of others and the selflessness of nurturing.

Two important factors emerge from this Freudian-based gender differentiation. One is the importance of developing scepticism of this analysis, recognizing the unhealthy way in which the extolling of *agape* (heedless love) by Niebuhr and others has become a means of oppression for women within the church, creating the expectation of self-effacement and self-negation, and leading to a loss of confidence and self-identity. The second factor is to recognize the importance of an alternative anthropology based on interdependence and mutual relationship, rather than limitless autonomy or self-denying sacrifice. This questions the supposed gender neutrality (or universality) of traditional Christian social ethics, which cultivates the 'culturally masculine qualities (of) individualism, autonomy, objectivity, mind, reason, culture, transcendence, violence and death' (2003: 22). In the past this mindset has dismissed 'feminine traits' such as 'interdependence, community, connectedness, body, emotion, nature, immanence, peace and life' (2003: 22). The challenge for feminist ethics (along with social ethics as a whole) is to ascertain the extent to which these opposing traits are genuine differentiations based on biological differences or are socially conditioned traits.

The second difference is a *feminist epistemology based on women's actual experience*, rather than universalizing theories of human development (such as Sigmund Freud's or Lawrence Kohlberg's analysis). Carol Gilligan's work, with women reflecting on their approaches to the ethics of abortion, found that they were as capable as men of conducting moral reasoning but, crucially, did so on the basis of different criteria and values. Graham summarizes thus: 'This "different" voice values specificity, particularity and relationship, in stark contrast to the norms of the western ethical tradition based on universal principles of justice and rules' (2003: 25).

Nel Noddings amplifies Gilligan's work to identify a relational ethic of care. She replaces Niebuhr's emphasis on the heedless, self-giving love of *agape* with an ethic based on *eros*, 'rooted in receptivity, relatedness and responsiveness' (Noddings, 1984: 2), in which 'relation will be taken as ontologically basic' (Noddings, 1984: 3). This is a direct move away from universalizing principles and theories (such as Rawls's theory on justice) towards an ethics 'based on the immediacy of the personal encounter which then expands into widening networks of connectedness and respect' (Graham, 2003: 24). This leads to a method of doing ethics based on a sense of being a person-within-community, a method that favour strategies of visibility and valorization of the role of women in public and well as private spheres.

Third, there is within feminist ethics the *cultivation of the moral imagination*, whereby as a response to the dangerous and oppressive systems of the day, women have developed the ancient literary tradition of imagining utopian worlds where the normal routines and values of everyday life are inverted. In these imagined worlds women free themselves from the psychological power of the given world and are enabled 'both to see and see through the structures and inevitabilities of this society' (Rose, 1994: 213, quoted in Graham, 2003: 28). More recent utopian women's fiction has paradoxically been dystopian in its portrayal of the rise of the religious right in the United States (for example Atwood, 1985), thus warning women and society in general of dangerous emergent political trends and providing 'the moral, didactic and political energy' by which pathways of transformation and resistance can be explored.

As we have seen earlier, the significance of utopian thinking is acknowledged as central to Sandercock's cosmopolis, 'a building site of the mind' rather than a totalitarian, masterplanned vision for cities. Emerging from the influences of the womanist tradition (as well as indigenous and other interdisciplinary sources), Sandercock's utopian vision functions as both a pragmatic and moral imperative to create more inclusive urban spaces that both men and women can work towards implementing.

Having identified the broad principles of feminist ethics, we will now take a closer look at the work of two feminist writers working within the Christian social ethics tradition who in different ways explicitly refer to the Christian Realist tradition. Beverley Harrison and Sharon Welch identify themselves *de facto* with the Liberation Theology tradition, which explicitly takes as its hermeneutical starting point the experience of women's oppression. They specifically refer to the silencing of women and the complicity of the church and other religious traditions in past oppressive acts that have damaged women and other subjugated minorities. There are certain key differences between these writers that helpfully illuminate the spectrum of thinking within Christian feminist ethical discourse, but also contribute significantly to what a reformulated Christian Realism might look like.

Sharon Welch and the Ethic of Risk

Welch represents the most radical movement within Christian feminist ethics that has not totally moved over to a post-Christian feminism (as exemplified, for example, by Mary Daly and Daphne Hampson). In an earlier work (Welch, 1985), she is highly critical of the liberal theology tradition for the moral inadequacy of Christian collusion with the atrocities of the twentieth century, and its inability to face up to the environmental and moral challenge of nuclear proliferation. This, in her view, is largely due to its inability to see through the distortions of scientific positivism and the pursuit of universalizing principles. She clearly articulates her sense of despair and her struggle to see signs of hope (Welch, 1985: 14), but nevertheless seeks some counter-narrative within the Christian tradition that will help foster these fragile signs.

In her search for this counter-discourse she acknowledges the thinking of Michel Foucault and his identification of the power that lies within the use of discourse, especially the *will-to-truth* (used, for example by academia, the media and science). Foucault identifies the 'insurrection of subjugated knowledges' from those social groups who find themselves low down in the 'hierarchy of scientificity' (quoted in Welch, 1985: 19). He refers to the task of *genealogy*, by which he means the lineages not of personal ancestors but of systems of thought and discourses of power, and of the resistance to them that was shaking Western epistemology to its foundations. Welch takes this concept of genealogy and links this to her understanding of the Christian faith as 'a commitment to eradicate oppression and establish justice' by similarly listening to the 'dangerous memories and heritage of women and other oppressed minorities engaged in the concrete struggle for justice' (Welch, 1985: 24).

This leads her to define 'truth' not as an ahistorical episteme located somewhere between the present day and an eschatological horizon, nor in any externalized doctrine of God, Christ or the Church, but to base her theology on Jon Sobrino's dictum that 'the quality of theodicy must be resolved in praxis, rather than theory', and Dorothy Solle's aphorism, 'Truth is something we make true' (quoted in Welch, 1985: 28). Welch herself writes, 'The truth of Christianity only exists as a concrete realization which means that theological statements contain as much truth as they deliver practically in transforming reality'. In terms of feminist liberation ethics, this means that the only worthwhile theology for women is that which is 'grounded in the liberating experience of sisterhood, in the process of liberation from sexism' (Welch, 1985: 29). This epistemology moves decisively towards postmodern suspicion of grand narratives and amplifies the intensity of Niebuhr's criteria for the outcome of social ethics: 'by their fruits ye shall know them'.

This thinking feeds into her later work, *A Feminist Ethic of Risk* (1990), which she constructs out of an extreme realism (what she calls a 'cultured nihilism') concerning the ability of faith-inspired human intervention to change the dual global pathologies of racism and the threat of global destruction wrought by nuclear war. Her ethic of risk is based on three elements: a redefinition of responsible action, grounding in community, and strategic risk-taking.

The redefinition of *responsible action* moves the basis of ethics from the accomplishment of targets and the implementation of programmes towards the creation of a matrix in which further actions of resistance are possible. This matrix of resistance she defines as any group or network where economic and political action is empowered by a spiritual tradition, and where lessons learned from experiences of small victories in the past are reflected upon in the present and worked through in the future. Drawing heavily on the literary works of womanist writers such as Alice Walker, Toni Morrison and Mildred Taylor, she defines this matrix primarily as the extended family.

Grounding in community builds on this idea of a matrix of resistance, by stressing the importance of a shared culture of memory and identity such as is contained within the broader civil rights movement – a culture that nurtures relationships and interdependence, and provides resources of continuing self-reflection in the light of setbacks. She quotes Martin Luther King, who calls this matrix the Beloved Community, and she identifies it as including 'the structures of church, school, family and community' (Welch, 1990: 81). However, Welch's overt references to the Church are few and generalized. Her general omission with regard to the Church puts her sharply at odds with the Christian Realist tradition, in which the Church is seen as a primary locus for the outworking of Christian public theology. This is because of her radical condemnation of the Church (particularly in its institutional guise) as a pernicious source of oppression within history.

Strategic risk-taking refers to the art of often small but symbolically significant actions in pursuit of resistance and justice, which inspire further action and have significance for the wider community. This idea represents a typical line of argument based on the experience of the peace movement in the United States, a contribution that Welch – as a white, middle-class feminist – feels is most representative of her experience. 'Even if we prevent nuclear war in our lifetime, the challenge of preventing such destruction will also be faced by another generation. We cannot make their choices; we can only provide a heritage of persistence, imagination and solidarity' (Welch, 1990: 22).

She acknowledges the dangers of romanticizing or absolutizing another's experience, because her relatively privileged position in Western society as a middle-class academic protects her from the same degree of oppressive experience as other women in the United States. However, her epistemology based on risk is a challenge to the liberal foundations of Christian Realism in the following ways.

First, there is the criticism of the 'eschatological reservation' (that is, the partiality attributed to human endeavour from the perspective of the Last Judgement), favoured by the liberal theologians we have already alluded to. Welch refers to the criticisms of Liberation Theology by an advocate of Niebuhr, Dennis McCann, who claims that Christian Realism is the more adequate basis for political action. This claim is based on Christian Realism's qualified hope, rather than the unbounded hope of Liberation Theology that leads proponents of the latter to naive conclusions about the operation of limits within human society. McCann claims that Liberation Theology cannot make the distinction between genuine limits and illusory ones, and that therefore it lacks the maturity that comes with a form of 'religious disinterestedness' as opposed to a 'revolutionary enthusiasm and solidarity with the oppressed'. McCann concludes, 'Genuine limit-situations must be accepted in faith, a response that leads, it is hoped, to repentance, and a measure of serenity in social conflict' (quoted in Welch, 1990: 109).

Welch's answer is to reiterate the methodology of Liberation Theology – namely the emphasis on truth as praxis – rather than a detached perspective of what is or is not possible in history. *Truth as praxis*, she contends, is a perspective from which one determines the current boundaries of human hope. Far from being naive and utopian, she argues, such a perspective questions the taken-for-granted, apparently neutral limits that circumscribe the quality of life of so many of the planet's inhabitants:

> Women of all races are questioning 'natural' physical and social limits, that is, women 'naturally' being defined socially and rewarded economically primarily through their relationships with men. Men and women of colour question the worldwide distribution of wealth and political power, and their questioning is grounded in a vital self-love.
>
> (Welch, 1990: 110)

Second, this definitive statement of epistemological difference between Liberation Theology and Christian Realism is reinforced by the concept of *standpoint epistemology*, which is based on the work of Sandra Harding and is a central methodology in much feminist ethics. Standpoint epistemology is a reaction to what Seyla Benhabib calls the 'generalized other' of the detached, universalizing perspectives of liberal ethics. Welch sums up Benhabib's argument thus:

> Within Liberalism, the 'generalized other', the partners in moral dialogue or the persons affected by decision-making are assumed to be fundamentally the same;

each individual is seen as 'a rational being entitled to the same rights and duties we would want to ascribe to ourselves'. There is no need to take account of 'the individuality and concrete identity of the other' for 'our relation to the other is governed by the norms of formal equality and reciprocity; each is entitled to expect and to assume from us what we can accept from him or her'.

(quoted in Welch, 1985: 127)

Benhabib develops Gilligan's work on the specificity of the moral standpoint of women, based on their experience, to advocate a communicative ethic that takes as its 'standpoint' the interaction between 'concrete others', and especially an awareness of them as 'an individual with a concrete history, identity and affective-emotional constitution' (Benhabib, quoted in Welch, 1985: 128). This means abstracting ourselves from preconceived notions of 'commonality' in order to relate to the 'concrete other' in terms of 'complementary reciprocity'. Benhabib defines this reciprocity as a form of behaviour by which we expect to give and receive the feeling of being 'recognized and confirmed as a concrete, individual being with specific needs, talents and capacities ... The norms of our interactions are friendship, love and care ... The corresponding moral feelings are those of love, care and sympathy and solidarity' (Benhabib, quoted in Welch, 1990: 128). This ethical stance of 'complementary reciprocity' resonates with the thinking of Lévinas and the encounter with the Other, which we examined in Chapter 1.

The significance of *standpoint ethics* for our argument is its strong resonance with Third Space hybridity's concerns, echoed in the planning and political philosophies of Sandercock and Young. They seek to explore the possibility of facilitating multiple publics and voices into speech, rather than constructing a vision of a democratic city or political system based on one universalizing concept of the 'common good' or 'public interest'.

The third relevance of Welch's Christian feminist ethic to our reformulated Christian Realism is her definition of an *epistemology of solidarity*. We have already seen this as a perspective offered by Kamergrauzis. Welch defines solidarity as a specific response to what she sees as the consensus-based discourse that Jürgen Habermas offers in his *Communicative Ethics* (1979). Welch is critical of Habermas's dismissal of some oral cultures on the grounds of their cognitive inadequacy (that is, their failure to test validity claims in the wider world) and contends that real resistance and change can only come from a perspective of solidarity rather than consensus. Her ethics of solidarity contains two strands: 1) granting each group sufficient respect to listen to their ideas and to be challenged by them; and 2) recognizing that the lives of various groups are so intertwined that each is accountable to the other (Welch, 1990: 135).

Discourse and respectful communication as defined by Habermas are important elements in bringing about inclusion, but real transformation will only occur if relationships reach the 'foundational' level articulated above, particularly if people are allowed to say things in anger that need to be expressed 'without the powerful people leaving the room'. Welch continues:

Transformation occurs when the reformer feels the pain of the people who are oppressed. He is open to examining different standards of justice, thus understanding why certain development projects were rejected by the oppressed group. Also, listening to the pain of others requires that the oppressor acknowledge his or her own pain, no longer accepting it as a necessary cost of a civilized order, but evaluating again its necessity and implications for a cultural and political system.

(Welch, 1990: 135)

Welch calls this interaction between new understanding and feeling a 'deepening spiral' of knowing, which enriches action and reflection.

Her feminist ethics based on the components of standpoint and solidarity amplify and enrich the concept of 'solidarity with the shaken' described by Kamergrauzis with reference to the work of Shanks.

Beverley Harrison and the Rehabilitation of a Reformed Radical Social Ethics Tradition

Beverley Harrison is a prolific feminist ethicist who has sought to apply her feminist critique to all areas of human life and social policy (for example, energy policy, homophobia, and the treatment of the elderly in society) as well as those of particular concern to women (such as abortion and sexism). She is more 'mainstream' within Christian feminist ethics than Sharon Welch in that, while recognizing the oppression and hostility suffered by women within the Church, she is committed to being in 'some continuity with the Christian tradition' (Harrison, 1985: 231) in the hope that some oppressive structures may be transformed. She still sees the Christian Church as a community capable of moral reflection, and therefore change. She defines herself as operating within the specific stream of 'socialist, feminist Christian theory', and as such has at least two direct points of interaction with the Christian Realist tradition.

The first is her concern for moral objectivity when it comes to endorsing universal principles such as justice. In line with other feminists she is keen to move from procedural understandings of justice to substantive ones, which address directly the need for the concrete socio-institutional changes that are required for women to live full and meaningful lives within Church and society. Where she differs from many feminists, however, is the circumspect way she approaches Gilligan's methodology and assumptions, which appear to her to devalue the usefulness of grounding principles. In a footnote to Gilligan's work she writes, 'My conviction regarding the irreplaceability of justice as a fundamental moral norm derives from my belief that no other moral norm, including "caring", adequately incorporates the structural-relational dimensions of life that justice illumines' (Harrison, 1985: 300).

The basis for this assertion is Harrison's belief that gender does not 'yield basic differences' in men and women's moral experience, or the norms to which they appeal (Harrison, 1985: xiv). She also rejects the notion that more objective understandings of fundamental moral principles such as justice necessarily lead to either 'emotional disinterestedness' or 'require us to assume a homogeneous reality' (Harrison, 1985: xv). This approach to Christian feminist ethics appears to offer a more substantive bridge into the Christian Realist tradition, because it seeks to derive guidelines for concrete actions from universal principles (for example, middle axioms). That being said, Harrison reserves some trenchant criticism for other aspects of Christian Realism, which leads us to our second point of interaction.

Her main critique of Christian Realism, especially as espoused by Niebuhr, has been its distortion of Marxist social analysis, which has had a profound influence on the sceptical way in which Christian social ethics has handled Marxist analysis since. This misanalysis has prevented Christian social ethics from formulating a sufficiently radical social theory to deal with the pernicious social consequences that flow from neoliberal global capitalism.

Her complaints about Niebuhr's reading of Marx are threefold. First, since Niebuhr was an idealist, he has chosen to read Marx as an idealist. This means, in her opinion, that Niebuhr deliberately chose to overemphasize Marx as an 'unqualified scientific positivist', misunderstood Marx's descriptions of 'economic activity' and his criticisms of the then-current mode of capitalist production, and then accused him of constructing, as the central basis of his work, a 'philosophy of history'. Second, Harrison maintains that a fairer reading of Marx would regard his use of social science as a way of providing the critical tools for people so that they could alter structures via political action, not technological change. The issue of class conflict in society was not a rallying cry by Marx for social ferment, but more a recognition that it was already endemic in society. His analysis of human labour was to critique the market-exchange functions that governed the economic institutions and political-economy theories of his day. He called instead for the recognition of the value of 'sensuous labour'. And finally, Marx simply had no interest in formulating a philosophy of history, since he believed that such theories 'were the fruit of mystification' that needed to be put aside along with other forms of 'ahistorical rationalistic speculation' (Harrison, 1985: 60–62). The need to construct a philosophy of history was, according to Harrison, Niebuhr's alone.

Harrison calls Niebuhr's political realism the 'anti-radical legacy' of social theories used in Christian ethics. She proposes the formulation of a more radical paradigm of social ethics that incorporates a more accurate reading of Marxist social analysis, an engagement with the recent proliferation in neo-Marxist thinking, and a move away from the traditional props of social ethics, namely 'realism, historical sociology and ... neoclassical economic theory' (Harrison, 1985: 75). There are four aspects to her renewed paradigm.

One, a reawakening to the existence of conflict and suffering that is emerging as a result of neoliberal capitalism (in line with the thinking of Adam Smith and David Ricardo, as well as Marx). We are beginning to see this realization being laid out in the work of Atherton on marginalization, and the 'wild facts' and experiences of global exclusion that social ethics needs to engage with. That is not to advocate a blanket condemnation of capitalism *per se*, since, as Marx himself recognized, capitalism creates some of the necessary conditions for economic democracy by productive innovation.

Second, there needs to be an active recognition that the political economy of late capitalism is not an ahistorical reality (see, for example, Fukuyama, 1992) but is in principle a socio-historical reality that is transformable. This would be achieved by the careful tracing and assessing of historical shifts in the way the mode of production is organized. Again, this is also the view of Atherton, who in response to the proponents of liberal democratic capitalism says that Christian ethics 'needs to persist with history as continuing narratives of change' (Atherton, 2000: 61).

Third, a reformed radical social theory with an acute sense of historical methodology would 'hold itself answerable to and accept responsibility for concretely illuminating the experiences of everyday life ... and for testing its theories by its practice' (Harrison, 1985: 77).

Finally, and connected to all the above, a reformed radical tradition would reaffirm that all dimensions of life, including the economic, are 'interrelated in a social whole' (Harrison, 1985: 78). Harrison admits this is not a new insight, but contends that its reiteration is vital within a political/economic climate that seeks, via the mechanism of the market, to 'segment' the social world into 'differing spheres of activity'. This segmentation 'camouflages' the role the market plays in shaping the ongoing issues of 'racism, sexism and classism', and prevents the emergence of human rights and proper democratic accountability. This proposal, written in the mid 1980s, is emerging two decades later in Atherton's call for the global market to be mainstreamed, or 'bent', towards a 'pro-poor, pro-environmental' agenda for reform.

The Contribution of Christian Feminist Ethics to a Reformulated Christian Realism

It is now time to apply the insights gained from feminist liberationist social ethics to Kamergrauzis's new thinking on Christian Realism. For his part, Kamergrauzis briefly alludes to the work of Harrison in his conclusion, but is unimpressed by what he sees as an optimistic anthropology at the heart of her writing when it comes to change, particularly of the oppressed. He writes of feminist ethics generally that 'it inspires propaganda for change in revolutionary contexts, but is hopelessly sentimental in everyday life' (Kamergrauzis, 2001: 238). In response to this criticism I would argue that a liberationist feminist perspective, where it directly engages with the Christian Realism tradition, deepens the latter's reformulation in at least four ways that help form a bridge of dialogue between Christian Realism and Third Space hybridity.

First, it redefines the concept of the epistemological privilege of the poor and marginalized by talking not in the category of ontology, but in terms of the view and perspective of the oppressed being an essential component of any effective moral critique (for example, Welch, 1985: 126).

Second, it articulates in greater detail the epistemological basis and rationale for moving towards an understanding of the need to engage in solidarity in ways that are concrete and specific. The theological emphasis within feminist ethics on the principle of love as *eros* (that is, reciprocal, mutual love) rather than *agape* (heedless, universal love), and the development of standpoint and solidarity ethics (a good decade before its use by Shanks) help give substantive credence to Kamergrauzis' reformulation of social ethics and his argument that it needs to move beyond its own boundaries in order to engage with plurality. Kamergrauzis doesn't acknowledge the influence of feminist ethics in these areas as perhaps he should.

Third, the feminist ethical perspective on matrices of resistance move Christian Realism away from an introspective interest (sometimes bordering on an obsession) with the status of the Church as a suitable locus for moral reflection. More will be said about this in the next chapter, but suffice it to say for now that the concept of a matrix of resistance is a useful way of acknowledging the imperative to work in partnership with others in a variety of different forms.

Finally, Harrison's reawakened understanding of the contribution of Marxist and neo-Marxist thought is one that has already come to fruition in the work of those engaged in post- or late-modern urban theology and political economy, whereby the work of neo-Marxist geographers, sociologists and planners such as Manuel Castells, David Harvey, Saskia Sassen and Doreen Massey is having a profound and energizing impact on public theology both in terms of analysis and in terms of an interdisciplinary methodology. Theology owes neo-Marxism a great deal, and that debt ought to be more graciously acknowledged. Where neo-Marxist thought is critically used within social ethics, then, it allows a closer dialogue and discussion with Third Space hybridity discourse, of which it is a central component.

Conclusion: Mainstream vs. Radical Christian Realism

What I have attempted in this chapter is to define the characteristics of a reformulated social ethics in the light of the insights and methods of Third Space hybridity. I am calling this a Third Space social ethics, and the main building block I am using in its construction is a radically reformulated Christian Realism.

The elements that we identified from Third Space hybridity epistemology and methodology (Chapter 1) that need to be carried over into Christian social ethics have been:

- an acceptance of diversity and plurality, and a willingness to embrace the concept of hybridity as a means of allowing them to express themselves
- a commitment to creating processes and spaces of hope and inclusivity that include insurgent narratives and practices while at the same time acknowledging the role of the state and the market in creating the right conditions for these processes, and working in dialogue with them at both local and national levels
- the fear of the Other has been identified as the problematic that carries the most potential for creating increasingly polarized spatial communities alongside the growing economic disparities associated with late (global) capitalism
- notwithstanding the above, a commitment to engaging hopefully with the future and the present, not returning to the past but using the past as a critical tool of analysis

- a focus on interdisciplinarity that combines perspectives from a wide variety of academic disciplines together with reflection on narrative and experience (that is, praxis)
- a suspicion of grand theories (metanarratives) and value-free versions of truth, including liberal (Enlightenment) models of urban planning, social planning, democracy and neoliberal economics.

We have suggested that a possible way of connecting social ethics to this postmodern epistemological agenda is to deploy a radically reformulated Christian Realist tradition. The Christian Realist tradition, as it emerged and developed from the mid- to the late-twentieth century in the UK and the United States, already had some of these elements in place. It was committed to interdisciplinary analysis (especially between theology, economics and Marxist social theory) and was committed to creating just political and economic structures via state regulation of the market (a hybrid form of political economy). It also held a realistically optimistic anthropology that stressed the value of human attempts in history to reflect the Kingdom of God on earth. It did so by balancing Augustine's doctrine of original sin with theologies based on creation and *imago dei* that stressed human potential for righteousness and creativity. It also stressed the need for provisionality when attempting to construct middle axioms as moral guidance for Christian individuals and communities. These were provisional in the sense that they were not universal and were dictated by the conditions of time and place.

The main criticism of this tradition that I am defining as mainstream Christian Realism, especially from liberation and feminist ethics, is that it was/is too embedded in Liberal/Enlightenment assumptions about the empirical priority of theory and data to understand the radical nature and experience of marginalization and oppression in contemporary society. This creates an ethical response characterized by an empirically dominant approach, and a commitment to liberal theology and consensual methodologies. Mainstream Christian Realism is content to adopt a narrower spectrum of stated outcomes, which would include working for incremental change within the *existing* economic and political structures. It is particularly poor at challenging structural oppression in the Church, and tends to overestimate the ability of the Church to change sufficiently radically and quickly enough to engage from a position of credibility with wider partners.

Later reformulations of the Christian Realist tradition have moved further away from a liberal to a post-liberal epistemology and methodology. In doing this I have combined Atherton's reformulated Christian Political Economy and his typology of *partnership* and *reconciliation*, along with Kamergrauzis's epistemologies of *plurality* and *solidarity*. Atherton's reformulated Christian Political Economy, for example, is far more hybrid than Preston's Democratic Socialist economy. It combines multi-faith perspectives, feminist insights, 'heretical' traditions, measure- ment systems, and 'mainstreamed' global capitalism. I have in turn built on this with the work of Graham, Welch and Harrison, which stresses the importance of standpoint and relational ethics and epistemology, and the need to form matrices of resistance in which the Church plays a significant but by no means dominant role. Finally, we have seen from Harrison the plea for a more radical paradigm of social ethics that rediscovers neo-Marxist analysis after its misrepresentation by mainstream Christian Realism.

A radically reformulated Christian Realism, I am proposing, while still committed to working in an interdisciplinary way, is less concerned with formulating Church statements that everyone can assent to. It is likely to be more propositional in its statements in order to provoke action and debate, rather than strive for consensual communiqués. It will be prepared to work with personal narratives as well as empirical data, be more critical of the assumptions behind liberal discourse and theology, be prepared to be more prophetic in its critique of the status quo, and have greater expectations of the levels of change required if systems are to be transformed according to a gospel agenda. It will often be comfortable with neo-Marxist analysis and be more connected to postmodern methodologies of analysis – including feminist, post-colonial, cultural and anthropological as well as economic. Its teleological perspective will be more concerned with practical outcomes rather than conforming to universal principles or theological patterns. In other words, the concept of *process* within a radically reformulated Christian Realism is as important, if not more important, than the outcomes. As the basis for evaluating the outcome of any political or economic programme, Niebuhr's famous biblical quote, 'By their fruits ye shall know them', could be supplemented with, 'By the *opportunities they create* ye shall know them'.

Much of what I am defining as a social ethics based on radical Christian Realism has clear overlaps with Liberation Theology ethics. The overlaps between the two are a commitment to narrative and experience as important bases for social ethics, and to exploring ethics based on solidarity and standpoint epistemologies. However, the differences are substantial. Liberation ethics defines truth as praxis in the service of the poor and oppressed, including the granting of an epistemological priority to the experience of the poor that makes it difficult for it to move beyond binary analysis. Radical Christian Realism would valorize the standpoint of oppressed and marginalized groups but would also seek a solution that would emerge from a partnership process that engages both the market and the state on the understanding that without the active involvement and engagement of these sectors, deeper and sustainable transformation is unlikely to occur. For example, the market needs to be allowed to operate a dynamic of competition and wealth creation, but needs to be persuaded to operate a fair and transparent system of trade that rewards locally based micro-credit initiatives and allows equal access to world markets for developing countries. Radical Christian Realism similarly endorses political engagement and influence from the state for the sake of defining, and where necessary implementing, fair policies to ensure that personal, ethnic or tribal rights to free speech and control over services does not impinge on the rights of others to live in relative peace and harmony. Radical Christian Realism recognizes the complexity of the problem of marginalization and the need for an interdisciplinary approach to its resolution.

Radical Christian Realism recognizes the simultaneous coexistence and need for a number of political strategies, including both participative and representative forms of democracy (see Chapter 3), as opposed to the over-reliance on participative forms that tends to be the hallmark of Liberation Theology. It also recognizes the need to maintain dialogue and communication between different strategies and partners. What it would articulate – and work to reduce – is the pernicious and ongoing exercise of power by the forces of the market in contexts in which *global* levers still overpower *local* consultation and attempts at decision-making.

A Third Space social ethics based on radical Christian Realism will not be worried by the loss of control it now has to dictate outcomes within a plural and diverse moral and political universe. What is lost in control is compensated by the commitment and ability to create spaces and processes of empowerment that includes many partners and discourses, and out of which new possibilities – though always grounded and with a clear sense of its own identity – will emerge.

Chapter 6

Towards a Third Space Church

In the previous chapter we made note of the characteristics of Third Space social ethics, which we also defined as a reformulated, post-liberal or radical Christian Realist position. The hallmarks of this emerging position are a commitment to partnership and reconciliation that nevertheless is prepared to adopt non-mainstream perspectives in the service of understanding power and how it perpetuates both global and local forms of exclusion (see John Atherton's political economy). It is also committed to working with plurality and diversity, but from the perspective of solidarity and relationship rather than abstract theory, even though the reformulation of theory and theology in the light of experience is an important ongoing task of Christian social ethics. To that end, it is a form of social ethics that will prefer to work with a provisional teleology that stresses the importance of establishing processes of inclusivity in order to prioritize the solution of the problems of increased polarization and marginalization that postmodernity has brought. However, this approach also welcomes the opportunities and possibilities to work in new and creative partnerships that postmodern society also brings, with the Church as part of a matrix of social, political, economic and spiritual transformation. We have summed this up by updating Niebuhr's famous dictum so that by the 'opportunities' for growth and transformation, as well as by the 'fruits' of any political or economic programme, 'ye shall know them.'

The purpose of this chapter is to test some of this theoretical understanding with reflection on actual church praxis in a variety of contexts. In particular we shall seek to address the potential problems associated with a post-liberal methodology – namely, what are the criteria by which one should evaluate 'good' outcomes from a Christian-based perspective, and what happens to questions of theological identity when one works in a pragmatic, interdisciplinary and partnership-based way. These agendas will emerge after we have observed some Church projects in action.

The Manchester Context

The following case studies emerge from the William Temple Foundation's three-year research programme into emerging patterns of Church-based engagement within rapidly changing urban and social contexts in Manchester (Baker and Skinner, 2005). We have already described the dramatic shifts in various types of urban space as Manchester vigorously pursues an agenda of transformation from a cottonopolis to an ideopolis. The Foundation's research has attempted to engage with a wide theological spectrum of Church-based communities, ranging from black-majority churches,

111

white-led charismatic community churches, mainstream denominational churches such as Anglican, Roman Catholic and Baptist churches and an ecumenical church-based project engaging in networks of urban regeneration and civil renewal. Membership of the church communities studied ranged from a dozen to four hundred. The research aimed not only to record the methods of engagement of these churches with the wider community, but also to listen to the experience of that engagement, with specific reference to the political and social agenda of the New Labour government (see Chapter 3). In this section we will briefly look at the methodologies of four contrasting types of church and the different ways they describe what they do.

The Church-Based Community Empowerment Network

The Community Pride Initiative was established as a local project by the national and ecumenically based organization Church Action on Poverty, together with the mainstream churches in Manchester. It is now an independent charity but retains a distinctive Christian ethos. Its main aim is to create and facilitate networks for local people to participate more effectively within regeneration processes set up by central government. This process of empowerment initially involved providing information on Manchester's regeneration schemes and government opportunities for community participation in language that grassroots communities could understand. It then developed into the creation of networks all over the cities of Manchester and Salford (with the use of government empowerment funding) for information-sharing and for strategy development, including piloting experiments in participatory budgeting with Salford City Council that were based on the Porto Alegre model from Brazil. Community Pride is now one of the three lead organizations for Manchester's Community Network, which feeds into Manchester's Local Strategic Partnership (LSP).

One of the key locations where they work, and where their office is based, is East Manchester. The area is emblematic of large capital-driven regeneration, focusing on major infrastructure projects – for example, a Wal-Mart/Asda hypermarket and the Commonwealth Games Stadium. The regeneration of this area relies on the development of mixed housing markets which, on the basis of new leisure and retailing facilities and good transport links to the city centre, will attract high-earning professionals to live alongside the existing and largely rehoused community. Some of these will be housed in the iconic new technopole (see Castells, Chapter 2) called New Islington, designed by Urban Splash and featuring redeveloped canal areas (including a new canal basin) to create a Venetian effect.

When asked to describe the impact of their work with the existing residents and tenants of East Manchester, the key workers of Community Pride defined their role as falling under the headings local–global analysis, bridge building and critical consensus.

1) Local–global analysis 'Our crunch points have been around this impact of globalization on local people and because after five or six years we've been able to critique externally what we've seen happening and how things have or have not *changed for people.'* (this and the following section-heading quotes are from Baker and Skinner 2005)

This quotation shows the importance of the *political and economic analyses of power* that are undertaken by some churches engaged in regeneration. The interface between global patterns of inward investment and locally used space is one of the key areas of critical analysis that needs to occur in any discourse on regeneration. It is an analysis that is almost entirely absent within the official regeneration discourses. The above quote implicitly acknowledges that some things have changed for the better for local people in East Manchester, but that other things have not, and the overall tone of the interview from which this quotation emerged suggests that more critical questions need to be asked concerning issues of change and empowerment, and the methods used to bring them about. Such statements can be characterized as asking the 'who, why and what' questions.

A harder-edged analysis of the local–global dynamic affecting East Manchester also emerges – one that critiques the regeneration process as a form of 'colonization'. This view articulates the connection between the physical demolition of urban environment (and its 'renaissance' as an attractive urban space for professional, higher-earning citizens) with a similar 'demolition' of the existing social norms and mores of working-class communities in favour of a more 'attractive society'. One key worker spoke of the regeneration industry having a 'missionary' approach, arriving in a new area and telling the existing residents and organizations how they should improve themselves and their lives (for example, prohibitions on smoking and eating meat pies as part of drives to improve health statistics). This 'neo-colonial' approach is personified in the reaction of the local community to a prominent regeneration professional working in their midst (known for the purposes of this extract as Mr X):

> … it as a colonial process, and I think that he deliberately implies within that a kind of missionary dimension … I mean there's no question to look at – well I don't mean this nastily, personally, but look at Mr. X at the New Deal for Communities … as a missionary kind of figure, you know, in all kinds of terms. The man that has come to save East Manchester, and the way the residents relate to him is like a priest in some respects, they defer to his wisdom. And he comes and presides at meetings, there's loads of imagery like that.
>
> (quoted in Baker and Skinner, 2005: 73)

2) Bridge building   'But also I think engaging with power structures … not being afraid to, I don't know, have lunch with a tax collector. It's not exclusively with the poor … there's a kind of bridging role I think within Christ's ministry, who certainly inspires me in my role.'

Despite hard-edged critical analysis of some of the social and economic dimensions of urban and community regeneration, workers in community-empowerment schemes see it as essential to building relationships of communication (as a prerequisite to building relationships of trust) between local communities and outside agencies seeking to implement regeneration schemes. This is so the outside agencies become more aware of the impact of their actions and are committed to trying to work in closer partnership with the existing local structures. The word 'bridging' carries with it clear connotations that distinguish it from the *bonding* social capital we discussed in Chapter 3. However, in the important task of facilitating communication between local networks and outside networks of power, there is also an important *linking* social-capital role evident in this project (as we saw in the previous example).

3) Working towards a critical consensus   'I think under the surface there isn't a consensus ... and I think that somewhere it's [conflict] got to come out. A consensus would only come from a really, really profound and deep engagement with people.'

The commitment to providing forms of bridging and linking social capital by this church-based initiative should not be construed as a strategy for ignoring issues of asymmetrical power that exist both within and between networks. The desired outcome of increasing the capacity of networks is to improve levels of communication and trust, and thus possibly to arrive at a consensus on key issues of strategy. This does not mean arriving at an uncritical consensus, which can result in the most powerfully represented view within a partnership holding sway. When this happens the silence of other partners might be suppressed expressions of frustration, exclusion or apathy rather than agreement. The above quotation expresses the commitment to pursue deeper levels of engagement, and acknowledges genuine diversity and plurality without diluting the integrity of any group (for example, the belief-based contributions of faith communities). This is, therefore, a commitment to a 'thicker' form of civil society than a non-controversial, surface form. A 'surface' form of consensus would possibly gain in expediency, but lose in terms of sustainability (that is, building networks and processes that will last for the future benefit of the community once the short-term funding dries up). This approach is particularly significant for the future of interdisciplinary partnerships such as the New Deal for Communities programme (described in Chapter 3), whose funding regimes are due to run out in the next few years.

The Black Majority Churches (BMCs)

The following three examples of church-based engagement with wider civil society come from two BMCs working in the Moss Side/Chorlton areas of Manchester. Both churches were established to meet the needs of the large number of Afro-Caribbean public-sector workers who settled south of the city centre in the late 1950s and early 1960s. Churches such as these helped create a sense of relative stability and identity, which survived until the early 1980s, when huge upheavals in these communities due to large-scale demolitions and economic poverty occurred. The 1990s onwards have seen further changes to the tapestry of these communities, with further immigration from African communities – many of which are Muslim in culture and practice – but also from Eastern Europe, as well as the occupants of an increasing numbers of student hostels that are being built due to the area's proximity to an expanding University. These churches have thus witnessed large changes in their local communities, and their own profile has also altered. Second- and third-generation British blacks are generally more wealthy and professionalized than their parents and grandparents, and appear to have a more liberal stance on matters of social living, if not theology (for example, admittance of remarried people to membership of the church, the role of women in leadership and so on). Increasing numbers of churchgoers are mixed-race themselves, as the younger generation form partnerships with the other racial groups. Their increased confidence and social profile means that churches such are these are more open to the wider community than they once were, not only attracting a significant minority of other ethnic communities (African, East European, British white) but also being thoroughly engaged in the social fabric of their communities. The three case studies we will now look at can be placed under the headings of bilinguality, arms length engagement and tithing.

1) Bilinguality   *'I think there need to be **bilingual facilitators and advocates** – those who actually come from the community and speak both languages.'*

This quote describes how one member of a BMC sees the need to ensure that when it comes to consulting the local black community on issues of crime prevention, or of planning (for example), the voices of black people – including their characteristic idioms and other cultural forms of expression – are properly heard and understood because there are 'a lot of times the voices of the people don't enter the arena'. This concept of bilinguality reflects a number of possible meanings, including a newfound confidence from within the black community to actively engage in public structures. Bilinguality also denotes a high degree of competence and skill in language, and explaining complex concepts. It assumes an intimate knowledge of two cultures; black, but also white; grassroots communities as well as professional regenerators. The concept is supported by two complementary roles: that of *facilitator*, denoting a neutral, listening and highly skilled understanding of group processes; and that of *advocate*, suggesting a tougher, more outspoken and politically committed stance within a public forum. This phrase suggests a sophisticated and subtle understanding of the complex processes involved in regeneration, and the need for a multi-faceted approach to it.

2) Arms-length Engagement   *'... because people just think about the church in terms of maybe a negative experience they may ... for example ... they see churches as hypocrites.'*

The members of BMCs that the Foundation worked with, while often expressing an explicit theology of God's love and redemption within public settings, also recognize the need for a more implicit understanding as part of their overall approach to civil society. One BMC has set up an umbrella organization called GIFT, which combines four existing community-based organizations into one loose entity in order to attract greater pots of funding and combine existing resources more effectively. The projects include initiatives providing counselling, mentoring and support to vulnerable black young people, and supporting victims of gun crime. This intra-partnership approach is designed to connect with secular agencies more effectively than projects with an explicit church-based identity. This is a form of arms-length initiative designed to present an implicit Christian identity for the sake of becoming more deeply involved in civil society initiatives.

3) Tithing One's Talents   One the key features of the methodology of church engagement that emerged during the William Temple Foundation's research has a strong resonance with the parable of the talents (see, for example, Mathew 25: 14–30) and the sayings of Jesus about the good tree bearing good fruit (for example, Matthew 12: 33–37). The communities where this resonance is most pronounced were the BMCs, with their strong emphasis on tithing (that is, giving at least a tenth of what you earn back to God via the church). The importance of tithing for these communities seemed to be related to pride associated with 'good housekeeping'; that is, that there is enough given by the members to support the running of the church as a self-sufficient entity, but also enough to give to others in need and to support the outreach of that church into the wider community.

There is evidence to suggest that younger church members are perhaps not as committed in their giving and patterns of attendance as their forebears. However, they do strongly perceive a moral duty to use their enhanced status in society as professionals and middle-to-high income earners for the benefit of those at the lower end of the social ladder. The roll call of professions represented by these churchgoers reflects a strong location within the caring public-service professions: housing benefits officer, housing association manager, probation officer, and regeneration and business enterprise adviser, as well as those working in the private sector as lawyers, solicitors and accountants. A key phrase used to describe this process by one church member is the activity of 'ploughing back' into the community the skills and influence they have now acquired:

> A couple of decades ago, our area was made up of a majority of semi-skilled blue-collar workers who struggled to make ends meet. Those same families now have children who are white collar professional workers like solicitors, lawyers, local government officials … all of whom are able to volunteer their services and sort of plough back into the community in terms of advising members of the local church and wider community with regards to maximizing any of the benefits entitlements, helping them to fill in forms, giving them legal advice, holding health and well being workshops, counselling and so on.
>
> (quoted in Baker and Skinner, 2005: 54)

Thus there would appear to be a strong concept of tithing one's talents as well as one's money – a concept that is a rich theological contribution to understanding the motivation and contribution of church-based civil society from this sector of the community. It reflects the importance of seeing one's life as an offering to God, and therefore being a blessing to others, both within, but also (crucially) outside of, one's kinship or ethnic boundaries. There is a strong emphasis on creating sustainable community in the sense that these local people, who have acquired skills, competence and economic power, are redistributing those resources into the local community rather than taking them elsewhere.

4) A Touchy-feely Gospel   *'I think we just need to take them on like Jesus took them really ... He met people where they were; they were hungry so he fed them; they were naked, he clothed them, he'd speak to them – it's a really touchy-feely gospel.'*

The context for this quotation was a nuanced observation of the fragmentation of identities and patterns of belonging within BMC church attendance. First-generation Jamaicans (in the case of this church) came to Manchester and created their own churches. '... people had stronger religious values back then, so they would come to church ... and then perhaps they weren't so readily accepted in the mainstream church.' This member, by contrast, is a second-generation churchgoer (a British-born Jamaican) whose cultural context is markedly different:

> Now we're reaching second and third generation who are not purely West Indian, most of us have intermarried, okay or mixed and you're reaching a different type of audience ... you can't sell it by saying we are a good traditional Jamaican church anymore ... you need to go to what is relevant in the community ... to understand where people are at.
>
> (quoted in Baker and Skinner, 2005: 51)

In the opinion of this church member, the context for sharing the gospel is not based on cultural purity (a 'good traditional Jamaican church') but on racial and ethnic diversity. The process by which this church member believes her church connects to the new hybridized generation is not through preaching certainty, but through an appeal to non-judgemental inclusivity that prioritizes a contemporary emphasis on emotional and physical connection (a 'touchy-feely' gospel). It is evidence that the church is having to learn new ways of connection. 'The message has always been the same ("redemptive love"), but what needs to happen is to recognize that the method needs to change' (quoted in Baker and Skinner, 2005: 51).

The Independent White-led Charismatic Church

The Eden Project is a collective name for a cluster of independent charismatic churches that were established in Manchester during the late 1980s under the auspices of the Message Trust with the specific aim of attracting young people to the message of the Christian gospel. Its methodology involves establishing a partnership with a sympathetic church in the area that will provide the physical base for intensive youth-focused evangelism in return for the free services of specialist youth workers. The distinctive feature of this youth-based project is the requirement that its trained and volunteer staff are committed to living in the community. This involves them buying a house in the area and using local services such as surgeries, schools and shops. They thus function as a locally embedded community within a community, and the church base acts as a centre that supports not only full-time youth activities and a worshipping base, but also the administrative base for activities such as youth work on the streets, mentoring in schools and so on. This broad template has been successfully transplanted to a wide variety of poorer communities in Manchester and beyond. The particular Eden Project that the William Temple Foundation worked with was based in East Manchester, which according to the government's own Indices of Multiple Deprivation (IMD), was at that time the 17th-most deprived ward (local government subdivision) out of 8,400 in England and Wales. The project has now been running for five years.

Two aspects of methods of engagement that emerge from this church typology are the significance of 'blurred encounters' and being active 'local residents'.

1) Blurred Encounters   References by the church leader to 'our evangelical heritage' are supported by explicit commitments to church growth, increased baptisms, and a commitment to alternative lifestyles, especially in relation to issues of sexual morality. However, interweaving this belief structure is a willingness to have the boundaries of identity blurred. As they live longer in the area, so church members are learning more about the complexity of drug- and alcohol-abuse issues, child abuse, poor education, long-term unemployment and chronic poverty. The issues of 'friendship' with the wider community, and becoming 'increasingly part of the community' are superseding traditionally understood roles and labels:

> We used to do a lot of detached youth, well that kind of gets merged when you walk down the shop and bump into a bunch of kids that you know on the street corner and they ask you something … before you know it you spend half an hour talking and you've walked down the shop to buy a bottle of milk when you think, 'What was that? Was that life? Was that shopping? Was that detached youth work?' …
>
> (quoted in Baker and Skinner, 2005: 63)

This 'blurring of identities' is pithily summed up later by the comment, 'we are residents first, Christians second' (quoted in Baker and Skinner, 2005: 61).

2) Being Active Local Citizens   *'Those are the kind of things that we need to be* **chivvying** *along and we need to keep saying, "But we need to make sure that my next door neighbour can actually have a house in the new estate".'*

'Chivvying along' is a deceptively deprecating phrase for a vital role this church finds itself playing with respect to the theme of housing regeneration. The context for the above quotation is the proposed demolition of 600 council houses in East Manchester to make way for mainly private housing. One of the original principles agreed between the local residents, developers and local authority was that 'the current community must be facilitated in all possible ways to stay together, to be the community that lives on the new estate'. The current value of each of the existing housing units had risen to £40–50,000 as of December 2004, and this is approximately what the local residents will receive under compulsory purchase order payments. However, it has recently emerged that the cheapest of the new family-sized units that will be offered by the developers will be in the order of £150,000, leaving a potential mortgage shortfall of £100,000, the sort of mortgage normally accessed by jobs paying salaries of £25–30,000 per annum. Such jobs are not available to the local community. Meanwhile, those who have already paid off the mortgage on their old houses face the prospect of having to take out another one, typically in the later stages of their lives or working careers. As residents themselves, the members of the church understand some of the implications of this process and consequently believe they will have fallen short in their collective responsibility to the neighbourhood if 'in five to ten years time this becomes just a suburban estate with a lot of sort of business people living on it' (quoted in Baker and Skinner, 2005: 56).

Hence the important role of 'chivvying' – reminding those who ultimately make the decisions of the need to base them on first principles, namely 'we need to make sure that my next door neighbour can actually have a house in the new estate'. The methodology deployed here is reminding others of important core values and principles and negotiating as subtly but powerfully as possible to ensure that these are respected.

The Anglican Parish Church

St Luke's parish church is situated in the Benchill area of the Wythenshawe estate, recently designated as the poorest ward in England. The church was built in 1935 to coincide with the inception of Wythenshawe as a new garden suburb for Manchester's skilled manual workers, built on the former land of the Tatton family in Cheshire, nine miles south of Manchester. Since then, the church's fortunes have been directly linked to the fortunes of the community. For example, from the 1940s to the early 1960s the church was a thriving centre in a well-established and stable white working-class community. However, during the spiral of sharp decline from the 1970s to the 1990s, the membership and fabric of the church also went into steady reverse.

The fragility of the community continues to this day, but with signs of hopeful change beginning to take root after a lot of focused work in the area centring on early-years provision for young families, and adult education. One of these signs of new hope was the institution of the Learn Direct scheme run from the church hall. The Learn Direct scheme is a government initiative to provide high-quality learning for those aged 16 and above with few or no qualifications, and who are unlikely to participate in traditional forms of learning. It also seeks to equip people with the skills they need for employability, and is delivered through the use of new technologies.

1) The Learning Community   'Come to me if you are hungry and I will give you something to eat ... it seemed that we were feeding people at several levels ... we were literally feeding them, but also feeding them in terms of spiritually, emotionally and intellectually.'

The Learn Direct scheme established at the church in 2003 was a success, and soon established a strong client base. However, numerous incidents of vandalism and burglary (including the theft of computers) resulted in the project being closed at the end of that year. The church decided to reopen the project in May 2004, and a party was organized to mark its relaunch to which all were invited. The party was an open buffet with clowns and community stalls. The new course now has 150 residents signed up, with long waiting lists. The current vicar expresses the impact of the closure and subsequent reopening in explicitly theological terms; as a death and resurrection experience:

I mean we had all these burglaries last year, and in that I was very aware of the cross and how, actually, we are called to be faithful in spite of the painfulness of that, and I suppose that when the Learn Direct Centre – which had been going so well – was closed down by the carjacking in January, that was a real sense of death and loss and brokenness.

(quoted in Baker and Skinner, 2005: 45)

After a period of soul-searching, members of the community started coming up to her and asking 'Is there anything we can do to get Learn Direct started again?' and it struck her that 'the whole point of the cross is that you accept the suffering, that you are involved with it, because there is something more important and better, and God's faithfulness about believing that God's goodness is stronger than the evil and destructiveness that people can show'. The church council, she recalls, were clear that if they reopened the Learn Direct centre, they were choosing to be burgled again. 'Reality is what that means – to take up our Cross, but that is what, as a Christian community, we're called to do' (quoted in Baker and Skinner, 2005: 45).

One apparent outcome of this close relationship between a secular agency and a church community is the way in which the church learns for itself a deeper understanding of its own faith tradition and mission. Learn Direct appears to have become a source of learning and wisdom to the church, and in this way ministers as much to the church as the church does to it. Another outcome of this relationship is the degree of empathy and identification the church allows itself to have with an organization outside its normal terms of reference, which allows such a learning transaction to take place.

The Valley Interfaith Experience, Texas, United States

The following case study comes from Robert Putnam and Lewis Feldstein's book *Working Together*, a collection of US-based case studies narrating methods and experiences from a wide range of social capital experiments. One such experiment involves a group called Valley Interfaith, a coalition of 45 churches and school groups whose aim is to improve the performance of schools in the Rio Grande valley close to the Mexican border. These schools are often situated among the poorest of communities in the United States, receiving children from unincorporated slum areas on the edge of towns and cities.

Valley Interfaith is part of a wider regional network of partnerships called the Southwest Industrial Areas Foundation, part of the national network of Industrial Areas Foundations (IAF) established by community development innovator Saul Alinsky in Chicago in the early 1940s. Alinsky believed that reform could be best achieved when the citizens of poor and neglected communities organized and exerted power on their own behalf. Attempts by outside agencies to achieve reform by undertaking action on behalf of local communities were less effective, and represented a form of welfare colonialism (see Putnam and Feldstein, 2003: 14). The main reason why poorer communities had failed to mobilize effectively in the past was not due to any lack of intelligence, skill or desire for a better life. Rather it emerged from a lack of connectedness to a critical mass – in short, isolation. At the heart of the IAF philosophy, therefore, were two principles. First, the iron rule of 'never doing anything for people that they can do themselves' (Putnam and Feldstein, 2003: 23). Second, the power of the one-to-one relationship and small group gatherings, which allows the sharing of narrative experiences.

In practical terms this means organizing groups of the local community into house meetings of six to ten people so that in the first instance stories can be shared and listened to. Often theses stories are painful. For example, in one of the Valley Interfaith house meetings attached to an elementary school, an elderly man bringing up a grandson on his own would regularly disrupt the meetings with angry tirades against the school, the district and the teachers. After while he was encouraged by the leader of the group to articulate the nature of his pain:

> For a moment, Mr. Ortiz stayed as he was, arms across his chest, body twisted in his chair. He dropped his arms and turned to face the group, his face softening. His voice, when he spoke was different too … He told about his other grandson, the one who had been hit and killed by a car outside his elementary school five years earlier. The group's frustration and impatience with Mr Ortiz melted away. They could see him as a man who had suffered a terrible loss and had had no way to express the pain except through his rage.
>
> (Putnam and Feldstein, 2003: 13)

A woman in the group empathized with the elderly man's feeling of 'powerlessness' through her experience of 'losing' a girl who had joined a drugs gang.

As a result of this process, the group fed through to the other networks of house meetings, and to the IAF regional network as a whole, their concerns about the lack of civic action to reduce the activities of drugs gangs and the need for increased safety procedures outside the school. This has resulted in positive action being taken with respect to both issues. Father Alfonso Guervera, Pastor of Christ the King Church in Brownsville, Texas, and the overall leader of Valley Interfaith, reflects on the power generated by these narratives, saying 'We make private pain public'. As Putnam and Feldstein remark, the expression of pain and suffering in the local group converts itself into the energy and commitment needed to bring that pain into a wider public stage, where officials would have to recognize and respond to it This is done via monthly accountability sessions with local public politicians, which are filled by 2,000 members of local poor communities. It also works 'horizontally' as a means by which relationships are formed within the house meeting, and individuals are knitted into powerful groups. Listening to stories also leaves the listener 'open to being changed by the conversation' while also enabling agendas for change to be accumulated from the bottom up rather than imposed from the top down. The nurturing of the house meetings, and communicating across the networks, is done via locally recruited leaders. It is through these structures that listening is moved towards intentionality.

The role of the churches in this broad-based political organization is crucial. When Alinsky was seeking to replace forms of social capital in poor communities undergoing deindustrialization and outward migration, his methodology was predicated on the following mantra: 'Find existing networks that can be recycled' (quoted in Putman and Feldstein, 2003: 288). This meant relying primarily on churches – an existing source of relationships and networks based on values of justice and political power. This is what Ernesto Cortes did when he set up the first IAF branch in Texas in the town of San Antonio in the early 1970s. 'Cortes worked closely with church congregations, rooting his organization in the networks and values of those institutions – an innovation that made it possible to tap into well-established ties of trust and mutual interest, as well as shared religious beliefs that supported justice and social action' (Putnam and Feldstein, 2003: 15).

The churches, however, also provided from the start the strong, experienced but 'invisible' leadership required to nurture and develop grassroots leadership, which, while not directly shaping the agenda, nevertheless enabled those agendas to be implemented.

The Churches in Chicago

The following cases are extracted from a report into the work of faith-based community projects and their contribution to 'what makes a good city', undertaken for the Church of England's Commission on Urban Life and Faith (CULF). CULF will produce an audit into the condition of British urban society 20 years on from the predecessors' *Faith in the City* report in the mid 1980s. Members of the Commission visited Chicago in order to get an international perspective on the changes to urban fabric and civil society, choosing the city precisely because of its associations with the work of Saul Alinsky and the Industrial Areas Foundation. We will look at two Chicago-based case studies. One explores the role of the Episcopalian Cathedral in the city, reflecting especially on the significance of its worship. The other looks at the work of the Albany Park Neighborhood Council, a neighbourhood empowerment scheme run by church-based resources and directly modelled on Alinsky's methodologies.

The City Centre Cathedral   The Episcopalian Cathedral of St James was built in the last quarter of the nineteenth century, following the great fire of 1871, which devastated most of central Chicago. It now lies at the heart of what is called the Magnificent Mile, which runs down North Michigan Avenue and is full of high-class hotels, restaurants and shopping malls. The Magnificent Mile is part of the reinvention of Chicago that took place from the mid 1980s onwards, as it moved from being an industrial city based on manufacturing to a post-industrial city based on new technology, financial services, tourism, leisure and heritage (see Chapter 2). Twenty years ago, the area was surrounded by inner-city neighbourhoods that were predominantly black and poor. Now, due to gentrification processes, including the construction of several thousand townhouses and condominiums for young professional workers, the area is increasingly prosperous and white, and beyond the economic means of existing workers and those on lower incomes. The present dean, Ralph Blackman, sums up part of the challenge to the cathedral of this new social configuration. 'We are faced with engaging with communities who are fifty or sixty stories high with doormen' (Blackman, 2005). But he also observes a growing trend in 'singledom', with over half those over 18 living in single households. 'People don't know their neighbours and therefore are alone' he says, and it has meant moving the cathedral worship away from an emphasis on family into an identity much more inclusive of single people.

The cathedral was originally built as a statement of power and prestige on behalf of its Anglican sponsors, but was also an expression of philanthropic concern, exemplified by programmes of service and outreach to poorer neighbourhoods. Once again, as the twenty-first century unfolds, the cathedral finds itself confronted with a juxtaposition of wealth and poverty on its doorstep, treading a delicate path between what Matthew Price has called 'the contradictory forces of city centre revitalization and urban decay' (Livezey, 2000: 58). Ralph Blackman observes this tension becoming more acute due to the rise in property prices, and the resulting potential for the congregation to lose its motivation to be involved in outreach to poorer communities (such as an AIDS task force and an affordable-housing project), settling instead for a more cosy, enclave existence with like-minded professionals. He regards the struggle as an ongoing resistance against 'homogenization' due to processes of suburbanization, and a maintaining of 'catholicity' – namely a diversity based on the local expression of many different cultures and identities that reflects the global significance of Chicago as a city built on over two centuries of immigration and urbanization. The congregation includes significant numbers of African-American, African, and Hispanic members. It also actively welcomes members of the city's gay and lesbian community.

He believes that St James' cathedral has the duty to 'speak truth to power' by engaging critically in the values of those economic and political forces who have now colonized the Magnificent Mile with their opulence and magnificence (quoted in Graham and Lowe, 2004: 22).

These contradictory forces and directions in which the cathedral feels pulled are, however, anchored – and given reflective expression – in the Sunday morning Eucharist. Here, according to Graham and Lowe, 'the values of inclusivity, hospitality and diversity are embodied in the liturgy' (Graham and Lowe, 2004: 23).In Ralph Blackman's own words, the cathedral exists to proclaim the 'outrageous and radical hospitality and inclusivity of the Gospel when one engages in the stories of what healing communities can be' (Blackman, 2005). Thus the homily and prayers provide a 'well-spring' of common values that inform the cathedral's presence in the wider community. The lectionary, for example, provides a resource for theological reflection that transcends the preferences of a preacher or worship team, and 'connects the community to an enduring narrative of faith'. In the sacraments, the bread and wine shared at the Eucharist remind the congregation of the importance for Christians of the doctrines of creation and incarnation 'amidst the ambivalence and change of the urban environment'. Finally, the make-up and participation of the congregation reflect the diversity of old Chicago before the gentrification processes, but also in a way that is inclusive of both the local and the global – the eclectic nature of the local congregation is held within a sense of belonging to 'the internationalism of the Anglican Communion' (Graham and Lowe, 2004: 23). At Pentecost, for example, the cathedral reverberates to the sound of African drumming and Nigerian dance. On other occasions, the Gospel is read in different languages, and the peace is proclaimed likewise. Children contribute drama in the service and bring the elements to the communion table in the form of a dance, and there are the occasional jazz masses.

Graham and Lowe summarize thus: 'It was an inspirational example of liturgy as harnessing the power of the aesthetic, the sacramental and the performative: a constructive and distinctive aspect of a faith-based contribution to the life of a city' (Graham and Lowe, 2004: 23).

Albany Park Neighborhood Council   The Albany Park Neighborhood Council is a resident-led coalition structured (like the Valley Interfaith) on the principles of Saul Alinsky, and with several faith-based individuals at it heart. Established in 2000, it covers four Chicago community areas with a combined population of around 200,000. The areas are all diverse in their populations, combining predominantly Asian, Hispanic and White groups, but with populations that are typically 50 to 60 per cent foreign-born. The areas are proud of their diverse traditions – represented in a myriad of family-run businesses, such as shops and restaurants – with evidence of tight and cohesive networks. The main areas of work in which the APNC have engaged are the rights of immigrants and asylum seekers, especially in relation to healthcare and education. Those who are 'undocumented' immigrants or who are unable to afford medical insurance are provided with free healthcare and substantially reduced tuition fees. The other pressing issue, however, is the rising cost of housing due to the gentrification taking place in the city centre (which we have already described). This is putting the cost of housing – in both the private and rented sectors – beyond the means of the existing working-class communities as well as those new immigrants arriving in the area. The APNC is pressing local councillors to establish an ordinance with private developers to set aside at least 15 per cent of new housing stock for affordable renting. An interesting aspect of the APNC is the way it has established a separate caucus, or conference, for faith-based groups looking at issues of immigration rights. The Immigrant Rights project (as it is called) has brought together local churches and mosques as well as immigrant aid organizations to help provide free legal services, as well as educating locally elected officials on the need to expand immigrant rights.

Another key feature of the work of the APNC is the overtly Christian-based value systems that lie at the heart of its work. Lying beneath the public contributions the churches were making in APNC is a deeper level of contribution that is concerned to make explicit the values and visions by which Christians were seeking to bring about transformation. This is exemplified in the approach of a Roman Catholic priest, Don Headley, who has been strongly influenced by liberation theology's approach to education and community development. At the heart of its methodology is the importance of allowing personal experiences of hardship and exclusion to connect with Gospel and other biblical narratives that speak to that experience (see previous discussion in Chapter 5) and thus provide an alternative source of encouragement and empowerment, especially when this 'reflection on personal experience' is done at a group or community level. As regards the work and mission of the APNC, Don Headley cites at least three biblical sources that reflect upon the local issues the network is trying to engage with – sources that he calls 'manna in the wilderness' (see Graham and Lowe, 2004: 24).

The first is Abraham's faithful response to 'Go and follow God into a world of uncertainty and risk' (Genesis 12: 1). Covenanting with God (that is, holding onto God's promises of new life and opportunity, especially for those who are wanderers and dispossessed) is at the heart of the 'walk of faith'. Second, there is the Pauline claim concerning baptism into the Christian family in the Letter to the Galatians (3: 28) – that whatever hierarchies and prejudices operate in the outside world, the Christian community is called, as part of its public expression of faith, to model an inclusive community in which there are no sexual, racial or economic barriers. Finally, in the Gospel of Mark, Jesus begins his public ministry by healing three individuals who represented – within his context, as well as our contemporary one – groups that are among the most marginalized within human society, namely those suffering acute mental health issues (the man 'possessed' by an unclean spirit), those excluded through social stigmatization (the leper); and those who are physically disabled (the paralysed man brought to Jesus through the roof by his friends – see Mark 1: 21 to 2: 12).

The main purpose of these reflections is to help especially lay people within the churches to get in touch with the spiritual and ethical sources of their own impetus towards engaging with, and on behalf of, the wider community, as well as creating what Graham and Lowe call 'a dynamic urban spirituality' (2004: 24).

Themes and Implications

The purpose of this final section is to draw together the threads of these representative case studies from both the United States and the UK. All these case studies emerge as a direct response to rapid urban and social change associated with the wider shifts identified in Chapter 2 (for example, the shift from industrial to post-industrial urban societies). Broadly speaking these shifts have produced urban cultures (or mosaics) of greater diversity, plurality and choice, while simultaneously producing cultures of greater social fragmentation and widening polarities of poverty and exclusion. The close proximity of these two types of world produces forces that both make for greater hybridization between cultures, but also greater separation between them. There is an emerging consensus that urban space is increasingly contested and negotiated between growing numbers of different groups who are having to learn to live in what Albrow has called 'globalized localities' (see Chapter 3).

The following themes that emerge from our church-based engagements with these broader urban and cultural shifts are aspects of what I am going to call Third Space ecclesiology; namely, ways of being a church that resist binary definitions both of itself and of the world, and instead place the church in that contested Third Space where new patterns, new forms and new thinking can emerge. The most significant feature of the Third Space ecclesiology is the construction of a local performative theology.

The Construction of a Local Performative Theology

On the basis of the case studies examined, I suggest that a *local performative theology* is one that is locally rooted, yet understands the nature of the global forces impinging on its locality. By 'locally rooted' I mean that it listens carefully to the experiences of those sharing a particular globalized locality, as well as having an overview and understanding of the history of that locality and the experiences, memories and ways of belonging that have shaped it in the past and brought it to the present moment.

Performative means a pragmatically based response that is committed to delivering outcomes; such a response is 'performative' in the sense that the knowledge and experience acquired locally is part of an analysis that will transform the locality at a political, economic, social and spiritual level. It is 'pragmatic' in the sense that it reflects the new understanding that no one agency has the ability or resources to bring about transformation. What is required is a strategic, multidisciplinary partnership that works with others to bring this about for the whole community, and a willingness to think creatively, take risks, be prepared to learn and adapt, and to live with a certain amount of dissonance and discomfort; in short, learning to live with a blurring of the edges.

But strategic partnership is not an uncritical partnership. The other side of a local performative theology is not simply being strategic, but being *reflexive* in the postmodern sense of the word (see the work of Giddens, discussed in Chapter 3). By 'reflexive' I mean reflecting in a self-critical way how one's identity is impacting on the wider network of relationships and outcomes, and whether it is better to act in ways that express a more explicit or implicit Christian identity. This requires a high degree of confidence and local autonomy to construct an identity that fits the local needs, but unlike the reflexivity associated with individualism (which tends to be the postmodern assumption), this reflexivity will be undertaken on the basis of what secures the 'best fruits and opportunities for delivering the fruits' (see the discussion of Niebuhr in Chapter 4) for the wider community.

Reflexivity also suggests a regular evaluation of methodology in the light of experience, and a broader analysis of how and why the local context is changing. Rapid change is now a fact of life, affecting all types of communities (not just urban ones), so strategic engagement at the local level will only remain if there is a high degree of reflexivity also built into the educational loop. The significance of the local will emerge as we explore some of the elements that make up the construction of a local performative theology.

Local and Global

As we have seen from previous chapters, the significance of the local is related to three important elements. First, as Sandercock, Putnam and UK government figures and reports have all pointed out, socially sustainable communities are those places that have a sense of place; some sense of a common identity and experience mediated through dense, rather than diffuse, networks of relationships and encounters, and which are built up over a long enough period for an individual to sense that there is a wider framework of memory, identity and belonging to which they can contribute. Ideally they should also be places where diversity is recognized and affirmed. Second, in relationship to the increased power of the global to dictate what happens locally in terms of prices, living conditions and even cultural identity, the local needs to be a commune or matrix of resistance (see Castells and Welch). This means creating a process that tries to redress examples of social injustice and exclusion that are manifest at a local level but are direct consequences of unaccountable decisions taken at the global level.

Third, the local is increasingly important as a locus of experimentation and learning, a space where new and collaborative partnerships are often formed to deal with locally expressed problems, such as the breakdown of trust between different religious and ethnic groups, racially motivated attacks, gun crime, and planning issues.

The centre (in the form of central government) now acknowledges that its role as expert provider is no longer paramount. Rather, it is expertise and good practice forged at the local level that now feeds its way back to the centre, rather than the other way round. The UK's New Labour government would claim, for example, that its policy of 'new localism' (that is, devolving power, for instance to levy taxes, to increasingly local levels in order to facilitate local solutions to local problems, and the provision of public services by local organizations that are attuned to the needs of 'local consumers') is an acknowledgment of the new age of post-bureaucratic and multi-level governance (see Chapter 3).

Critics of the government point out that the terms and conditions under which local 'initiative' is allowed to flourish are still heavily controlled by procedures and targets issued by central government and enforced by regional and local government. However, the fact remains that on all three ways of understanding the continuing importance of the local (identified above), churches see themselves, and are in turn seen by others, as making important contributions to the economic, political, social and spiritual well-being of people living in geographically proximate arrangements.

However, a focus on the contours of a local performative theology does not rule out the possibility of the church being an agent of transformation at regional, national and global level. Regionally in the UK, since the creation of regional development agencies (RDAs) and regional assemblies, formal structures exist for the churches and other faith groups to make a contribution to debates concerning the direction of economic and social policy. We have seen, for example, the pioneering work undertaken by the Northwest Development Agency, with its secular-funded research into the economic impact of the social contribution of all faith communities in that region. A similar report was produced by the Yorkshire and Humberside region, which highlighted the important social and economic contribution by churches and other faith groups to rural and market town economies (CRCYH, 2002).

Nationally, the Church struggles to make its collective voice heard. As we have seen earlier, the days when William Temple, as an Archbishop of the Church of

England and thus leader of a national established church, would have the moral and political authority to fundamentally shape the political and economic structures of national life have disappeared for good. Despite the rhetoric of the Third Way, most observers believe that the political era of welfare consensus and macroeconomic intervention has wilted forever in the face of the global restructuring brought about by the market. Recent concern at terrorist atrocities in London and other European capitals suggest that national religious bodies will have important contributions to make in terms of advising the drafting of new 'anti-terror' legislation in relation to its impact on human rights laws and trying to promote, at national level, dialogue and further understanding of the causes of religious-based tension. However, it remains uncertain to what extent religious groups will be able to step outside the strong political pressure being exerted by national government to maintain the necessary semblance of a consensus or united front. It is also reasonably clear that national governments of all political persuasions are relatively powerless to prevent globally networked terrorism that finds its devastating impact and recruiting grounds always at the local level.

It is perhaps at the global level that faith groups still provide a meaningful and potentially beneficial framework of influence. As we saw in our case studies, the claim to catholicity – genuine diversity and plurality – that is expressed by churches at the local level is lent considerable credence by the fact that local groups are directly linked to global networks; for example a 70-million-strong worldwide Anglican communion, the 1.5-billion-strong Roman Catholic communion, and the significance of the *ummah* or international 'brotherhood' of Islam. Politically, the global Church, as an institution, remains weak. However, it is an important source of recruitment and resourcing of global civil society in which coalitions of different churches join globally based coalitions of other faiths and non-governmental organizations to lobby for change on issues such as trade justice, often by participative democratic means. The holding in tension of local and global identities is therefore an important form of hybridity to develop in a global society in which the global–local axis continues to dominate the national–regional one. However, it is important to remember that church-based engagement at the local and global level can work as much against the common good as for it. The local faith community can be an expression of inward-looking insularity that expresses itself in mistrust and tension between cultures and religions at the global level also.

Implicit and Explicit

As we saw in the previous chapter, John Atherton, in his book *The Changing Face of Public Theology*, identifies three political and theological eras during the last two centuries (for more detail see Chapter 4). The first was the age of Voluntarism and Atonement, which saw the emergence of an evangelistic message of individual salvation within the context of laissez-faire and colonialist economics during the nineteenth century. The second was the post-war age of consensus, the Age of Incarnation and the State. With the impetus to create a more just society after the suffering of global warfare and the apparent failure of capitalism during the depressions of the 1930s, the expertise of the State as both provider of social welfare and controller of the economy emerges as the major context setter.

Atherton's third era was ushered in during the late 1970s and 1980s, with the collapse of state control of the economy and the ascendancy of the market. Atherton calls this current period the Age of Partnership and Reconciliation. This age confirms the continuing weakness and marginalization of the institutional Church, but sees hope in the possibility of constructing effective partnerships and making creative connections. However, there are basic principles involved in forging new partnerships which the church needs to be aware of. The first is that partnerships should only be engaged in if they create added value to the wider community. Second, partnerships should only be engaged in if they are a means to achieving outcomes that, as a partner, one feels should be accomplished in accordance with one's own values system. Third, true partnership, founded on acceptance of diversity and honest disagreement, can only be achieved through a measure of explicit identification of the values and motivations that churches and other faith groups bring (that is, their faith).

However, the right to express your own value base also comes with it the responsibility of listening to and respecting the values and identities other partners bring to the table. This requires careful and open listening by all parties, and a skilled facilitation of processes so that minority perspectives are not simply ignored or suppressed by the majority ones. This point is reinforced by, for example, the case study of the church empowerment network and their reference to the need to build up a critical (rather than uncritical) consensus (see above). The building of a critical consensus, however, is costly, risky and time-consuming, and the need for space – so that real difference can emerge – can inhibit the sense of quick outcomes being achieved. Thus, when working in partnerships, sharing and expressing the more explicit dimensions of theological identity needs to mixed with a flexible approach that sometimes works with a more implicit identity in order to help achieve results. We saw examples of this with the BMCs in Manchester and their use of an arms-length umbrella organization to attract funding for causes they were committed to, and which predominantly affect young black people in the UK. The creation of this implicit identity project was in recognition of the 'bad press' that BMCs had with some of their potential clients and partners, based on perceptions of over-moralizing and judgemental attitudes.

We also saw implicit theological identities at work in the concept of tithing – laying one's skills and resources open to the benefit of the local community. Tithing is a practice that has explicit roots in New Testament theology and traditional church teaching, but which is nevertheless implicitly expressed via community networks for the benefit of those in the larger community.

Solid and Liquid

I am indebted to Pete Ward's work on 'solid' and 'liquid' ecclesiologies in his book, *Liquid Church* (2001), in which he argues for the need to facilitate the emergence of liquid forms of church to connect more closely with liquid forms of modernity (a concept borrowed from Zygmunt Bauman's book, *Liquid Modernity*). According to

Ward's typology, the solid Church shares the structures associated with institutional modernity. These revolve around the need for gathered forms of expression (where everybody, regardless of age or background, does the same thing at the same time in the same place), hierarchies and formal procedures to conduct business and initiate new members, a stress on loyalty to the institution, and a prioritizing of long service in terms of benefits and prestige over those who have joined more recently. Because of this way of working, institutional or solid churches tend to absorb energy inwards rather than send it spinning outwards. At their most moribund (but not necessarily numerically or financially weak), Ward suggests that they become sites of Heritage, Refuge and Nostalgia (Ward, 2002: 28).

The liquid Church, on the other hand, can reflect some of the dynamics of liquid modernity. Thus it expresses itself in movement and flows, relying on networks and nodes to keep the energy flowing. Nodes, those points of connection that supply power to the next part of the loop, can (in the liquid Church) be individual people or events (for example, the Spring Harvest, New Wine and Greenbelt festivals in the UK). Relationships are the central organizing principle of the liquid Church – what Ward refers to as 'networked informal contact between individuals and groups, rather than monolithic and structured meetings' (2002: 34). The liquid Church will also feel comfortable with the notion of the Christian seeker and believer as a *consumer* – someone who has the right to exercise choice over when and how to belong to which networks. He or she will also be encouraged to consume the product the network offers as a way of communicating information or conferring a sense of membership and identity, which might come in the form of CDs, DVDs, manifestos, fashion accessories and so on. The emphasis in the liquid Church is on a form of communication rather than a gathering, and there will therefore be fuzzy edges to the definition of who is an insider and who an outsider. Ward also suggests that leadership in the liquid church will be more diffuse, but I think that depends on the type of networks being described. Some 'networks' are so well established they are almost institutional, and will probably have strongly embedded leaderships.

However, Ward is not advocating that the liquid model replaces the solid model for the Church. His book simply articulates a plea that the solid and institutional parts of the Church reflect on and learn about the importance of more fluid forms of expression. Not only that, but he suggests that the role of the solid Church is to support or facilitate experiments in liquidity, often at the local level. The relationship between the liquid and the solid definitions of the Church is possibly a symbiotic one. They both need each other. For example, the solid will often have greater access to strategic resources to invest in supporting innovative and experimental initiatives that emerge at the local or liquid level, whereas the good practice and ideas that emerge from the local will hopefully feed back into the centre and modify some of the assumptions and practices at the institutional or solid level. More work needs to be done in this area, but similar findings have emerged from research work by Nicholls and Beaumont, who have explored the development of what they call 'justice movements' within urban settings. They pose the question whether cities can actually be places where justice movements can flourish, given the contested nature of urban space and the increasing amounts of regulation imposed by both civic authorities and business. In some cities, grassroots or participative movements were stifled, while in other urban societies justice movements seemed to flourish better.

The optimum conditions for participative democracy to work, they suggest, are when justice movements manage to maintain what they call 'light forms of interaction and affiliation' (Nicholls and Beaumont, 2003: 27) between national and local organization networks, without resorting to more formal and hierarchical norms. It helps, for example, when local networks can be financed by resource-rich anchor institutions within other areas of civil society, such as trades unions, national churches and universities. National funders must be prepared to allow well-proven local ways of working and networking to continue. However, their default position is often to control the local by dictating outcomes, as we have seen in relation to the relationships between New Labour and local communities described in Chapter 3.

My own research into how churches organized themselves in English New Towns also showed that local innovations in civil society struggle when national or regional funders impose too much control. In this case, the regional and national funders were church authorities who preferred to impose centralized ecumenical structures that were top-down in nature and stifled more organic ways of church organization for the early and very needy New Town communities (Baker, 2002). Thus, institutions such as central government or national or regional church bodies can inhibit local and contextual ways of working. National organizations such as churches and NGOs need to understand the importance of encouraging enthusiastic and creative local initiatives if their structures are to be replenished by new ideas and new personnel (especially younger ones).

Within the case studies we have examined, we have seen many instances of how churches operate within the hybrid space that lies between the solid and the liquid. The community empowerment network in East Manchester, for example, has been allowed to develop its own strategic response for those residents who were seeing huge changes being proposed for their neighbourhood. However, it was initially managed and financially supported by a national ecumenical NGO called Church Action on Poverty, and it plays a significant role in piloting government-led empowerment schemes at the local level. The work of the IAF is similarly predicated on creating networks of story and information-sharing as a means of creating a critical mass of participative democracy that can be called upon at strategic moments of political change. For example, the Valley Interfaith network can now summon 2,000 people, via a series of mobile phone calls, to turn up to rallies, marches or 'accountability sessions', as well as mobilize 75,000 voters to use their vote in a strategic way (see Putnam and Feldstein, 2003: 31). It also tries to run itself on the minimum of administrative support and infrastructure, thanks to the efficient working of local volunteer leaders. A network that contains 45 churches and public schools representing 60,000 families is supported by a paid staff of just two organizers, a trainee and a secretary (Putnam and Feldstein, 2003: 25). However, the support nodes for this network are based around institutions such as churches and schools, or personnel who are paid and housed by those institutions and who are 'seconded' by them to engage in a 'network-support' role (such as priests and those in religious orders).

Third Space Ecclesiology

I have attempted to show, via the case studies of local churches operating in rapidly changing urban societies, how the construction of a local performative theology is an exercise in methodological hybridity. These churches are operating in the spaces between the local and the global, between the explicit and the implicit, and between the solid and the liquid. This blurring of the boundaries emerges from a growing recognition of the need to adopt flexible, multidisciplinary and partnership-based approaches within increasingly contested, rapidly changing and polarized spaces, and to achieve solutions that work in the absence of overarching methodologies or ideologies. Churches and other voluntary institutions are finding that they have to adapt quickly to the changing social and cultural landscapes, and are sometimes at the forefront of generating creative initiatives at the local level.

However, for some churches, this hybrid way of working cannot be restricted to that of methodology. The hybrid encounter has also wrought a significant change in outlook and identity, characterized by an expanding of boundaries and a deepening of understanding. In other words, they are, through a willingness to take risks, an openness to learning and a conscious relinquishing of power, being changed by their encounter with the Other.

Spectrum of Hybridities: From Assimilationist to Destabilizing Hybridity

A more sophisticated way of analysing the hybrid nature of Third Space ecclesiology is to work with the idea that there are spectrums of different types of hybridity. These are useful because they suggest that change and transformation comes in a variety of ways. In the mid 1990s Jan Pieterse devised a continuum of hybridities. At one end was what he called *assimilationist* hybridity, which 'adopts the canon and mimics the hegemony' (or dominant class/tradition). These are hybrid forms that superficially represent the bringing together of two or more different elements, but they never change the political status quo (see also *bricolage* theory in Chapter 2). The status quo thus continues to operate in favour of those who already have the greatest power. At the other end of the continuum is what Pieterse calls *destabilizing* hybridity, one 'that blurs the canon, reverses the current and subverts the centre' (1995: 56–7). These are forms of hybridity that upset the existing power structures and so bring about more substantial change. We shall return to this concept of destabilizing hybridity when we look at post-colonial reflections on the nature and person of Jesus Christ in our final chapter.

From the case studies presented above, it would appear that the churches' occupation of the Third Space is possibly more towards the destabilizing end of Pieterse's spectrum. As we have seen, several church-based projects, with their pro-poor, liberation theology or neo-colonial critiques are, at an intellectual level, more inclined to subvert the dominant hegemony – as represented, for example, by regeneration rhetoric or the mantra of the neoliberal market. However, at the level of practice, even those with a radical political critique are committed to building bridges between the different levels of civil society in the interests of constructing a more just consensus by engaging with those in power and acting as translators and bilinguists between the actors and the acted upon.

Negotiation and Translation

We observed in Chapter 1 how Homi Bhabha and others have identified the ideas of *translation* and *negotiation*, the means by which new and hybrid forms of political and cultural expression are brought into being. Translation referred to the way in which a totally different critique is introduced into the prevailing discourses (or hegemony) deeply unsettling it and highlighting the fluid and unstable elements upon which it is based. Thus, for Bhabha, translation meant radically questioning the metanarratives of capitalism and Marxism (for example) which had a view of history as a type of preordained master plan that simply rolled itself out over the course of time. From the perspective of post-colonial immigration and its impact on urban society and literature, we can see, however, that history is now an 'open-ended and non-teleological' space in which the experiences and perspectives of the Other reject and disrupt definitions based on binary assumptions, and open up instead new possibilities based on hybridity that 'alienates our expectations' and changes the way we recognize events.

One example among our case studies, in which churches engage in *translation* to disrupt the majority view of the world, would be that of the church empowerment network in Manchester. This church-based project engages in a critique of urban regeneration as a form of neo-colonialism, thus calling into question the benign assumption that all people benefit from regeneration and there are no hidden winners or losers. However, their willingness to engage with people at all levels of the regeneration matrix means that they don't simply falling into the trap of producing a simplistic critique that continues a form of binary analysis. Instead, they help create a new space where pragmatic solutions can emerge based on genuinely creative partnerships that would never have been able to occur under the old hierarchical conditions, in which the residents knew nothing and the local city council were the experts.

Negotiation refers to the way in which different voices and discourses are brought into (or indeed push themselves into) the Third Space to negotiate with one another on how best to accommodate different perspectives. If translation involves introducing a destabilizing critique, or carrying out a symbolic action that radically questions either/or categories, then negotiation seems to refer to the nitty-gritty array of discussions, alliances, arguments and protests by which one actually brings about transformation on the ground. Two key words Bhabha uses in association with this concept of negotiation are *agonistic* and *pragmatic*. Agonistic, according to dictionary definitions, has its roots in the Greek word *agon*, which means competitor. It therefore refers to an attitude that is competitive or 'eager to win a discussion or argument' (Collins Dictionary, 2003: 32). At one level this adjective seems the complete antithesis to ideas about negotiation, where one imagines people sitting around a table listening carefully and seeing where they can possibly make concessions for the sake of the common good.

However, as we have seen both in this chapter and the previous one, sustainable partnerships and truly just mechanisms for change can only be brought about through honesty and transparency about one's identity, one's values and motivations and what one needs to achieve out of a joint process. It reflects something of the insistent call from Sandercock, Young and others that true diversity and the move towards making our 'mongrel' cities work is based on an acknowledgement of difference, rather than a denial of it (see Chapter 2). Competitiveness therefore needs to be seen as an asset rather than a hindrance.

Of course, if what was being advocated by Bhabha and others was agonistic politics for its own sake, then that would be needlessly destructive. So that is why the word *pragmatic* is important, because it locates the proper place of assertiveness and competitiveness within a larger framework of seeking workable solutions at local and global levels that will deal with seemingly intractable problems at a multi-level, and in a multidisciplinary, way. This emphasis on the pragmatic reminds us that Third Space hybridity is not particularly interested in creating mechanisms for a liberal consensus based on metanarratives of justice or multiculturalism or shared notions of Britishness, for example. What is more significant is creating local conditions that allow people from different backgrounds to come together to achieve outcomes that will be in their best interest, in such a way that the rights and needs of others are also respected.

If in the course of achieving modest but successful outcomes in the short term, longer-term relationships of trust and understanding can be built, then clearly that is desirable. The concept of negotiation implies that short-term pragmatism is an initial phase that involves at least the willingness of different partners to recognize the rights of others from a position of having stated their own rights and needs. This methodological hybridity might then produce a deeper level of hybridity that, as we have seen with church groups, revolves around a willingness to take risks, learning from others and being vulnerable to the possibility of change.

In terms of negotiation within our church-based case studies we have observed, for example, the way that Valley Interfaith worked. Its networks among the poorest communities, and the voices and experiences they held, were brought together at 'accountability sessions' with the voices of those who had the power to change things according to the wishes of those usually excluded. This process of negotiation allowed everyone in that room to listen and explain the degrees to which they felt able to move along the agendas that everyone required. Sometimes this resulted in most agenda items being agreed, sometimes only a few. But the important principle behind these negotiation sessions was that the processes are apolitical in the sense that no one is either endorsed or vilified according to their political affiliation. What counts particularly in the eyes of the more marginalized is *who delivers what* in terms of workable solutions. Valley Interfaith has a policy of 'No permanent allies, no permanent enemies', and it works with whoever can help it achieve its goals (Putnam and Feldstein, 2003: 19). Some BMCs in the UK are keen to act as translators for those within the black community who are especially vulnerable to being marginalized by planning and criminal justice systems, but they are also keen to embrace a wider vision of the common good that sees them as one of the fastest-growing sectors of social-capital provision in the community. These case studies seem to me to be good examples of agonistic yet pragmatic hybridity, and ones that churches are increasingly recognizing the value of in respect of a Third Space ecclesiology

Chapter 7

Towards a Theology of the Third Space

The aim of this concluding chapter is to identify some of the main strands of a theology of the Third Space. These strands will help show where hybridity is already emerging within recent Christian thought, both implicitly and explicitly. They will thus become the critical tools by which to explore the concept of the Third Space as a new device that can not only help create some guidelines by which to measure the effectiveness of church praxis in local communities, but also provide some dynamic theological principles that will support and encourage innovative church-based practice in the future. Some of these strands will be harvested from the previous chapters, which have explored a Third Space social ethics and a Third Space ecclesiology. Others will emerge from sources not yet encountered in this book. What will appear is an original and creative synthesis of new and existing ideas that will begin to construct a practical theology based on the principles of hybridity and Third Space practice and thought.

The main strands will be:

- a theology of blurred encounters – a theological reflection on the significance of the encounter with the Other, based on the thinking of Lévinas and Jacques Derrida, and for which I am indebted to the creative thought already applied to this topic by John Reader (2005)
- a theology of hospitality, and the risks of eating well or being eaten
- a theology of a new catholicity that stresses the need to avoid confusing the concept of hybridity with syncretism, and which argues for a sympathetic understanding of the earliest inculturation of the gospel within different cultures, an inculturation that continues to shape and unsettle it to this day
- a Christology emerging from post-colonial and feminist readings that emphasizes the hybrid nature and identity of Jesus Christ
- a theology of creation based on sharing in God's creative and redemptive activity along the lines identified in Chapter 4 as a post-liberal, multidisciplinary, solidarity- and standpoint-based Christian social ethics
- a Pentecostal theology that stresses the importance of difference and diversity as signs of the Kingdom and reminds the church that it must be constantly reborn into new and challenging contexts.

A Theology of Blurred Encounters: The Importance of Derrida and Deconstruction

Jacques Derrida's ideas of deconstruction were both influenced by and influenced the thinking of Lévinas on the relationship between the Saying and the Said, which we explored in Chapter 1. According to Lévinas, any encounter with the Other carries within it a residue of depth that can never be fully described by the Said (the person who is attempting to define the nature of the encounter). This is because of the inadequacy of language to fully define or articulate a particular experience or encounter with another person or culture. This idea links closely with Derrida's theory of deconstruction, which emphasizes the fluidity and instability of language and meaning following the collapse of colonialism. Colonialism, with its linear views on the evolution of human history in the name of rationality, religion and the market, was one of the great metanarratives of modernity.

According to Derrida, the very need to create these hierarchies, systems and metanarratives with which to organize reality suggests that *instability* is actually the default position of human reality. This has both positive and negative affects. He writes:

> It becomes necessary to stabilize precisely because stability is not natural: it is because there is instability that stabilization becomes necessary; it is because there is chaos there is the need for stability. Now this chaos and instability is fundamental, founding and irreducible, but at the same time it is a chance to change and destabilize. If there were continual stability, there would be no need for politics, and it is to the extent that stability is not natural, essential or substantial that politics exists and ethics is possible. Chaos is at once a risk and a chance.
>
> (Derrida, 1996: 64)

One implication of this 'chaos theory' refers to language and definitions; as soon as one attempts to define a term or concept, this represents an attempted stabilization of its meaning. All words and definitions are culturally defined and invariably represent the definitions that reflect the most culturally powerful discourses. There is no pool of universal ideas 'out there' that would imply some corresponding meaning between different languages, or suggest that equivalent transferrals from one to the other are possible. Rather, meaning is *negotiated* somewhere between the general and the specific, and the work of negotiation is ongoing. We make our own meaning based on encounter. Derrida's theory of deconstruction actually allows more of the essence of the Other to be released, as deeper levels of meaning and information are exchanged between the two sides or parties engaging in the encounter. As Reader says; 'deconstruction ... is the intention to bring to the surface that which is "other", that which has been forced underground once language takes over. This process can never be completed, but remains an obligation and responsibility' (Reader, 2005: 35).

This then brings in the theme of *hospitality*, which is a key motif within Derrida's thought. Like Lévinas, Derrida is keen to define our relationship with the Other, and he mediates his discussion through a reflection on the processes of migration and urbanization, which we explored in Chapter 2. Within the mechanisms of a highly mobile, increasingly deterritorialized global market, what are the practical criteria by which cultures and societies should set boundaries, and attempt to control the flow of the Other into their domain? Derrida is not arguing against the idea that host communities should create appropriate limits to the hospitality they offer to the outsider in terms of practical politics. However, he is clear that once one sets boundaries, quotas or criteria to one's hospitality, there is a danger that those in genuine need will be rejected, and that both religious and secular ideals of hospitality or fundamental human rights to a dignified life, based on the ability to provide for oneself and one's family, will be contravened. His argument is that in a world of increasing deconstruction and relativity, the ideal of unconditional hospitality is necessary as a benchmark against which to guide 'our sense of our relationship with those who might need our help' (Reader, 2005: 39). Derrida thus argues:

> We have to be aware that, to the extent that we are looking for criteria, for conditions, for passports, borders and so on, we are limiting hospitality ... as such, if there is such a thing. I'm not sure there is pure hospitality. But if we want to understand what hospitality means, we have to think of unconditional hospitality, that is, openness to whomever, to any newcomer. And of course, if I want to know in advance who is the good one, who is the bad one – in advance! – if I want to have an available criterion to distinguish between the good immigrant and the bad immigrant, then I would have no relation to the other as such. So to welcome the other as such, you have to suspend the use of criteria.
>
> (Derrida, 1993: 133, quoted in Reader, 2005: 39)

Eating Well or Being Eaten?

This idea of risky hospitality resonates strongly, as we have seen, with some of our church-based case studies in Chapter 5. For example, in the Anglican-based 'learning' project we discovered that the image of the feast, at which all were being fed at different levels, was a powerful symbol in the life of that community. The image of the feast to which all are invited is a powerfully recurring biblical metaphor of God's unconditional love for humankind. It also expresses the practical action of grace (a sensation of being released from the grip of the past and empowered to grasp the future) that lies at the heart of the New Testament gospel and the way it presents the ministry of Jesus. In Jesus' physical act of sharing food (such as the feeding of the five thousand, or the feeding of the disciples at breakfast by the lake) and the sharing in meals (such as with the tax collector Zaccheus), not only are the physical needs of people met, but their spiritual needs as well in the positive regard and blessing they experience in the course of that sharing. The experience of receiving regard and blessing, especially when unsolicited, releases within people a new energy and sense of purpose; in short a feeling of inner liberation which is the direct fruit of grace.

However, to act upon this idea of unconditional hospitality as expressed within both Derrida and certain elements of the New Testament, is to engage in risky action.

To open oneself unconditionally to the Other is potentially to allow one's own identity to be deconstructed, thus allowing the normal boundaries that separate, indeed protect yourself from the demands and cultures of others to be *blurred*. Reader refers to another of Derrida's key metaphors in this area; that of eating well (2005: 38). Within any hybrid encounter that emerges from blurred edges, there is a new opportunity to eat well. In other words, there is an opportunity to enjoy new experiences and ideas that deepen and refresh your own identity and sense of mission or purpose. This would appear to be the case for many of our church-based communities who have chosen to move beyond their 'comfort zone' – predicated on rigid boundaries and old methodologies – in order to engage in new partnerships that have taken them into uncharted territory.

The downside of entering into new, hybrid ways of working based on partnership, and more fluid ways of engaging, is that instead of eating well, one gets *eaten*. In other words, one's identity and mission is overwhelmed by the Other and one is left feeling disempowered by the experience of working in new partnerships and new forums of participation. This would suggest that one has not been clear enough about the aims and outcomes one wants to achieve before embarking in new and risky ways of working. It could also suggest that the values and principles by which one is prepared to work have been ignored or devalued by others, which would in turn suggest that one has entered into a new arena with an insufficient sense of personal identity. Thus, a theology of blurred edges or encounters that is central to a Third Space theology highlights both the potential and the risks involved in this way of working. It stresses what we discovered in previous chapters on hybridity. That is, the importance for churches and theology to have a strong enough critique of some of the values and methods at work within a local or global context, and to communicate this critique effectively (the work of translation), while reacting with the flexibility and creativity to work for pragmatic solutions to intractable problems (the ongoing work of negotiation).

Hybridity and Catholicity

If Reader's reflections on *recent* postmodern philosophy allows him to construct a theology of mission based on blurred encounters (an aspect of what I am calling hybridity), then further foundations for constructing a Third Space theology emerge from much older sources – the doctrine of catholicity, from which is derived the traditional formulation of the 'catholic' church. For this insight I am indebted to the incisive thought of Roman Catholic theologian Robert Schreiter, who in the late 1990s argued persuasively for a reformulated understanding of the doctrine of catholicity to reflect the globalized nature of the world. For him, there are three features of globalization that have led to the need to reformulate the doctrine of catholicity (Schreiter, 1997: 26).

The first is the idea that local context has become deterritorialized. This is due to the compression of time and space that has been brought about by the technological drivers of late global capitalism, namely electronic flows of information and knowledge, and cheap air travel. What boundaries are left are those associated with difference, not territory. It is at these points of connection between boundaries of difference (what Sandercock refers to as 'the borderlands', see Chapter 2) that the greatest amount of activity takes place to change established meanings. It is in these liminal spaces that the greatest amount of what Derrida would call deconstruction takes place. It is at these faultlines that established identities also become most fluid and unstable, and it is difference rather than commonality that becomes the basis for identity. It is these points of difference, and the new hybridities that they create, that for Schreiter now become the raw material for the construction of new contextual theologies.

The second feature of globalization highlighted by Schreiter is contained within the concept of *multiple belonging*. This is caused 'by the compression of time, the world of cyberspace and the movement of peoples which mean that people are now participating in different realities at the same time' (Schreiter, 1997: 26). This feature is connected to the first in that identity is now made up of multiple cultures interacting simultaneously. Schreiter suggests that this new form of identity involves struggle as people 'find a way of dealing with a variety of cultures, or fragments of cultures, occupying the same space' (1997: 26).

This leads to his third feature of globalization, which is that contexts are 'more clearly hybridized' (1997: 27). Within a globalized world, concepts about the purity of culture (which is his opinion was 'always more of an aspiration than a reality') become increasingly untenable. The intense 'interaction' (a favourite word of Schreiter) brought about by globalization destabilizes culture to create increasingly hybridized forms. Schreiter's conclusion is that 'hybridity has to be embraced more consciously in contextual theologies: we need to realize that most of our attempts to reach an ideal point will always be but approximate' (1997: 27).

These three strands of globalization contribute to Schreiter's reformulated definition of catholicity. He starts off his reformulation by noting the origins of the term, which was first used by Ignatius of Antioch in 110 CE to define both the Church's universality and its orthodoxy. These definitions were reinforced judicially and geographically by the spread of Christianity throughout the Roman Empire following the conversion of Constantine in the fourth century and the growth of the see of Rome as the epicentre of a new global faith culminating in the colonization of the New World at the end of the fifteenth century. After the Reformation of the sixteenth century, the concept was reinforced to describe uniformity and obedience to the creeds of the Roman Catholic Church.

In Reformation and Orthodox traditions, the word carries connotations of a mystical sense of a perfect church order, which will only be manifested at the end of time, but which infuses the direction and impetus of the earthly Church.

We can see that the concept of catholicity emerged over several hundred years of tradition (especially within the Roman Catholic one) to symbolize a sense of universality, homogeneity and conformity reinforced by centralized systems of dogmatic obedience and pastoral sanction in cases of apostasy or moral dereliction.

However, under the conditions of post-colonialism and globalization, this 'solid' and institutional understanding of catholicity has fragmented into a set of new and emerging propositions. Schreiter notes Avery Dulles's definition of a catholic ecclesiology, which refers to the 'ability to hold things together in tension with one another' (1997: 128). Siegfried Wiedenhofer talks about a new understanding of catholicity based not on hierarchies and uniformity, but on a sense of wholeness deriving from 'exchange and communication' (quoted in Schreiter, 1997: 128).

Schreiter then adds his own elements to the mix. The fragmentation of cultures and identities exacerbated by globalization is often reinforced by what he describes as 'the asymmetries of power, the experience of loss through forced migration (and) the sense of risk and contingency in a world threatened ecologically and in other ways' (1997: 129). A new catholicity should include the ability and commitment of the universal Church to both stand in solidarity with, but also be advocates for, those communities and societies caught up in the pain and misery of exploitation and fragmentation. This solidarity would also need to acknowledge the differences of experience and culture between the churches of the North and South. This approach will contribute to a new global wholeness that must be one of the marks of the new catholicity.

Another such mark involves holding out a vision of an outcome for the *whole* of humankind; a form of realized eschatology that stresses the need for a new humanity based on a commitment to the full dignity of humankind and a genuine peace and reconciliation. This is based on Pauline theology, with its vision of a new creation (2 Corinthians 5: 17), and these Christian-based values and principles could be offered by a global and catholic church as guidelines for a *telos* or outcome for human society, as a way of mitigating some of the unchallenged values and assumptions of global capitalism. Within this section of Schreiter's book, entitled 'Fullness of Faith', I believe he is attempting to make a connections with the gospel imperative based on Jesus' self-defined mandate to bring fullness of life (such as in John 10: 10). In other words, the new catholicity adds to the dimension of orthodoxy (a prominent feature of the old-style catholicity) the commitment to *orthopraxis*. Truth is not simply a commitment to an epistemological proposition; it is also revealed in a commitment to action. As Schreiter says, 'Many cultures will not believe what one says until they have seen what one does'. He continues, 'Because such understandings of truth are not simply an ideological choice, but are deeply embedded in many cultures, the power of orthopraxis becomes even more salient for a new catholicity' (1997: 132).

In this reformulation of catholicity, Schreiter has amplified many of the themes we explored in Chapter 4. He stresses the need for churches to devise pragmatic solutions within local contexts that focus on the theme of reconciliation and the need to establish inclusive processes of dialogue and exchange, but which start from the standpoint of suffering and exclusion. Like Atherton, he is keen that the catholic church should work on behalf of all humankind to produce *a reformed and reconstructed person in community*. Like feminist theologians such as Welch, he stresses the need for the church to practise its own orthopraxis – that is, a commitment to wholeness, inclusion, exchange and communication within its own structures. What he adds to Third Space theology is the global dimension; the sense that the Church's great gift and potential is to offer a role model to the wider world in which local diversity and difference is held and affirmed within a global network. The local does not fragment (as in the more dystopian views of postmodernity), but its experience and identity is affirmed (though not controlled) by a global community (the catholic church) linked by a common sense of purpose (life in all its fullness) and shared values (the commitment to unconditional hospitality).

Hybridity and Syncretism

Before we move on from Schreiter's thinking, we need to address a key accusation that has emerged within theology in its nascent engagement with concepts of hybridity. That accusation centres on the charge of syncretism – namely that a positive engagement by churches and Christian theology with hybridized contexts of thinking will 'dilute' the purity of the gospel and the Christian tradition, so that its distinctive identity and message is lost.

This argument goes to the heart of a recurring theme in this book, namely the negotiation of identity and the transmission of the Christian message within a postmodern world characterized by competing truth claims and fluid cultural foundations.

Schreiter, as part of his strategy for helping the church engage creatively with hybridity, argues for a more positive assessment of syncretism. This he does via a number of arguments.

First, he traces the historical fluidity of Christianity from its earliest roots as a reform movement within the Judaism of its day, in which it looked both backwards in an attempt to repristinate Jewish life, and forwards to see the Lord coming again. As a reform movement, Christianity has always had 'a certain asymmetry, a certain restlessness' (1997: 65).

This initial impulse towards reform has in fact reoccurred throughout Christian history; the desert dwellers of the fourth century, monastic founders, leaders of lay movements, sixteenth-century reformers and the Second Vatican Council are all examples. This ethos of reform, of *ecclesia semper reformanda*, is both a positive and a negative phenomenon with regard to syncretism. As Schreiter points out, the 'restlessness' inherent within Christianity can raise anxiety within some parts of the faith for whom 'an addition or amendment is potentially encumbering to pure faith' (1997: 65). On the other hand, as the Chinese feminist and post-colonial theologian Kwok Pui-lan points out, syncretism (the ability of Christianity to adapt to its cultural context and to change as circumstances required) is what has ensured its viability as a faith tradition. She cites, by way of example, the way early Christianity interacted with the Hellenistic culture and philosophy in which it was embedded, including dualistic notions of darkness and light, and in particular how the doctrines of the early church fathers were influenced by the thinking of Plato and Aristotle (Pui-lan, 2005: 129).

Second, Schreiter points out the wide divergence of historical forms of Christianity in spite of a common canon and a largely common profession of faith. He quotes the work of James Russell, who conducted a survey of early medieval

Christianity and the substantial differences between East and West. Russell hypothesizes that 'the world-view of the Indo-European, Greek, Roman and Germanic religions was essentially folk centred and "world-accepting" whereas the world view of the Eastern mystery religions and early Christianity was essentially "soteriological and eschatological, hence world-rejecting"' (Russell, 1994: 4, quoted in Schreiter, 1997: 66). The point Schreiter is making is that the diversity of cultural contexts into which Christianity has been embedded has created significant differences in theological outlook, without this being interpreted as a crisis of syncretism.

Finally, Schreiter reminds his readers that perceptions, and therefore fears, about syncretism always emerge from those parts of the faith community that are in power. He links this part of his argument with the colonial era of Christianity, when the Word of God was transmitted as part of the cultural and economic colonialization of the world by European powers. He recounts the amusing story of an evangelist in northern India who wanted to convey to a local village that he was there to win 'souls for Christ'. Within the speaker's universe this was intelligible evangelistic rhetoric. To his listeners, however, the phrase 'winning souls for Christ' had a different resonance within their cultural universe. 'Winning' souls sounded like 'snatching' souls, which was the activity of witches. The evangelist and his wife had a cat, a familiar symbol associated with witches. Therefore, the villagers surmised that the evangelist and his wife must be witches on the prowl for their souls. Schreiter concludes the story, 'The puzzling thing, of course, was why would the witch announce this rather than undertake his heinous crime surreptitiously? And what was this Christ going to do with their souls anyway?' (1997: 69).

Schreiter uses this story to remind his readers of the different hermeneutical tasks undertaken by the proclaimer of the message (especially if they believe that they represent a superior culture) and the listener. The proclaimer will perceive any different interpretation to his message as a dilution of its integrity and purity. She will be therefore be alert to the processes of syncretism (as she would interpret it). The listener (or the Other to whom the message is proclaimed) will probably be engaged in the task of attempting to embed the new message into their existing world view. Rather than syncretism, therefore, the listener is more likely to be engaging in the task of synthesizing (Schreiter, 1997: 71). Thus the true meaning of the encounter probably lies somewhere between, reinforcing the points we have already made with reference to Derrida and Lévinas, namely, the unstable gap between the Saying and the Said. The point Schreiter makes is that syncretism and synthesis are two aspects of the same hermeneutical loop, but if one sees the gospel from the underside of history, as his new catholicity would suggest, then it should be possible for the church to reinterpret a lot of what would, under the old order, have been dismissed as syncretism, as in fact a form of synthesis, which one view of church history would suggest has been part of the genetic blueprint of Christianity since its earliest incarnations.

Perceived from this perspective, synthesis becomes a more positive way of viewing the interaction between the gospel and postmodern culture, rather than seeing it in terms of an uninvited syncretism. In order for a synthesis to occur, both cultures have to move from a position of rigid separation to one of partial accommodation and understanding. In other words, both are changed by the encounter. From a gospel perspective this is right, because at its heart is the call to change – what the original Greek of the New Testament describes as *metanoia*, or change of heart and a change of knowledge. 'If the culture does not change, the Gospel has not been preached!' (1997: 71). However, the converse is that the Gospel itself is also developed by the encounter, because it never comes to a culture in a pure form. As Schreiter says, 'it is already embedded in the less-than-pure culture of the speaker, the treasure carried in vessels of clay' (Schreiter, 1997: 71).

Schreiter's point about the connection between power and perceptions of syncretism is reinforced by Kwok Pui-lan. From her perspective, there is a close connection between gender, religion and colonialism; in particular, the way that orthodoxy becomes synonymous with male control, and heresy becomes closely identified with the denial of the place of women in the early church and the suppression of texts describing the pivotal role of women such as Mary of Magdala. She discusses these dynamics of power in relation to the formation of the Bible via a series of increasingly powerful councils, as Christianity became the adopted religion of the Roman Empire in the fourth century. The Bible, or canon scripture,

> ... cannot be naively seen as a religious text reflecting the faith of the Hebrew people and early Christians. Instead, it must also be seen as a political text written, collected and redacted by male ... elites in their attempts to rewrite and reconcile with history and to reconceptualize both individual and collective identities under the shadow of the empire.
>
> (Pui-lan 2005: 8)

By which she means:

> The Christian missionary movement, which at its beginning represented an alternative vision and social structure in the Greco-Roman society (i.e. a discipleship of equals) adapted to the Greco-Roman patriarchal household structure and Roman bureaucracy. The episcopacy became the centre of unity of patristic Christianity, as women's authority as official prophets and teachers of the church was eliminated and repressed. The ascendancy of the Roman papacy in the fourth century also placed the centre of the church in the capital of the state.
>
> (Pui-lan, 2005: 10)

The contemporary point she makes from this perspective is that the insights of Christian women, especially those from the South who incorporate insights of shamanism, Taoism or Buddhism into their theology and liturgy, continue to be labelled as syncretistic (2005: 69).

Schreiter concludes his debate on hybridity and syncretism with the observation that when it comes to exploring new forms of religious identity, it is all too often the case that the churches of wealthy nations align themselves against the emerging churches of poor nations and 'deliver pronouncements of syncretism upon them'. This will be done despite the churches from wealthy societies often refusing to see their own 'perversions' of the gospel (1997: 72). This could also be argued as an expression of neo-colonialism within the church.

The Hybrid Christ: An Open-ended Christology

Charges of syncretism, which emerged in previous eras of Christian history, especially during the colonial era, may surface again as awareness of the hybridity and fluidity of the post-colonial and postmodern era begins to emerge within mainstream theological debate. They will possibly be fuelled once the radical and creative Christology of Kwok Pui-lan reaches a wider audience in her book *Postcolonial Imagination and Feminist Theology* (2005).

Pui-lan begins her exploration of the hybrid Christ with the question Jesus himself asks of his own disciples – 'Who do you say I am?' – and states that that question 'is an invitation for every Christian and every local faith community to infuse that contact zone with new meanings, insights and possibilities' (2005: 171). From her feminist and post-colonial perspective she spends much of her book rehearsing the arguments we have already explored concerning the fluidity of cultural and linguistic spaces, following the deconstruction of traditional points of reference based on modernity, colonialism and patriarchy. For her, the local is the context from which hybridity should be allowed to emerge:

> The richness and vibrancy of the Christian community is diminished whenever the space between Jesus and Christ is fixed, whether … as a result for the need for doctrinal purity, the suppression of syncretism, or the fear of contamination of native cultures, or … on account of historical positivism and its claims of objectivity and scientific truths about Jesus.
>
> (2005: 171)

That last reference refers to the nineteenth and early twentieth century quest for the historical Jesus epitomized by Albert Schweitzer's book *The Quest for the Historical Jesus* (1906). For Pui-lan this attempt to present a scientific and historical account of Jesus was symptomatic of the time, a project deployed by colonialism in its need to locate Christ away from his Jewish and Middle East origins into a more European model of humanity, thus showing the superiority of Christianity to the other so-called primitive religions it was now coming into contact with (2005: 62–64). This fixed, static, Eurocentric understanding of Jesus' role and identity, with its power of representation over and against other cultural perspectives, is now being replaced, in Pui-lan's opinion, by what she terms the Quest for the Hybridized Jesus (2005: 170).

However, like Schreiter, she is keen to point out that the quest for the hybridized Jesus is not a post-colonial phenomenon. In fact, in her opinion, the hybridized Christ emerges clearly from the pages of the New Testament, which describe situations that are highly pluralistic and hybridized, arising out of the 'intermingling' of the cultures of Palestine, the Hellenistic Jewish diaspora, and the wider Hellenistic world. She quotes the work of Indian biblical scholar George Soares Prabhu, who articulates not only the continuous evolution of hybrid Christologies, but the methodology of openness and pluralism that seems to come more naturally to theological communities in India, reflecting the polytheistic legacy of Hinduism:

> New Testament Christology is inclusive and pluriform. Every community evolves its own understanding of Jesus responding to its own cry for life. And because life changes, christologies change too. The New Testament preserves all these christologies, without opting exclusively for anyone among them … Its pluralism indicates a *christological open-mindedness*, inviting us to discover our own particular Christology, that is, the specific significance of Jesus for our situation in the Third World today.
>
> (Prabhu, 1994: 146, quoted Pui-lan, 2005: 172; emphasis mine)

An open-ended and fluid Christology, it seems to me, lies at the heart of the Third Space theology. It suggests that hybridity is located at the very centre of the Christian faith, by reminding us that the Incarnation of the Christ (the divine and eternal Logos or Word of God) was not confined to the point in time and culture some two thousand years ago, but is a continuous event whereby the love of God for creation takes the risk of being born into human cultures in a way that both translates and negotiates with those cultures from the underside of human experience, but also is itself translated by that experience. It is a risky, kenotic theology which will often lead to messy or blurred encounters, and will potentially subvert the status quo; but it will always point towards the *telos* of justice, inclusivity and reconciliation.

Pui-lan finds all the powerful transforming mystery of the Incarnation not in the words Jesus or Christ (which could be argued are the two binary symbols at either end of the human–divine spectrum), but in the tiny hyphen or slash sign that one could insert in between (Jesus-Christ, or Jesus/Christ). In a memorable passage, she says:

> The space between Jesus and Christ is unsettling and fluid, resisting easy categorization and closure. It is the 'contact zone' or 'borderland' between the human and the divine, the one and the many, the historical and the cosmological, the Jewish and the Hellenistic, the prophetic and the sacramental, the God of the conquerors and the God of the meek and the lowly.
>
> (2005: 17)

Pui-lan offers five examples of hybrid Christologies emerging from the South (2005: 174–82). One of these is a theological reflection on the person of Christ within the framework of the significance of the Corn Mother within Native American culture; she is a ritual figure symbolizing Mother Earth and the interconnectedness of all living things, whose suffering and self-sacrificial death offers food and sustenance for all her children. In dying she returns to the soil, and because of her suffering and death, all food is sacred and to be shared. These elements resonate strongly with the Christian symbolism of Jesus being laid in the earth and the Eucharistic sharing of food in 'memory of him'. The revival of the Corn Mother figure within Native American theology not only begins to rescue Christian theology from its colonial overtones for Native American believers, but also reconnects them with their Native traditions and rights.

From within the UK post-colonial experience, we return to Robert Beckford and his attempts to create a liberation theological praxis for British black Christians from both the dread and Black Pentecostal traditions. Central to this praxis is the emergence of a dread Christ, and a dread Christology. Beckford is careful to draw out the limitations of constructing a Christology in this way. For example, the category of dread, although a symbol of 'emancipation-fulfilment' is not a synonym for all divine activity. 'It cannot encompass the fullness of the divine' (Beckford, 2000: 201). He also recognizes that the symbol of dread has a 'limited lifespan; it will grow and die when the time is right'. However, he identifies three emancipatory dimensions to this hybrid Christology. First is what he defines as the importance of nurturing 'self-love' among black Christian communities. Having often internalized the image of a white Christ, black people counter its negative psychological effects through a 'pneumatic [purely spiritual] Christ who becomes experientially Black' (2000: 198). According to other black commentators, the tension between these two elements is 'negotiated' within a worship experience that synthesizes the two (quoted in Beckford, 2000: 198).

Second, 'a dread Christ is one who equips Black folk to face and destroy all structures of oppression ... to say that Christ is 'dread' is to unveil a Christ of Black uplift, Black empowerment and Black progress' (1998: 151). This translates the synthesis of worship into a more explicit political and spiritual agenda for social change and transformation. Finally, dread Christology engages creatively with traditional atonement theologies based around the centrality of the cross in Christian belief. On the one hand, the cross is a helpful symbol within a dread Christology because it presents a Christ who understands what it means to suffer at the hands of the oppressor. 'Within African Caribbean history, this view of Jesus resonates with the suffering of Africans during slavery and in a different form with the first generation of African Caribbean people in Britain' (2000: 202). However, the cross has also represented the centrality of unmerited suffering (the penal atonement theory), which black women theologians in particular have recognized as harmful in encouraging black women, who suffer discrimination both within their own church and wider society, to see such discrimination as in some way 'redemptive'. Womanist theologians such as Delores Williams and Karen Baker-Fletcher instead propose a 'cross theology' that stresses the healing and new life aspects of Jesus' Passion. It is a difficult balancing act to fulfil, which Beckford summarizes thus: 'Primarily, a dread Christ must be one that encompasses the life and death of Jesus, and finds ways of making sense of the cross of Christ (atonement) without neglecting or glorifying the cross. While signifying suffering, the cross also signifies that Christ came to give life' (2000: 203).

I would like to return to Pui-lan's powerful and evocative definition of a hybrid Christ quoted earlier. If we overlap Pui-lan's hybrid Christology with Bhabha's theories about different forms of hybridity that emerge in literature and culture to unsettle and interrogate the static binary labelling of powerful hegemonies, then we could describe Jesus as 'a truly insurgent act of cultural translation' (Bhabha,

1994: 6). That seems to me to be a genuinely interesting idea that should inform the praxis of all locally based Christian communities.

A Reoriented Theology of Creation

So far we have proposed three strands that could form part of a Third Space theology tapestry. These include a praxis-based or practical theology of the blurred encounter based on notions of hospitality, a reformulated understanding of catholicity, and a hybrid Christology that functions as a radically open and interrogatory symbol of all human cultures at all times.

We now move onto a reformulated theology of creation, some of which we have already identified in Chapter 4. In that chapter we looked at the work of Normunds Kamergrauzis in relation to the persistence of Christian Realism, and how a renewed emphasis on the doctrine of creation is a foundation of that persistence. Traditionally, the doctrine of creation has been based on the opening chapter of Genesis, which presents the image of God first creating light, and then the other orders of creation, out of the formless void and darkness that covered the face of the deep. Thus God creates out of nothing (*ex nihilo*) and the radical otherness of God from the rest of creation allows God to stand outside it and act in a completely autonomous fashion. Creation therefore has traditionally been presented as a one-way process in which all made things, including humankind, are utterly dependent upon God for their existence. This was later reinforced by Thomist theology which stressed the role of God as the First Cause, the prime mover; a theology later elaborated in Enlightenment theology in the image of God the divine watchmaker, who set the universe on its timeless and balanced course.

Within the Genesis 1 account, more recent focus on the doctrine of creation has concentrated on the controversial statement contained in verse 28, commonly translated as God giving man and woman '*dominion* over the fish of the sea and over the birds of the air, and over every living thing that moves upon the earth' (NRSV, emphasis mine).

In the past, this was commonly assumed to mean that humankind's role as the top species in the order of creation was essentially a passive one; one of management in accordance with the 'boss's' requests. The word 'dominion' also did little to mitigate the idea that nature was there as a resource to be plundered and manipulated in the interests of the human species. However, recent theological trends since the 1970s have radically questioned the so-called divine command to have dominion over creation, citing the growing awareness of the various ecological disasters now facing Planet Earth, threatening its very existence. These disasters also remind us powerfully of our dependence on other networks of nature (such as water and pure air, up to now supplied freely and bounteously by Mother Nature).

The language of dominion has therefore been superseded by the idea of *stewardship*. Instead of the passive management role based on strictly hierarchical notions of the relationship between God, humankind and the rest of creation, we see in Kamergrauzis's notion of stewardship a growing awareness that God is calling humankind into a creative relationship with regard to creation, rather than a management hierarchy. Humankind actually shares with God both the responsibility for and the creativity in evolving new responses to new situations, and ensuring that the proper balances are kept whereby the earth can indeed 'be fruitful and multiply'.

More specifically, Kamergrauzis sees this stewardship 'as the exercise of social responsibility in engagement with the economic and political sphere within the context of plurality as part of the creative activity of God in the world' (2003: 214). The implication of this important phrase is that *plurality and diversity* are God-given principles of creation. Just as God desires to see creation teeming with colour, life and diversity, so does God wish to see those conditions replicated in the human order, whereby diversity and plurality also flourish under favourable economic, political and social conditions. As we have seen, Kamergrauzis sees this co-creative act best implemented via a commitment to a Christian social ethics based on solidarity with those who are shaken, and to the learning and acceptance of diversity such a standpoint takes. This doctrine of stewardship as a positive encouragement of diversity and plurality is thus a further important perspective in the construction of practical theology informed by hybridity, since when we allow diversity and plurality to flourish (rather than be suppressed), hybridized identities are inevitably created.

Another important contemporary insight into the doctrine of creation is offered by British theologian Tim Gorringe, who reminds us of the importance of applying the principles of creation to the way we construct urban environments. He contrasts the difference between what Lewis Mumford called *organic* vs. *mechanistic* forms of urban development (Gorringe, 2002: 202). In ancient times urban development tended to follow an organic route, tracing features already present in the landscape, such as cows' paths, and slowly adding onto things that were already there, often in a way guided by the existing contours of the surroundings; in some parts of the world such a model of development still occurs. This organic development tended to relate buildings and public spaces to the human dimension, as well as offering the potential for surprise; one literally never knew what lay around the corner.

The mechanistic dimension of urban planning was expressed, for Mumford, in the rational and geometric forms of classical antiquity, later returned to by eighteenth-century city plans such as for Bath and Edinburgh, and then the modern architectural movements of the early twentieth century, epitomized in the style of Le Corbusier and his notion of the city as 'a machine'. The philosophical rationale behind modernism was the idea that one could tame nature and impose the human will upon it. The organic model, by contrast, was built in sympathy with nature. The clear conclusion that Gorringe comes to is that, where possible, organic principles of planning are those most likely to reflect a theology of creation based on stewardship rather than dominion. They are also most likely to be environments of 'grace', whereby the human spirit is nurtured. He writes:

> There is an artistic correlate to 'sin' and it is all around us, in our tedious estates, our boring shopping centres, in our tower blocks. Likewise, there is an expression of grace in the form of the built environment, wherever forms give pleasure, raise

the spirit or proclaim the world home, in suburban gardens, in city streets and parks, in the alleys and narrow lanes of villages. In the creation of such form the work of redemption is forwarded.

(2002: 221)

One might justifiably accuse Gorringe of a more than a touch of nostalgic romanticism, and it is hard to grasp the logic of Mumford's idea that would elide tower blocks and 'boring shopping centres' with such well-loved urban landscapes as Edinburgh New Town and Georgian Bath, but the main point he raises is a valid one. He is reminding us that we have a choice, as co-creators of the environment, to create urban spaces that nurture and engage the human spirit. Or we can create urban spaces that dehumanize and even destroy it. The choice we tend to make in Western societies, based on criteria of cost, expediency and the desire to separate from the other, is the latter.

Celebrating Pentecost in the Heteropolis

The account of the emergence of the early Church by the author of Luke and Acts is beset by scholarly disagreements about the historical veracity with which it presents events, edits themes and shapes characterization of the main protagonists. Fortunately, there is no need for this book to get embroiled in these fascinating debates. What is generally agreed, however, is that the author of Luke and Acts presents a rich and compelling narrative of the emergence of the early Church, containing many powerful themes and events that have resonated with succeeding generations of Christian communities. The purpose of the final section in this chapter is to allow some of these well-known themes to further deepen and inform our understanding of Third Space theology.

Christian Mission and Identity in Heteropolis

The birth of the early church, as recorded in Acts, starts in Jerusalem and finishes in Rome. In the course of that journey, the gospel is preached in other prominent urban centres of the first century Near East, including Athens, Philippi, Corinth and Antioch. Most of these cities were ports, and represented urban sites of considerable wealth, power and culture. They would also have been the *heteropoli* of their day – cities composed of diverse cultures and religious practices brought in by immigrants and traders. For example, first century Antioch, a Roman garrison city built at the intersection of trade routes between India and Egypt, would have been composed of populations made up of Greek, Jewish, Arabic, Asian and North African communities as well as Germans, Gauls and Romans.

Of course, the spectrum of difference represented by these cities in no way approaches the scale of size and diversity of global cities today. We reflected in Chapter 2 that Charles Jencks identified heteropolis on the basis of the Los Angeles of the mid 1990s, with its 140 incorporated cities, 13 ethnic groups and 86 languages.

We also reflected on the even greater diversity of a truly global city like London, with its 300 languages and citizens from most countries of the world.

Nevertheless, these first-century cities of the Near East were expressions of diversity and therefore hybridity, and it was in this context that the Christian church and its message were born. At one level, therefore, Christianity should 'feel a home' in the plural and diverse heteropolis.

A Locally Shaped Message

A prominent feature of the way the author of Luke and Acts presents the account of earliest church history is the attention paid to the different proclamations (or *kerygmata*) of the gospel. These different proclamations show evidence of being 'tailored' to communicate as effectively as possible in a wide variety of encounters with the Other. The core of the *kerygma* remains essentially the same, namely the proclamation of the resurrection of Jesus, the response to that proclamation in the form of repentance and faith in this Jesus, and the promise of forgiveness, salvation and the gift of the Spirit to those who 'turn around' in this way. But the contextual proclamation of this message is notably diverse. Thus Paul, in presenting the gospel to the intellectuals of Greek society in Athens (an audience that included both Stoics and Epicureans) starts his argument with reference to the sacred monuments the Greeks have erected to the Unknown God. He commends his listeners for their already existing religious sensibilities (Acts 17: 16–34). However, when addressing a Jewish synagogue in Antioch, Paul is careful to offer a view of salvation history that roots Jesus in the kingly succession of Judah, and shows how the ministry of Jesus was a fulfilment of prophecy (Acts 13: 13–52). Some commentators speculate that this particular occasion is a traditional *midrash* (or exposition) on 2 Samuel 7: 6–16, which describes Nathan's prophecy to David concerning the building of the Temple in Jerusalem and the perpetuation of his royal line.

In another type of encounter, this time in a rural area, it appears there are strong elements of a pagan folk religion (nature worship) mixed with Roman mythology (Acts 13: 8–20). Paul and Barnabas heal a paralysed man and are promptly hailed as 'gods from the sky' by the local villagers – Barnabas being identified with Zeus, and Paul with Hermes – and in honour of the miracle the villagers offer to sacrifice an ox to them. Paul and Barnabas resist the worship aimed at them by stressing to their rural audience that the God they worship is not an 'empty idol' but is the living God who makes himself shown and communicates his love by sending 'rain from heaven and seasons of fruitfulness', thus filling the villagers' stomachs with food and their hearts with joy. The author of Luke and Acts suggests that Barnabas and Paul skilfully use a situation to their advantage by appealing to the concepts and practices of divine worship that their audience would understand – namely, seeing God working through the beauty and fruitfulness of Nature.

In the light of Schreiter and Pui-lan's sharp analysis of the way the Bible has been used as a hermeneutical tool for the colonization of other cultures, I offer these case studies from Acts with considerable caution. It is clear that they are typologies of encounter, rather than specifically remembered and recorded events. However, these case studies effectively make the point that the *kerygma* of the gospel was contextualized in order to communicate with diverse and hybrid cultures, a task that, as I have argued in this book, continues to lie as a challenge at the heart of Third Space ecclesiology and praxis.

Speaking many Languages: Communicating with Diversity

The central symbolic image of Pentecost is the tongues of fire descending on the disciples gathered in Jerusalem, who then address a large crowd of Jewish citizens of the city as well as proselytes from other nations who may have been gathered for a major festival, possibly the Feast of Weeks. The gathered throng who are addressed by the disciples are symbolically representative of 'every nation under heaven' (Acts 2: 5). The author of Luke and Acts then proceeds to list the nations and peoples representing all four points of the compass. This global throng is amazed to hear the disciples addressing them, each in their own language, about the marvels of God. Just as, in the previous section, where we saw the *kerygma* of the gospel communicated in many different contexts, so now we see it communicated in many different languages.

We are back to the context of heteropolis again. The significance of the Pentecost account for Third Space theology is that we have within the Christian tradition a theology of mission that respects diversity, which is prepared to communicate effectively and powerfully to local communities within an overall context of urban plurality in terms and idioms they understand rather than in a universalized and homogenized discourse. Charles Jencks, in his description of heteropolis, uses a key phrase to describe the different languages or vernaculars that are expressed in the architecture and design of postmodern cities such as Los Angeles. The *monoglossia* of the modernist city, obsessed with rectangular forms and linear purity (summed up in the symbol of the skyscraper or tower block) has given way, he says, to the *heteroglossia* of the postmodern city, with its ironic use of eclectic styles and forms. This reference to heteroglossia (or 'different tongues') from a secular and postmodern source provides a fascinating resonance with the central idea of Pentecost; that many different languages and vernaculars come together in the post-colonial, postmodern city to demand anew a radical manifestation of the Good News of forgiveness, regeneration and life in all its fullness.

We have already seen elements of this heteroglossia within our church-based case studies. We have seen churches taking the time and trouble to translate their communications and negotiate meaning between different levels of people engaging in regeneration and political governance, so that those without power might understand their potential better, and that all might listen and understand the perceptions of the Other.

Finally, we should not abandon a sense of God's Spirit at work, both within the church but also the wider world, which is a major theme of Pentecost. Engagement with plurality and diversity, and the commitment to working with fluid and hybrid identities, requires careful discernment and some courage. A Spirit-based approach reminds us of the importance of balance between action and listening; that in the midst of creative praxis, time needs to be set aside for simply being, and listening to the still small voice of the Spirit, which within the biblical tradition helps give a sense of guidance, discernment and perspective. A Spirit-based approach also expresses a theological strand that emerged in the 1960s, and which was crystallized by the Second Vatican Council, but which since has been submerged. That strand speaks powerfully about 'discerning the signs of the times', of actively seeking and expecting to find the activity of God beyond the confines of the church and the narrow ecclesial subculture. As we have discussed in Chapter 2, there is evidence of the re-emergence of the sacred in our 'unsecular cities' (Davey, 2004) and the opportunity presents itself to engage as never before in co-creating spaces of hope and inclusivity. The Pentecost event challenges the church and theology alike to engage creatively with the heteroglossia of the heteropolis, to listen to the many voices, and engage the *kerygma* of the gospel within many different contexts.

The Paradox of Third Space Thinking

A final coda to this book is a reminder to those who are beginning to think about hybridity in terms of praxis as well as theology (as laid out in this book) just how countercultural and hard it can be to have the courage and foresight to engage in Third Space thinking. I hope that this book has been honest about the challenges confronting out postmodern 'mongrel' societies; for example, of how, embedded within the very fragmentation and dissolution of the engrained prejudice and will-to-power within our modernist and colonialist structures, new forms of exclusivity, and the perceived need for purity of cultural form and identity, are beginning to re-emerge. These re-emerging forms provide a strong and necessary 'reality check' to the concepts and praxis of hybridity. This is the paradox of the Third Space; that just as it creates new potential identities and methodologies for all sections of society, but especially churches and other faith groups, so that potential creates the climate of fear of encountering the Other, who is now more in our midst than ever before. I am very clear that these dangers exist, and that there will doubtless be voices who counsel either caution or dismissal of Third Space thinking.

However, I am also very clear that there is no turning back to the static labelling of binary systems, and that the world in which we now live is rapidly evolving in economic, political, cultural, scientific, but above all urban ways that are increasingly disconnected from any past we might have known, and in ways that are defying any sort of predictive outcome. As a person of faith from within the Christian tradition, I am also clear that this world unfolding before us is still God's world, and the Spirit of God is still challenging the church (and indeed all human society) to be hopeful, to be clear about its place in society, but above all to be creative in the way we opens ourselves to engaging with our world. I hope in this book to have begun to show how the Third Space is often a difficult place to be; a place where we must have the courage to face the Other in a mutual encounter, rather than hurling platitudes or insults from a safe space across the binary divide. It is, however, as I hope I have showed, and particularly in the case studies I have shared, a space of renewal, excitement and new opportunity – to learn, to encounter, but above all, to create new hybrid forms of church.

Bibliography

Agulnik, P. et al. *Understanding Social Exclusion*. Oxford and New York: Oxford University Press, 2002.

Albrow, M. *The Global Age: State and Society beyond Modernity*. Cambridge: Polity Press, and Stanford, CA: Stanford University Press, 1997.

Allen, J. and Turner, E. *The Ethnic Quilt: Population Diversity in Southern California*. Northridge: Center for Geographical Studies, 1997.

Amin, A., 'Ethnicity and the Multicultural City: Living with Diversity'. *Environment and Planning A* 34 (2002): 959–80.

Amin, A, and Thrift, N. *Cities: Reimagining the Urban*. Cambridge: Polity Press, 2002.

Atherton, J. *Public Theology for Changing Times*. London: SPCK, 2000.

——. *Marginalization*. London: SCM, 2003.

Atherton, J., Baker, C., and Graham, E. 'A Genius of Place?', in E. Graham and A. Rowlands (eds), *Pathways to the Public Square: Practical Theology in an Age of Pluralism*. Münster: Lit Verlag, 2005.

Atwood, M. *The Handmaid's Tale*. Toronto: McClelland and Stewart, 1985.

Baker, C. "Towards A Theology of New Towns: The Implications of the New Town Experience for Urban Theology". Unpublished thesis. Manchester: University of Manchester, 2002.

——. 'Going with the Flow: Can Christian Faith Communities in the UK Flourish in Non-institutional Civil Society', in *Political Theology* 6/1 (2005): 113–16.

Baker, C. and Skinner, H. *Telling the Stories: How Churches are Contributing to Social Capital*. Manchester: William Temple Foundation, 2005.

Bakhtin, M.. *The Dialogic Imagination: Four Essays*, translated by Caryl Emerson and Michael Holquist. Austin: University of Texas Press, 1981.

Beckford, R. *Jesus is Dread: Black Theology and Black Culture in Britain*. London: Darton, Longman and Todd, 1998.

——. *Dread and Pentecostal: A Political Theology for the Black Church in Britain*. London: SPCK, 2000.

Bender, T. *Community and Social Change in America*. New Brunswick, NJ: Rutgers University Press, 1978.

——. 'Opinion' section, *Los Angeles Times*, 22 December 1996.

Bhabha, H.K. *The Location of Culture*. London and New York: Routledge, 1994.

Blackman, R. Interview with the author, September 2005.

Blair, T. *Faith in Politics*. London: Christian Socialist Movement, 2001.

——. Untitled speech to Faithworks conference, March 2005, available at www.number-10.gov.uk/output/Page7375.asp

Brah, A. and Coombes, A. (eds). *Hybridity and its Discontents: Politics, Science, Culture*. London and New York: Routledge, 2000.

Castells, M. *The Informational City: Information Technology, Economic Restructuring, and the Urban–Regional Process*. Oxford: Blackwell, 1989.

——. *The Rise of the Network Society.* Oxford and Cambridge, MA: Blackwell, 1996.

CENTRIS. *Unravelling the Maze: A Survey of Civil Society in the UK*. Newcastle: Centre for Research and Innovation in Social Policy and Practice, 2003.

Chapman, M. *Blair's Britain: A Christian Critique*. London: Darton, Longman and Todd, 2005.

CRCYH. *Angels and Advocates: Church Social Action in Yorkshire and the Humber* Leeds: Churches Regional Commission for Yorkshire and the Humber, 2002.

——. *Sowing the Seed: Church and Rural Renaissance in Yorkshire and the Humber*. Leeds: Churches Regional Commission for Yorkshire and the Humber, 2003.

Dale, G. *God's Politicians: The Christian Contribution to 100 Years of Labour*. London: HarperCollins, 2001.

Davey, A. 'On the Faultlines of the Global City' (editorial). *Crucible* (July– September 2004).

De Gruchy, J. (ed). *The Cambridge Companion to Dietrich Bonhoeffer*. Cambridge and New York: Cambridge University Press, 1999.

De Tocqueville, A. *Democracy in America*, 2 vols. New York: Knopf, 1945 (originally published 1835–40).

——. *Journeys to England and Ireland*, translated by George Lawrence and K.P. Mayer. London: Faber, 1958 (written 1833–35).

Denham, J. *Building Cohesive Communities: A Report of the Ministerial Group on Public Order and Community Cohesion*. London: Home Office, 2002.

Derrida, J. 'Remarks on Deconstruction and Pragmatism', in S. Critchley et al., *Deconstruction and Pragmatism*. London and New York: Routledge, 1996.

Douglass, M. and Friedmann, J. (eds.). *Cities for Citizens: Planning and the Rise of Civil Society in a Global Age*. Chichester and New York: Wiley, 1998.

Durkheim, E. *Suicide: A Study in Sociology*, translated by George Simpson and John A. Spaulding. Glencoe, IL: Free Press, 1951; London: Routledge, 1952 (originally published 1897).

Engels, F. *The Condition of the Working Class in England*. London: Panther, 1969 (originally published 1844).

Field, J. *Social Capital*. London and New York: Routledge, 2003.

Florida, R. *The Rise of the Creative Class: And How it's Transforming Work, Leisure, Community and Everyday Life*. New York: Basic Books, 2002.

Forrester, D. *On Human Worth: A Christian Vindication of Equality*. London: SCM, 2001.

Fox, R. *Reinhold Niebuhr: A Biography*. New York: Pantheon, 1985.

Friedman, J. 'Global Crises, the Struggle for Cultural Identity and Intellectual Porkbarrelling: Cosmopolitans versus Locals, Ethnics and Nationals in an Era of De-hegemonisation' in P. Werbner and T. Modood (eds), *Debating Cultural Hybridity: Multi-cultural Identities and the Politics of Anti-racism*. London: Zed Books, 1997.

Fukuyama, Francis. *The End of History and the Last Man*. New York: Free Press, and London: Hamilton, 1992.

Furbey, R. and Macey, M. 'Religion and Urban Regeneration'. *Policy and Politics* 33/1 (2005): 95–116.

Garreau, J. *Edge City: Life on the New Frontier*. New York: Doubleday, 1991.

Giddens, A. *Modernity and Self-identity: Self and Society in the Late Modern Age*. Cambridge: Polity Press, and Stanford, CA: Stanford University Press, 1991.

——. *The Third Way: The Renewal of Social Democracy*. Cambridge: Polity Press, and Malden, MA: Blackwell, 1998.

Gorringe, T. *A Theology of the Built Environment: Justice, Empowerment, Redemption*. Cambridge and New York: Cambridge University Press, 2002.

Graham, E. 'Different Forms of Feminist Ethics', in C.-H. Grenholm and N. Kamergrauzis, (eds), *Feminist Ethics: Perspectives, Problems and Possibilities*. Uppsala: University of Uppsala, 2003.

Graham, E. and Lowe, S. *What Makes a Good City? The Chicago Experience: Report on a Trip to Chicago, August 2004*. Unpublished paper. London: Commission on Urban Life and Faith, 2004.

Graham, S. and Marvin, S. *Splintering Urbanism: Networked Infrastructures, Technological Mobilities and the Urban Condition*. London and New York: Routledge, 2001.

Hall, S. 'Blue Election, Election Blues' *Marxism Today* (July 1987): 30–35; reprinted in his *The Hard Road to Renewal: Thatcherism and the Crisis of the Left*. London: Verso, 1988.

Halpern, D. *Social Capital*. Cambridge and Malden, MA: Polity Press, 2005.

Harrison, B. *Making the Connections: Essays in Feminist Social Ethics*. Boston: Beacon Press, 1985.

Harvey, D. 'From Managerialism to Entrepreneurialism: The Transformation in Urban Governance in Late Capitalism', *Geografiska Annaler* 71B (1989): 3–17; reprinted in his *Spaces of Capital: Towards a Critical Geography*. Edinburgh: Edinburgh University Press, and New York: Routledge, 2001.

Hauerwas, S. *A Community of Character: Toward a Constructive Christian Social Ethic*. Notre Dame, IN: University of Notre Dame Press, 1981.

Hills, J., Le Grand, J. and Piachaud, D. *Understanding Social Exclusion*. Oxford: Oxford University Press, 2002.

Home Office. *Community Cohesion: A Report of the Independent Review Team*. London: Home Office, 2001.

——. *Working Together: Cooperation between Government and Faith Communities*. London: Home Office, 2004.

Hirschman, A. *Exit, Voice and Loyalty: Responses to Decline in Firms, Organizations, and States*. Cambridge, MA: Harvard University Press, 1970.

hooks, bell. *Yearning: Race, Gender, and Cultural Politics*. Boston: South End Press, 1990.

Huntington, S. *Who Are We?: The Challenges to America's National Identity*. New York and London: Simon and Schuster, 2004.

Hutnyk, J. 'Adorno at Womad: South Asian Crossovers and the Limits of Hybridity-Talk', in P. Werbner and T. Modood (eds), *Debating Cultural Hybridity: Multicultural Identities and the Politics of Anti-racism*. London: Zed Books, 1997.

Jacobs, J. *Edge of Empire: Postcolonialism and the City*. London and New York: Routledge, 1996.

Jencks, C. 'Hetero-architecture and the LA School', in A. Scott and E.W. Soja (eds), *The City: Los Angeles and Urban Theory at the End of the Twentieth Century*. Berkeley: University of California Press, 1996.

Kamergrauzis, N. *The Persistence of Christian Realism: A Study of the Social Ethics of Ronald H. Preston*. Uppsala: University of Uppsala, 2001.

Keating, A. and Connor, R. 'In Memory: Gloria Evangelina Anzaldúa, 1942–2004', available at http://gloria.chicanas.com/keatingobit.html

Kegley, C., and Bretall, R. (eds). *Reinhold Niebuhr: His Religious, Social, and Political Thought*. New York: Macmillan, 1956.

Kraniauskas, J. 'Hybridity in a Transnational Frame: Latin-Americanist and Postcolonial Perspectives on Cultural Studies', in A. Brah and A. Coombes (eds), *Hybridity and its Discontents: Politics, Science, Culture*. London and New York: Routledge, 2000.

Küng, H. *A Global Ethic for Global Politics and Economics*. London: SCM, 1997; New York: Oxford University Press, 1998.

Leadbeter, C. *The Rise of the Social Entrepreneur*. London: Demos, 1997.

Lefebvre, H. *Critique of Everyday Life*, translated by John Moore, 3 vols. London: Verso, 1991–2005.

Lévinas, E. *Totality and Infinity: An Essay on Exteriority*, translated by Alphonso Lingis. Pittsburgh, PA: Duquesne University Press, 1969.

Lewis, P. *Islamic Britain: Religion, Politics and Identity Among British Muslims*. London: I.B. Taurus, 2002.

Livezey, L. (ed.). *Public Religion and Urban Transformation: Faith in the City*. New York: New York University Press, 2000.

LGA. *Faith and Community: A Good Practice Guide for Local Authorities*. London: Local Government Association, 2002.

Lovin, R. *Christian Faith and Public Choices: The Social Ethics of Barth, Brunner, and Bonhoeffer*. Philadelphia: Fortress Press, 1984.

MacIntyre, A. *After Virtue: A Study in Moral Theology*. London: Duckworth, and Notre Dame, IN: Notre Dame University Press, 1981.

Milbank, J. *The Word Made Strange: Theology, Language, Culture*. Oxford and Cambridge, MA: Blackwell, 1997.

Müller, H. 'The Identity and Formation of Dietrich Bonhoeffer', in R. Smith (ed.), *World Come of Age: A Symposium on Dietrich Bonhoeffer*. London: Collins, and Philadelphia: Fortress Press, 1967.

Nicholls, W. and Beaumont, J. 'The Urbanisation of Justice Movements? Possibilities and Constraints for the City as a Space of Contentious Struggle'. *Space and Polity* 8/2 (August 2004): 119–35.

Niebuhr, R. *An Interpretation of Christian Ethics*. New York: Harper, 1935; London: SCM, 1937.

Niebuhr, R. *Faith and History: A Comparison of Christian and Modern Views of History*. London: Nisbet, and New York: Scribner, 1949.

NWDA. *Faith in England's Northwest: Economic Impact Assessment*. Warrington: Northwest Development Agency, 2005.

Papastergiadis, N. *The Turbulence of Migration: Globalization, Deterritorialization, and Hybridity*. Cambridge: Polity Press, and Malden, MA: Blackwell, 2000.

Parsons, T. *The Social System*. Glencoe, IL: Free Press, 1951; London: Tavistock, 1952.

Peck, J. and Ward, K. *City of Revolution: Restructuring Manchester*. Manchester: Manchester University Press, 2002.

Pierre, J. and Peters, G. *Governance, Politics and the State*. Basingstoke: Macmillan, 2000.

Pieterse, J. 'Globalization as Hybridization', in M. Featherstone, S. Lash and R. Robertson (eds), *Global Modernities*. London: Sage, 1995.

Plamenatz, J. *Man and Society: Political and Social Theory*. London: Longman, and New York: McGraw-Hill, 1963.

Preston, R. *Church and Society in the Late Twentieth Century: The Economic and Political Task*. London: SCM, 1983.

——. *Religion and the Ambiguities of Capitalism*. London: SCM, 1991; Cleveland, OH: Pilgrim Press, 1993.

Pui-lan, K. *Postcolonial Imagination and Feminist Theology*. Louisville, KY: Westminster John Knox Press, 2005.

Putnam, R. *Bowling Alone: The Collapse and Revival of American Community*. New York and London: Simon and Schuster, 2000.

Putnam, R, and Feldstein, L. *Better Together: Restoring the American Community*. New York and London: Simon and Schuster, 2003.

Ram, M., Edwards, P., and Jones, T. *The Employment of Illegal Immigrants in SMEs*. London: DTI Central Unit Research Report, 2002.

Reader, J. *Blurred Encounters: A Reasoned Practice of Faith*. St Bride's, Vale of Glamorgan: Aureus, 2005.

Rose, H. *Love, Power and Knowledge: Towards a Feminist Transformation of the Sciences*. Cambridge: Polity Press, and Bloomington: Indiana University Press, 1994.

Ross, E. *Social Control: A Survey of the Foundations of Order*. Cleveland, OH: Case Western Reserve University Press, 1969; New York: Johnson Reprint, 1970 (originally published 1901).

Rothstein, B. 'Social Capital in the Social Democratic Welfare State'. *Politics and Society* 29/2 (2001): 207–41.

Rushdie, S. *The Satanic Verses*. London: Vintage, and New York: Viking, 1988.

——. *Imaginary Homelands: Essays and Criticism, 1981–1991*. London: Granta, 1991.

Said, E. *Orientalism*. New York: Pantheon, 1978; London: Routledge, 1979.

Sandercock, L. *Towards Cosmopolis: Planning for Multicultural Cities*. Chichester and New York: John Wiley, 1998.

——. *Cosmopolis II: Mongrel Cities in the 21st Century*. London and New York: Continuum, 2003.

Sassen, S. *The Global City: New York, London, Tokyo*. Princeton, NJ: Princeton University Press, 1991.

Schreiter, R. *The New Catholicity: Theology between the Global and the Local*. Maryknoll, NY: Orbis, 1997.

Selby, P. 'Christianity in a World Come of Age', in J. De Gruchy (ed.), *The Cambridge Companion to Dietrich Bonhoeffer*. Cambridge and New York: Cambridge University Press, 1999.

Shapins, J. 'From the Tortilla Curtain to the Former East Berlin: The Performances of Guillermo Gómez-Peña and the City In-Between Identities and Times', available at www.columbia.edu/cu/museo/6/gomez-pena/index.html, 2003.

Soja, E. *Postmetropolis: Critical Studies of Cities and Regions*. Oxford and Malden, MA: Blackwell, 2000.

Stoker, G. *Transforming Local Governance: From Thatcherism to New Labour*. Basingstoke: Palgrave Macmillan, 2004.

Stone, R. *Reinhold Niebuhr: Prophet to Politicians*. Nashville, TN: Abingdon, 1972.

Temple, W. *Christianity and Social Order*. London: SPCK, 1976 (originally published 1942).

Tomlinson, D. *The Post-Evangelical*. London: Triangle, 1995.

Townsend, P. *Poverty in the United Kingdom: A Survey of Household Resources and Standards of Living*. Harmondsworth: Penguin, 1979.

Veldhuis, R. *Realism versus Utopianism? Reinhold Niebuhr's Christian Realism and the Relevance of Utopian Thought for Social Ethics*, Assen: Van Gorcum, 1975.

Visser 't Hooft, W.A., and Oldham, J. *The Church and its Function in Society*. London: George, Allen and Unwin, and Chicago: Willett, Clark, 1937.

Wainwright, H. *Reclaim the State: Experiments in Popular Democracy*. London and New York: Verso, 2003.

Waldinger, R. and Bozorgmehr, M. (eds). *Ethnic Los Angeles*. New York : Russell Sage Foundation, 1996.

Ward, P. *Liquid Church*. Carlisle: Paternoster Press, and Peabody, MA: Hendrickson, 2002.

Welch, S. *Communities of Resistance and Solidarity: A Feminist Theology of Liberation*. Maryknoll, NY: Orbis, 1985.

——. *A Feminist Ethic of Risk*. Minneapolis: Fortress Press, 1990.

Westwood, A. and Nathan, M. (2002) *Manchester: Ideopolis? Developing a Knowledge Capital*. London: Work Foundation, 2002.

White, S. 'Interpreting the "Third Way": Not One Road, but Many'. *Renewal* 6/1 (1998): 17–30.

Wirth, L. 'Urbanism as a Way of Life' (1938), reprinted in A. Reiss Jr (ed.) *Louis Wirth on Cities and Social Life*. Chicago: University of Chicago, 1964.

Young, R. *Colonial Desire: Hybridity in Theory, Culture and Race*. London and New York: Routledge, 1995.

Index

Florida, Richard 40
    New Bohemians 35, 39
    creative class 35
    city of liveability 35, 37
Forrester, Duncan 85, 93
Foucault, Michel 99
Fox, R. 92
Freud, Sigmund 98
Friedman, J. 24
Friedmann, J. 47, 53
Fukuyama, Francis 105
Furbey, Rob 64

Garreau, Joel 28
Gemeinschaft, Gesellschaft (*see also* Ferdinand Tönnies)
Giddens, Anthony 58, 126
Gilligan, Carol 98, 102, 103
Globalisation 26
    immigration 26
    mixed populations 30
Gómez-Peña, Guillermo 33, 34
Gorringe, Tim 150, 151
Graham, Elaine 97, 107, 123, 124
    feminist epistemology 98
    feminist moral imagination 98
    feminist social ethics 97–9
    renewed moral anthropology 97
Graham, S. 31, 41
Greenbelt 130
Guervera, Alfonso 121

Habermas, Jurgen 102
Hall, Stuart 23
Halpern, David 47, 48, 49, 53, 55
    decline in UK civil society 54
Harding, Sandra 101
Harvey, David 27, 36, 37, 38, 39, 40, 106
    managerialism 36
    entrepreneurialism 36, 39
Hampson, Daphne 90, 99
Harrison, Beverley 89, 92, 99, 107, 108
    distorted Marxist analysis 104
    reformed social ethics 103–6
Hauerwas, Stanley 69
Headley, Don 124
Hegel, Georg 21
Heidigger, Martin 90
Heteroglossia 153, 154
Heteropolis 30, 31, 44, 151, 152, 153, 154
Hills, John 80
Hirschmann, Albert 56
hooks, bell 19, 33
Huntingdon, Samuel 14

Hutnyk, John 45
Hybridity (*see also* Third Space) 26
    assimilationist 132
    bricolage theory 45, 46, 47
    British-born identities 23, 26, 68
    colonial constructs 13–14
    curry mile, Manchester 6
    destabilising 132
    historical concepts 13–14
    interrogatory 24, 149
    liminality 18
    mixed race – discrimination 14
    mongrel cities (*see also* cities)
    negotiation (*see also* Homi Bhabha) 21, 135
    organic 46
    social impact 2
    translation (*see also* Homi Bhabha) 21, 135

Ideopolis (*see also* Manchester) 40, 41, 111
India 83
Indices of Multiple Deprivation (IMD) 118
Industrial Areas Foundations (IAF) 120, 121, 122, 131
Internet, the 27, 31, 52, 54
Islam (*see also* Salman Rushdie) 1, 7
    African 114
    British-born Muslims 1–2, 6–7, 46
    economics 1, 84
    terrorist cells 1, 7, 64, 128
    Ummah, the 128

Jacobs, Jane 44, 45, 46
    neo-colonialism 46
Japan 84
Jarl, Ann-Cathrin 85
Jencks, Charles 30, 151, 153
Jenkins, David 85
Jesus Christ (*see also* Hybrid Christ) 75, 76, 77, 78, 87, 91, 132, 137, 147
Judeo-Christian tradition
    Cross of Christ 87, 147
    Genesis 1 90, 149
    Genesis 12: 1; 125
    Hebrew prophets 87
July 7 (2005) 1, 2, 7, 46

Kamergrauzis, Normunds 70, 80, 81, 92, 102, 103, 105, 106, 149, 150
    ethics of solidarity 96
    redeveloped Christian Realism 95–7
    stewardship and creation 96, 149, 150
Keating, A. 34
Kegley, C. 88

ANALYSING CONVERSATION

Also by Beatrice Szczepek Reed

PROSODIC ORIENTATION IN ENGLISH CONVERSATION